YOSHIKO UENO—MÜLLER

# SA KE

## THE ART
## AND CRAFT
## OF JAPAN'S
## NATIONAL DRINK

PRESTEL

MUNICH • LONDON • NEW YORK

# Foreword — The World of Sake

As President of the Japan Sommelier Association and organizer of the Sake Diploma International, I would hereby like to congratulate Ms. Ueno-Müller upon the publication of this book about Japanese sake.

People in Japan started making sake around 2,000 years ago, and since the early 1990s in particular, the quality of sake has increased at a tearing pace. Numerous factors have contributed to this development: the isolation of yeast strains from the best breweries, their culture and distribution, the introduction of the yamahai brewing method, and the use of lactic acid in the starter culture; the development of the vertical rice polishing machine around 1933; the use of brewing alcohol; and the improvement in quality of varieties of rice cultivated specifically for brewing sake.

Sake is an alcoholic brewed product made in Japan. Traditionally, it was enjoyed before consuming a rice dish; its effects encourage communication with the people you are sharing your table with. However, in the past, sake was—unlike wine—not consciously paired with food. This has changed. These days, we know that different types of sake can also be paired well with various dishes and that they excellently harmonize with each other, so whole menus are now offered with corresponding sakes for each course. Anyone who loves pairing wine with food can also learn to enjoy sake pairing.

We thought that sommeliers, whose main task is to combine wine with food dishes, should be the ones to spread the word about this new way of enjoying sake, which is why we decided to launch a sake diploma examination, organized by the Japan Sommelier Association.

One of the big advantages sake has when being paired with food is that, unlike wine, combining it with egg-based dishes is entirely unproblematic. This is because no sulfur is added during the production of sake. Sulfites react negatively with egg yolk, which can lead to unpleasant changes in their flavors.

In fact, sake even makes egg-based dishes creamier and tastier, thanks to the balance between its mild sweetness and umami, as well as the aroma that is added to the rice by its lactic acid. This balance also elegantly enhances the natural sweetness of raw salad, cucumber, and other types of green vegetables. Sake underscores the sweetness and flavor of fish roe, such as caviar and bottarga (mullet roe), without the negative notes that can sometimes be detected when one combines these products with wine. The same applies to raw oysters.

Furthermore, sake harmonizes well with the flavors of animal fats and oils (including otoro from tuna fish) and emphasizes the fine, buttery notes of marbled meat, such as Kobe beef. Thanks to these properties, sake pairs well with dishes made with cream, butter, and cheese.

As it ages, sake acquires a brownish color. This change is not caused by oxidization, however, as is the case with wine, but is mainly due to the Maillard reaction between the sugar and amino acids it contains. For this reason, sake pairs well with dishes made with soy sauce and miso, which age through a similar reaction, as well as with the aromas of washed-rind cheeses (e.g. Munster). It can even be combined with veal stock and dishes made with Madeira wine, since in these, too, a Maillard reaction has taken place.

We are confident that this book will inspire you to experiment with various types of sake and food combinations, and thus create new taste experiences every day.

**Shinya Tasaki**
President of the Japan Sommelier Association

# Preface by the Author

*Ichi-go ichi-e* (一期一会) is a Japanese concept referring to the unrepeatable nature of every moment—and it is perfectly suited to the topic of sake.

One single sip of sake will give you a taste of the whole of Japan. Sake is the elixir of the Japanese soul; it reflects the history, landscape, culture, and culinary practices of the country just as much as the philosophy and art of its brewers. In this book, I want to introduce you to the many different facets of the world of sake.

My first book about this traditional Japanese drink was published back in 2013. But since then, the public perception of sake has fundamentally changed: once viewed as an exotic curiosity among alcoholic drinks, it has now become a globally celebrated accompaniment to many meals. I therefore would like to invite you to join me on a journey through time—a journey involving myths, craftsmanship, and delectation.

Time unfurls in a single glass of sake. It tells the stories of all the people who have helped refine this rice wine for the past 2,000 years, of the raw materials and various techniques that have been used to produce and further develop it, and of the joy it brings to these people and others.

How and where is the rice used to produce sake cultivated? What is koji? How long does the brewing process last? What roles are played by water and yeast in this process? How is sake stored and drunk? Who or what determines what it will taste like? What different styles of sake exist? In this book, I will take you with me to visit a rice farmer, a cooper, a glass and ceramic artist, a Kobe beef breeder, holy shrines—and, of course, exceptional breweries. You will also follow me into izakaya sake bars to partake in their relaxed sharing menus, and I will introduce you to restaurateurs who choose to enhance their culinary art—distinguished with Michelin stars in some cases, and based on the traditional principle of kaiseki—by offering the appropriate kind of sake as an accompaniment.

In addition to my personal encounters and emotional experiences within the Japanese world of sake, this book also contains a wealth of information for anyone who wants to dive deeper into the topic. You will learn technical details about the production of sake, ways to describe and enhance your sensory experience, and the art of combining sake with various dishes—from Japanese cuisine and other world cultures, too.

I will also introduce you to a selection of the best sakes that represent Japan, teaching you all you need to know about the various styles—from sparkling to aged—and I will take you on a tasting tour of a dozen or so stations, including the employee canteen of a brewery and an oyster stand in Sendai Market. Get ready for a few surprises!

Take a little break from your daily routine and enjoy a glass of sake. Explore it with all your senses; let your thoughts flow through the time unfolding within it. This unique experience will mark your palate and your memory forever.

*Kanpai* – cheers!

**Yoshiko Ueno-Müller**

# Contents

## 18 I. ORIGINS

— **MYTH. HISTORY. DRINKING CULTURE.**

20    What is Sake?

24    From Sacred Rice to a Modern Delight

30    A Feast for the Sake God

40    **MASAYUKI** — Mimurosugi Brewery in Nara

— **RICE. WATER. KOJI.**

46    KEY INGREDIENTS AND FERMENTATION

48    ELEMENTS OF WATER

50    **TSUSHIMA** — Shichiken Brewery in Yamanashi

58    A YEAR IN THE RICE PADDY

60    VARIETIES OF RICE

62    THE SECRET OF KOJI

64    THE POWER OF YEAST

— **MASTERS. CRAFT. TIME.**

66    How is Sake Made?

84    **YASUYUKI** — Tedorigawa Brewery in Ishikawa

94    **KIICHIRO** — Toji in Toyama

98    **TAKESHI** — Barrel Maker in Osaka

104    SAKE CLASSIFICATION AND VARIETIES

292    *Sake around the World*

295    *Glossary — Japanese Words and Technical Terms*

302    *About the Author*

303    *Acknowledgments*

**110** **II.
THE
COUNTRY
AND THE
PEOPLE**

—— **TERROIR. CULTURE.
KURAMOTO.**

112 Satoyama: The Home of
Japanese Gastronomy

122 TOPOGRAPHY, GEOLOGY,
AND CLIMATE

124 TERROIR AND
SAKE CULTURES

126 **SHOZO** — Rice Farmer and
Cattle Breeder in Hyogo

132 **RYUSUKE** — Tatsuriki
Brewery in Hyogo

138 Regional Varieties:
30 Breweries

156 **YASUHIKO** — Niida Honke
Brewery in Fukushima

162 **RICHARD** — IWA Brewery
in Toyama

**168** **III.
A FEAST
FOR ALL
THE
SENSES**

—— **AROMA. FLAVOR.
DIVERSITY.**

170 **RYUICHIRO** — Masuizumi
Brewery in Toyama

182 AROMAS, APPEARANCE,
AND FLAVOR

187 STYLES OF SAKE
AND FLAVOR PROFILES

206 **SHIGERI** — Daruma
Masamune Brewery in Gifu

212 DRINKING VESSELS
AND DINING CULTURE

216 ENJOYING SAKE
ALL YEAR ROUND

—— **SAKE. FOOD. PAIRING.**

218 WHAT IS SAKE PAIRING?

222 HARMONY WITH FOOD

226 WASHOKU — KEY ELEMENTS
OF JAPANESE CUISINE

230 **HIRONORI** — Oryouri Fujii **
Restaurant in Toyama

240 **YOSHIHIRO** — Narisawa **
Restaurant in Tokyo

246 Tokyo by Night

260 Japanese Sake Journey

# I.
# ORIGINS

According to Japanese mythology, the sun goddess, Amaterasu, sent ears of rice down to Earth. The "sacred grain," grown in small rural settlements, was used with the best water and koji to brew a heavenly potion. The following chapter is dedicated to the mythical origins of sake, the festive Shinto ceremony associated with it, and the ancient craft of sake brewing.

# What is Sake?

How is a non-Japanese person to approach Japan's traditional drink? What do we need to know in order to understand sake, this drink of the gods that brings happiness to human beings, this brewed, rice-based "wine" that reflects the Japanese soul? The most important factors are the different types and aromas, brewing styles, and price ranges, but it is also important to understand the raw materials involved in sake production, influences of particular regions, and the roles of master brewers.

## Elixir of the Japanese Soul

"Every ancient civilization in world history has its own particular, beautiful alcoholic beverages," wrote Kinichiro Sakaguchi, the father of modern fermentation science, in his 1964 volume, *Nihon no Sake* (Japanese Sake). Sake has represented the culture, history, and landscapes of Japan for around 2,000 years. The beverage used to be made in every village, but nowadays there are only around 1,200 sake breweries left in Japan, most of which have remained in the hands of their founding families over the generations. For Japanese people, sake is pleasure in liquid form.

## The Drink of the Gods

Good water makes for good rice, and good rice makes for good sake: a wonderful natural cycle that Japanese people have known to honor and cherish since time immemorial. According to the ancient Japanese Shinto religion, divinities live in every occurrence and in every object—in claps of thunder, in rivers, in a grain of rice—and therefore also in sake. In order to appease the wild spirits of the natural gods and thank them for their gifts, sake is brewed as a sacrificial offering. But sake also brings people closer together: To this day, festive occasions and religious rituals are not complete without some sake. In addition, workers in every brewery pray before a miniature holy shrine before starting their work.

## Rice and the Japanese People

Rice was introduced to the country from ancient China around 3,000 years ago, and ever since then, both Japan's land and society have been shaped by the grain's cultivation. Satoyama, a cultivated landscape of rice paddies and woods, represents the complex coexistence of human beings and nature.

# Sake brings people together: Festive occasions and religious rituals are not complete without some sake.

Rice was even once used as a means of payment. During the Shogunate period, until about 150 years ago, the power and performance of feudal lords and samurai were measured according to the amounts of rice produced under their rules. And sake is the best you can make out of rice; an abundance of special sorts of rice are now used to produce premium sake.

## Koji and Sake

Japan's humid, warm climate provides optimal conditions for mold cultures used to ferment soybeans for soy sauce and miso, and rice for sake. There is no sake without koji (fermented rice), which was initially produced under the supervision of the Japanese imperial court by the world's first biotechnical companies in the fourteenth century. In the Middle Ages, Buddhist monasteries took on a major role and eventually monopolized koji production. Now, anyone can produce koji themselves, but koji spores are produced by only a handful of companies (see p. 63).

In addition to koji, yeasts and other microorganisms also play a big role in the fermentation of sake rice. The Japanese state has been supporting the development of powerfully fermenting yeasts for around 100 years, and one sake brewing process, called the kimoto method, was developed 300 years ago. This involves repeatedly pounding koji rice and adding water, which produces natural lactic acids, protecting the sake mash from contamination. Sake brewers have a lot of respect for the work of these microorganisms. The legendary toji (master brewer) Koichi Sanpai said, "I believe it is the yeasts and the koji that make the sake, and the people involved are simply creating the environment within which these are able to work well."

## The Craft of the Toji and Philosophy of the Kuramoto

Sake breweries (sakagura) are part of Japan's traditional industry. The oldest of these companies was founded around 850 years ago, most breweries can look back on several centuries of history, and many are still in the hands of their founding families. Each brewery has at least one brand named after the family's lucky symbol or the philosophy of its kuramoto (owner) and produces around 20 different kinds of sake. The toji (chief master brewer) is responsible for their brewery's individual taste and quality.

Originally, sake was only brewed in the winter, and this remains the case in many places throughout Japan, where the work is carried out by seasonal contractors over the course of about 60 days. Because of the innumerable factors involved—from the choice of rice and its polishing ratio to how the koji is produced and the sake is aged—many breweries have chosen the motto, *wajo ryoshu* ("harmony brews good sake, and good sake brews harmony").

## Fruity Aromas and Umami

Creamy banana, green apple, honeysweet melon—thanks to its complex brewing process, sake can have over 500 different aromas and nuances of flavor. And Japanese people can get quite poetic with their descriptions of this national beverage, using language like this: "Pure mountain water gently flows down my throat and fills up my soul and my body, leaving behind beautiful fruity aromas . . ."

Sake is considerably less acidic than wine; it tastes full-bodied and mild. Its alcohol content is around 15 percent, a little higher than that of wine, and just like the grape-based brew, sake comes in a wide range of different qualities and prices. Premium types comprise the six classes of honjozo, junmai, ginjo, junmai ginjo, daiginjo and junmai daiginjo. These make up just under half of total production in Japan. However, because the term *sake* is not yet protected in other countries, cheap liquor of dubious origin can also be sold as sake outside of Japan.

## The Pleasures of Sake Pairings

Sake is not just an exquisite soloist, but also a multifaceted talent in the orchestra known as pleasure. With its nuanced aromas and full-bodied taste, high-quality sake shines as an excellent accompaniment to food. But it is not just a wonderful pairing for traditional Japanese specialties—it also goes perfectly with dishes from Europe or other parts of the world.

Like different types of wines, various sake varieties can complement just about any flavor, depending on the style, drinking vessel, atmosphere, and one's personal taste.

## Sake Conquers the World

More and more people outside Japan are enriching their palette with sake, and handcrafted premium sake, with its refined flavor, is particularly sought-after, resulting in export market growth. Such high-value types of sake are served in New York, Sydney, Hong Kong, London, and Berlin to accompany all types of haute cuisine. As a result, many sake lovers have now also started producing the rice wine in their own homelands: There are currently about 60 breweries operating outside of Japan, half of which are based in the United States. In Europe, there are sake producers in the United Kingdom, Spain, France, Austria, and Switzerland, among other countries. Sake rice is cultivated in the USA, and the country has even seen the foundation of a sake brewers association. In the beverage's country of origin, this momentum from abroad is viewed positively, and these international exchanges have raised true Japanese sake to a new level of prestige. —

# From Sacred Rice to a Modern Delight

Long before Japan acquired the names it is known by today—Nihon and Nippon—ancient Japanese people called their country Toyoashihara no Mizuho no Kuni ("the country where the reeds grow and crops prosper abundantly"). According to mythology, when the sun goddess Amaterasu's grandson Ninigi no Mikoto was to descend to Earth, she gave him ears of rice that had grown in the fields of the heavens where the gods lived. Rice is a holy object, a gift from the gods that contains their spirit—that is why it is deemed to make the best offering for the gods.

## Rice Cultivation and the Origins of Sake

Japan's history, economy, society, and culture were all developed hand-in-hand with rice cultivation, so rice has always been an important topic for Japanese people.

It is assumed that the paddy rice cultivation method that is widespread in Japan today came to the country around 3,000 years ago from Korea and other parts of East Asia was initially introduced to the northern region of Kyushu. In the seventh century BC, rice cultivation then spread to the region of Kinki, and later on it made its way to the northern tip of Honshu. Japan changed from a hunter-gatherer society to an agrarian one between the fifth century BC and the middle of the third century AD, and people established communal settlements in order to cultivate rice together.

Small villages thus appeared in various parts of the country. In the Kinki region, powerful clans emerged over time, and the central power that united them took shape. The ancient state of Yamato promoted policies that made rice the foundation of its economy. However, since agrarian societies were vulnerable to climate variability and natural disasters, its rulers were given a very important role in conducting sacred rituals. Sacrificial offerings were made to appease the wild spirits of the gods and ask for a good harvest.

When exactly the production of sake began has not been documented, but before koji was used to make sake, kuchikami-no-sake was produced by

Omiki: The power of the gods lives in sanctified sake.

priestesses. For ritual purposes, they would start by cleansing their bodies with water and their teeth with salt, then chewing rice inside their mouths before spitting it out into containers and leaving it to ferment.

In addition, the national chronicles *Kojiki* and *Nihonshoki*, written in the eighth century AD, include a myth from the Izumo region, according to which Susano no Mikoto, the divine brother of Amaterasu, produced yashioorino sake, a strong ferment that was brewed eight times in order to make the eight-headed monster, Yamata-no-orochi, drunk and kill it. There are also further legends to be found in regional chronicles. One of them says that Kusunokami, who is worshipped in the sake shrine of Izumo, would brew and serve sake to the eight million gods who had gathered there from the whole country. This is why some Japanese people view Izumo as the cradle of sake.

## Sake Gods and Sake Brewing at Shrines

Shintoism and Buddhism are the two main religions of Japan. Shinto—the Way of the Gods—is the (mainly orally transmitted) ethnic religion of the Japanese people. It has some features of ancient animism, in which nature and natural phenomena are deified and worshipped, including wind and thunder gods and the sun god, Amaterasu, and all the divinities that embody the mountains and rivers of various regions. It also includes some aspects of popular belief, such as the veneration of ancestors' spirits and of the gods of paddy fields. Nature and divinities are acknowledged as one and the same, and there are no doctrine or gurus.

When Buddhism reached Japan via China and Korea in the middle of the sixth century, the rulers of the time promoted this faith, too, and henceforth both religions existed alongside each other. There are around 88,000 Shinto shrines all over Japan, where various divinities are worshipped, but three jinja are particularly venerated as sacred sites of the sake gods: Omiwa Shrine, in Nara, and the Umemiya and Matsunoo Shrines, both in Kyoto.

In the past, people brewed their own sake for festive occasions at many of these sites. During the Meiji Era (1868 to 1912), when the government started to control the brewing of alcohol and used its alcohol tax as a major source of income, the brewing of sake at the shrines was considerably restricted.

Now, there are only four jinja left in the country with a license to produce sake, of which Ise Jingu Shrine is the most famous. Several emperors already worshipped their mythical ancestor goddess Amaterasu there, and it is the highest-ranked and largest of all shrines in Japan. Every day, morning and evening, sake brewed there and rice and produce grown there are offered up in sacrifice. All foodstuffs, items of clothing, and ceramics for the shrine are also manufactured there according to ancient production methods.

## Omiki and Mike

Sake that is offered up to the gods is called omiki. It has been an essential component of Shinto rituals since antiquity and is so important that it is ranked in the middle of the uppermost tier of the mike, the daily meal offered up to the gods, which also includes other foods essential to human life, such as rice, salt, water, vegetables, and meat. In Shintoism, great value is placed on harmony with nature, because people believe that the gods live inside mountains, in the sea, and in certain foods. And if each grain of rice contains a divinity, think of how many divinities a glass of sake contains! Dotted around the grounds of most shrines are barrels of sake: offerings made by the breweries to thank the gods. Omiki, sanctified sake, is also offered to the faithful during devotions and on occasions such as New Year celebrations.

## Sake Connects People to the Gods and to Each Other

After a Shinto ceremony usually comes the naorai, a shared meal that brings together all participants and the priest, during which sake is offered as an oblation. Sake is also offered up on people's everyday alters at home and work, it is sprinkled on the earth at groundbreaking ceremonies to symbolize purification before new construction projects begin, and it is drunk at various festivities to signify the link between gods and human beings.

During the Edo period (1603–1867), sake rituals were held with the aim of sealing anew the master-servant relationship between the samurai, daimyo, and shogun, and were governed by strict rules. The most typical contractual ritual involving sake is the san san kudo, performed by the bridal couple during a Shinto wedding. During this ceremony, the bride and groom each take three sips from three different-sized flat cups of sake. Three is a sacred number in Japan—so the number nine means triple good luck. Parents and relations also drink sake with the bridal couple, in order to strengthen their bond.

## Kanpai and Sacrificial Offerings

The term *kanpai* (cheers!) comes from China, and clinking sake cups is a relatively new custom that was imported to Japan from the West in the middle of the nineteenth century. Unlike the Chinese custom (literally, to dry the sake cup), in Japan one is not expected to drink it all in one go. Instead, you hold the cup with both hands at eye level. When this rite is carried out at memorial services or on sad occasions, the term *kenpai* (devotement) is used instead of kanpai: this expresses respect or commiseration.

## Nominication

Up until the Heian period (794–1185), sake was mainly consumed by the privileged classes. It was not until the Kamakura period, which followed, when sake breweries started to flourish and the larger public was given access to this refined drink during official events. How this public was expected to handle sake appropriately is reflected in the shudo ("way of drinking") ritual that emerged in the Ashikaga period (1573–1568), the aim of which was to develop politeness and spirituality through the drinking of alcohol. Its fundamental idea was "not to aim to be drunk, but rather to make drinking more graceful and wonderful."

Then, during the Edo period (1603–1867), rice wine, which was brewed in a way almost identical to modern methods, was distributed in large quantities, and the common people began to enjoy it every day. Sake from Nada and Itami came across the sea to Edo, where it was sold by the cup out of barrels or served alongside simple dishes such as sushi, tempura, and soba. It was purchased most commonly by single samurai and craftsmen who had settled in Edo as followers of the Shogun.

Following the Meiji restoration (around 1867), beer, wine, and whisky spread across Japan along with Western food. However, sake remained the most popular alcoholic drink in the country through to the 1970s, with the exception of phases during and shortly after World War II.

Enjoying sake with other people—with colleagues after work or on other occasions—is now often referred to as nomination (from *nomi*, "drinking together," and "communication"). The aim here is to encourage solidarity within a group: newcomers are taught how to drink by their elders or superiors, and they learn how people within the group communicate with each other. In Japanese culture, aside from the formalities of day-to-day professional meetings, the way colleagues interact with each other is relaxed, and drinking is intended to further people's understanding of and relation to each other.

Another typical Japanese custom is enjoying sake while admiring flowers, birds, the wind, and the moon of each of the four seasons—for example, during cherry blossom season or when leaves change color in the fall.

## Sake Brewing with Koji

The practice of brewing sake using koji, as we know it today, seems to have arisen by accident nearly 3,000 years ago. In the *Harima Fudoki* manuscript, written in the eighth century, there is a description of sake being brewed with moldy (fermented) rice and then served at sake feasts. And, indeed, the position of Mikino-Tsukasa (imperial office for sake) already existed in courts during the Nara and Heian periods (eighth to twelfth centuries). Whoever held this position was responsible for both the brewing of sake and the preparation of ceremonies and sake banquets. The *Engishiki* manuscript, which dates back to this same period, describes the production of up to 15 different types of sake by the Mikino-Tsukasa and already includes brewing recipes for sake using koji, but a safe way of producing koji (using wood ash) was not developed until the Muromachi period (1336–1573).

## The Temple Sake of Nara

During the second half of the sixteenth century, basic techniques for brewing sake were developed,

> **Rice is a holy object, a gift from the gods that contains their spirit—that is why it is deemed to make the best offering for the gods.**

including rice polishing, straining the mash, and the separation into kasu (lees) and sake, as well as the method of heat sterilization (hi-ire), which would later be scientifically explained by Pasteur. And the big temples and shrines of Nara played important roles in these advancements. The bodaimoto method was developed in what was then Shoryakuji Temple, and the preparation of the mash in several stages was also practiced from this time on in the region's temples. This is also why Nara Prefecture is described as the birthplace of Japanese sake. Thanks to the wooden barrels of Nara, sake could be brewed and stored in larger quantities—before this period, people used ceramic containers, which could only hold a maximum of 540 liters.

## Sake Brewing and Distribution in the Edo Period

During the Edo period (1603–1867), industrial sake production grew ever more popular. In order to prevent the rice wine from being spoiled, producers began adding alcohol, which was produced, among other methods, by distilling the kasu (lees). The Edo period also saw the introduction of rice polishing using water wheels, the kimoto brewing method, and the promotion of sake brewing during wintertime so farmers and fishers could work for sake breweries during their slow season. The toji system was also developed during the Edo period, and many new breweries were established in famous brewing regions such as Fushimi, Ikeda, Itami, Nishinomiya, and Nada in order to produce large quantities of sake for Edo, the ruling metropolis.

With around one million inhabitants, Edo (now known as Tokyo) was the largest city in the world at this time. Five major overland roads departed from it in a radial pattern. However, these roads were not suitable for transporting large quantities of heavy goods such as rice out of the direct zone of influence of the Shogunate in the North to the capital city. People thus preferred to take the sea route when transporting such goods over long distances. Soon, around the middle of the seventeenth century, a western route from Sakata to Osaka was developed, as well as a southern route from Osaka or Kobe to Edo. At that time, Osaka was known as the "kitchen of the nation"; it was a major economic center and commercial hub. A system of maritime trading companies developed, and kitamae ships transported goods such as rice, sake, kelp, other sea products, fertilizers, and clothing. From the port of Osaka, a fast and inexpensive system was set up for the regular transport of sake in particular, using tarukaisen sailing boats, named for the taru (small casks) used for storing sake.

## From the Technical Innovations of the Meiji Era through to the End of World War II

The Meiji era (1868–1912) marked the end of the Edo period and the modernization of the country's political and economic systems. It became easier to obtain a sake license during this time, so numerous sake breweries were founded—more than 27,000 in 1881 alone. Also, thanks to the emergence of modern microbiology, sake yeast was isolated for the first time at the end of the nineteenth century. Since the alcohol tax was the state's most important source of revenue, scientific research into sake brewing, aimed at avoiding microbiological contamination, became a national strategy. 1904 saw the foundation of the National Research Institute of Brewing, and people began to develop new ways to brew sake (sokujo and yamahai methods, p. 75) and distribute cultured yeast. In the 1930s, the invention of vertical rice polishers allowed for a higher grade of polishing. During World War II, however, rice was used primarily as a foodstuff, limiting sake production and sales, and labor shortages led to the consolidation of breweries. In order to meet the demand for sake, breweries created recipes for gosei seishu (synthetic sake) and sanzoushu (thrice-diluted sake).

## An Economic Boom After the World War II, and a Transition from Mass Consumption to Modern Quality Concerns

The post-war economic rebound also brought with it an increase in sake consumption. Techniques developed before World War II, such as the sokujo method and the use of kyokai yeast (cultured yeast), as well as the use of enamel tanks instead of traditional wood casks, became more established, and a steady production of sake commenced. In addition, mechanization was pushed further, for example with rice steamers and automatic koji production machines. The major breweries in Nada and Fushimi expanded their production and increased their revenue. A rice quota system was in place until 1969, so it was common practice for large breweries to mix sake produced by small and medium-sized breweries with their own production and to sell it under their own brands.

After the 1973 oil crisis, the consumption of sake dropped sharply, leading to a corresponding reduction in the number of sake breweries. While Japan still counted 4,000 breweries in the 1960s, there were only around 1,200 by 2020. In order to survive, producers now emphasized quality over quantity. Smaller breweries advertised jizake (local sake), which contrasted the uniformity of sake made by big-name breweries. The 1990s then saw a ginjo boom, a diversification into nama (raw) sake, an increase in popularity of sparkling and aged sake, and increases in exports of sake abroad. At the same time, the number of brewers who worked on a seasonal basis decreased, leading breweries to rely on permanent staff instead. Today, many kuramoto (brewery owners) also act as toji (master brewers) due to staffing restraints. In addition, breweries are developing a wide range of products that reflect their own strengths and the taste of the market. Still, half of total sake production in Japan is attributable to the country's 10 largest sake breweries. —

# A Feast for the Sake God

SAKURAI

Every November, brewers and merchants pay tribute to the holy Mount Miwa, also known as Mimuro-yama or Omononushi, during a ceremony of dancing, singing, and praying at the Omiwa Shrine in Sakurai.

On the side of the busy main road of Sakurai, a concrete archway stretches several meters above my head. This simple and elegant construction marks the access road to Omiwa Jinja, Japan's oldest sacred shrine, which appears in numerous ancient myths. I walk slowly through the grey stone otorii (large gate). The cobbled road leading to the vast, densely wooded shrine area at the foot of Mount Miwa, which is worshipped as the divinity Omononushi, is lined with souvenir shops for the faithful, shops selling Shinto shrine necessities, and restaurants serving somen noodles. On this day of the Sake-Jozo Anzen Kigan-sai festival, reserved for sake brewers and merchants, it is relatively quiet here. However, when a major festival is held at the shrine, the roads are usually lined with food stands selling not just yakisoba, takoyaki, oden, and other hearty delicacies, but also ama sake—and the scent of this sweet, low- or nonalcoholic sake mixes with the smell of soy sauce burning on the cooking grates.

A white, wooden torii (gate) seems to act like a gracious barrier separating the commercial out-side world from that of the shrine. Behind this gate, groves of evergreen trees line a gravel walk and form a kind of plant corridor. Once we have bowed to the torii and stepped through it, we are surrounded by cool, clean air. I walk slowly along the right side of the wide path—the middle of it is reserved for the gods. A brook runs through the whole area around the shrine. A small wooden bridge takes us over it and leads us into an even darker green. We are getting close to the steps to the prayer hall; at first, though, all we can see of it is its roof, with the shimenawa (holy straw rope). This rope and the torii separate the normal world from the territory of the gods.

On my left side, I soon discover a washbasin filled with water from the sacred Mount Miwa. This is where the faithful wash their hands and rinse their mouths before entering the prayer hall. When you climb further up the steps, your gaze falls onto the low hall, covered with cypress bark in front of the green mountain landscape. This well-proportioned ensemble, which manages to combine an air of generous festivity with one of simple naturalness,

A sugitama ball made out of cedar branches is hung up in the prayer hall.

The prayer hall in front of the sacred Mount Miwa

The color and shape of festive hair jewelry are full of symbolic meaning.

**"**

The air is cool and refreshing, and the wind blowing through the pine trees is so clear and sacred that I can feel the presence of a divinity. I have now arrived in the kingdom of Omononushi.

reminds me of a falcon that has just landed and still has its wings spread out.

Most Japanese shrines have a closed room (honden) that houses a special object (mitamashiro or goshintai) that is assumed to contain a divinity. This object might be a mirror, sword, magatama (curved bead), statue, or something else, and it is typically concealed from human eyes. Nevertheless, if one prays in the direction of the mitamashiro or goshintai, one can feel the presence of the divinity. In the case of the Omiwa Shrine, the goshintai is Mount Miwa itself, with its luscious covering of deciduous and coniferous trees. The mountain has been worshipped as the god of sake since antiquity. And the mitsu-torii behind the prayer hall that opens up onto the mountain is seen as holy, a shine unto itself.

The sound of low-pitched taiko drums echoes through the air, and priests in white medieval Japanese robes enter the prayer hall, in which around 80 sake brewers, toji, sake merchants, and other people working in the sake industry wait in silence. At the beginning of the brewing season in November, sake prayer festivals are held at shrines in various regions of Japan; the Omiwa Shrine is even mentioned in the *Nihon Shoki*, one of Japan's oldest official chronicles. One day, this text claims, when the country was being plagued by an epidemic, Emperor Sujin, the 10th tenno (emperor) of Japan, received a message from the god Omononushi-no-Okami in a dream; this god ordered him to appoint a man called Otataneko as priest of the Omiwa Shrine and to bring an offering of sake to this shrine. The emperor immediately summoned the brewer Takahashi Ikuhi no Mikoto, who created a very good sake overnight. His creation was used to perform a ritual in honor of Omononushi, and soon afterwards, the epidemic came to an end.

Ever since then, Ikuhi no Mikoto has been worshipped by sake brewers across Japan as the country's first toji and Omononushi has been worshipped as the great tutelary god of sake brewing. The land at the foot of Mount Miwa does not, however, only house the Omiwa Shrine and the smaller Ikuhi Shrine—it is also the location of the Iwakura Shrine, whose goshintai is a cliff upon which rests a divinity, and the Sai Shrine, which is known as a healing shrine.

One of the priests in the prayer hall has now stood up and is passing a staff hung with white strips of fabric over the heads of everyone present: once from the left, once from the right, and again from the left. After this cleansing gesture has been performed, the actual ceremony can start. A ceremonial gagaku sounds out with hichiriki flutes and drums. This ancient Japanese courtly music goes back almost 1,000 years, and its sound and rhythm are unique. It gives listeners the feeling that they are leaving the world outside and entering into the realm of the gods.

Eleven mike (sacred offerings) of rice, salt, sea bream, vegetables, fruit, and other foodstuffs have now been laid out, one at a time, before the mitsu-torii on vermillion-painted platforms. Underneath them are two heishi carafes containing sake. Sake has been an essential element of Shinto rituals since antiquity, and thus it is important for it to be in the middle of the upper row of the mike—the meal that is brought to the gods every day, the composition of which varies according to the region.

Once all preparations for the ceremony are complete, one of the Shinto priests says a prayer to express gratitude for this year's plentiful rice harvest and to ask for the protection of all people involved in the brewing process. His words are presented to the mountain god in loose, lyrical sentences.

I eavesdrop on the brewers' ceremony's prayer with my head bent low. I feel myself fill with reverence, and I pray with all my heart and soul together with the other worshippers. I feel a great gratitude for being here: I am very thankful to be able to explore the world of sake. I pray that good sake will be

Sacred sugi cedar trees surround the shrine.

brewed once more this season all over Japan. Suddenly, a fresh breeze comes down from the mountains and gently blows around me. *What is that?* I wonder. An inexplicable feeling of safety rises up within me. I ask the priest about it later on, and he tells me it was a sign that the god dropped in on us.

Four shrine maidens (miko) wearing traditional red and white robes, their hair in tight bundles, now enter the prayer hall. Each one of these miko carries a sake carafe on a thick, table-like wooden tablet and places this on the table of offerings. As gagaku music plays, the quartet then performs the Umashi Sake no Kuni Miwa, the dance of the beautiful country of Miwa sake. As they do so, the four charmingly swing branches of the holy sugi cedar tree, which also adorn the front of their heads. Then, a man sings a song about miki, the divine sake. It goes something like this: "This is holy sake. It is not my work, but rather brewed by Omononushi." I wonder whether the gods enjoy watching the dance of the four shrine maidens and listening to a man singing while they eat and drink. The wind from the mountains, the one I felt earlier on, slips gently between the miko's movements.

With this dancing and singing, the official ceremony of Sake-Jozo Anzen Kigan-sai nears its end. As a conclusion, the priests and their attendants offer up a tamagushi (also known as the "jewel skewer"), a further offering for the mountain god. This is a small branch of the evergreen, holy sakaki tree.

Then begins the naorai, the moment when the priests and all other people present drink the sake dedicated to the mountain god and eat a little food. A priestess pours the sake out of a golden pot into a white sakazuki cup, which I hold stretched out toward her with both hands. Its inside is decorated with the symbol of the three holy cedars of the Omiwa Shrine. I hold the cup up at eye level and thank the gods, then take a sip. The cool sake soon lights up my mouth and fills me with warmth. This is the moment when the tension of the ritual is released. But I am no longer the same person as before the ceremony: I feel galvanized, as though a calm power is animating me from the inside.

The day before the Sake-Jozo Anzen Kigan-sai, a large ball of cedar branches (sugitama) was hung up in the middle of the entrance to the prayer hall. These cedar balls, which get their shape from woven bamboo baskets, often have a diameter of 1.5 meters (5 feet) and bring the scent of fresh, green cedar from the sacred Mount Mira into the shrine. New balls of cedar, in various sizes, are also given out to sake brewers from everywhere in the country; they then hang them up with a wooden sign bearing the inscription "Omiwa Myojin" under the eaves of their breweries. The green balls of branches are a sign that the brewing season has begun. They are supposed to watch over the sake brewery day and night, guaranteeing its employees divine protection. When the sugitama grows brown, months later, this is a sign that the freshly-produced sake is ready to be enjoyed.

After leaving the prayer hall, I climb up a narrow path through the woods, together with the other sake industry visitors to the shrine, to visit the Ikuhi Shrine and pray there for another year of good sake production. Further up the hill is the starting point to climb up Mount Miwa, which rises up about 460 meters (1,509 feet). Because this is a sacred site, strict rules apply: taking photographs is forbidden, as are eating and drinking. The path to the summit is steep and lined with moss-covered cliff-faces, towering cedar and pine trees, and wild sasa lilies, which are used to produce yeast for a particular local type of sake. We are accompanied by birdsong and the sound of flowing water. The air is cool and refreshing, and the wind blowing through the cedar trees is so clear and sacred that I can feel the presence of a divinity. I have now arrived in the kingdom of Omononushi. —

# Masayuki

MIMUROSUGI BREWERY
SAKURAI, NARA PREFECTURE

SAKURAI

Crystal clear water flows out of a bamboo cylinder into a stone basin, its patter mixing with the voices of the brewery workers, diligently at work at the back of the building. I am in the Mimurosugi Sake Brewery, one of the oldest continuously operational sake breweries in Japan. It was founded in 1660, barely a stone's throw away from the sacred Mount Miwa, the reputed cradle of sake brewing. The brewery building is on Ise Kaido, the road that has connected the commercial city of Osaka with the holy Ise Shrine since antiquity. To this day, the typical old houses with dark brown wooden fences, white plaster façades, and black tiled roofs have been preserved here.

Masayuki Imanishi, the 14th kuramoto of Mimurosugi Brewery, has welcomed me at their entrance, which is adorned with a cedar branch ball. Now we are standing in front of the water basin and Masayuki explains, "For our sake, we use this water from the sacred Mount Miwa as a base and add to it the flavor of tsuyuhakaze, a local variety of rice, which is farmed in the same water." I take a sip to taste it. The cool mountain water is mild and soft on the tongue, leaving behind a slightly sweet impression.

We walk into the building, where the rice for the Mimurosugi sake is washed and soaked in the pure water—which is available in abundance on these premises. Across from it is a small building with four cedar wood barrels (oke), each around 2.5 meters (8

feet) tall, arranged in the room in a U shape. Their staves are bound together with bamboo straps, five at the bottom and two at the top. If you come close to the barrels, they exude a scent of fresh cedar. Each oke is inscribed with the name Wood Work in Osaka, a company belonging to Takeshi Ueshiba, one of the last wooden barrel manufacturers in Japan.

"We use Ueshiba-san's oke to produce super-natural sake," explains Masayuki, "by which I mean that we do not add in any yeast. This is the bodaimoto method, which was developed in the fifteenth century in Shoryakuji Temple in Nara. With this method, fermentation is supported by natural lactobacilli. Bodaimoto became a prototype for modern sake brewing methods. Nara, where relics from prehistoric times can still be found today, is not just the place where the first central government of Japan was founded in the third century, but also probably the birthplace of sake."

We walk from the wooden barrels to the back part of the 170-year-old production hall, which contains over a dozen state-of-the-art, precisely temperature-controlled containers. The shiny black columns are coated with antibacterial kakishibu (a tanning agent extracted from the kaki fruit) and are supported by earthquake-proof steel frames. Mimurosugi is thus an exemplar of both medieval sake brewing and ultramodern production methods.

Masayuki Imanishi, a 14th generation kuramoto

Different varieties of rice are sourced from local farmers.

Three types of sake, from classic to modern, are ready for tasting.

Fermentation in cedar wood barrels gives the sake unique notes.

Its current kuramoto, Masayuki, studied management at a prestigious university in Kyoto, then lived in Tokyo, where he worked at a recruitment company. "When my father died suddenly in 2011, I came back to Nara and took over the brewery. I had just turned 28 years old. Back then, the company only employed two brewers, and we produced low-quality sake in an old facility. The structure of the company, which also included several restaurants, was also a disaster, and the books showed that my father's brewery was on the edge of bankruptcy. I immediately closed down the restaurants, and from that point onwards I focused on sake production."

In order to produce sake that would sell well, Masayuki continues to explain, he tried to imitate the trend for sakes with aromatic yeasts, ordering different sorts of rice from throughout the country. "During the first two years, I was basically lost as far as brewing was concerned. When I brought my sake to a famous sake dealer in Tokyo, I received nothing but criticism—even my inner voice was telling me that this sake was definitely not good enough. I kept asking myself, 'What kind of sake do I want to make, and who am I?'"

Masayuki was, in his own words, brought back from his profound despair by the words of the priest at the nearby Omiwa Shrine. "'You have a calling, a task given to you by God. God teaches you to work for the good of the world through your work,' the priest told me. These words still keep me grounded today."

Masayuki Imanishi lets himself be guided by this priestly piece of advice, which is why, since 2013, the slogan of his brewery has been "drink Miwa."

"We wanted to use the water and the rice which the gods live in to create a sake that would match this culturally and historically rich place: a clear sake with a smooth, gentle aroma and fresh taste."

Ever since then, the philosophy of the brewery has been "pure, proper sake brewing." "'Pure' means expressing the purity of Mount Miwa. 'Proper' means that when we brew our sake, we always do things properly," explains Masayuki. "We place a lot of value on asking ourselves whether we are doing the right thing at every stage of the brewing process. Our main goal is to brew without contaminating the rice with bacteria and without damaging it. This is why we carry out all preparations for the rice by hand, regardless of how much time and effort this involves."

When Masayuki Imanishi took over the brewery following his father's death, its two former brewers resigned of their own accord because they could not adapt to the new structure. So, the young kuramoto found a partner in Tokyo who shared the same passion that animates him. "Although we were both amateurs, from our first collaboration in 2013 we produced a sake with a convincing, trailblazing flavor."

The Mimurosugi Brewery now has 22 employees and produces around 1,500 koku per year, equivalent to about 2.7 million hectoliters (71 million gallons) of "pure and proper sake." Usually, a brewery business producing such amounts would about employ six or seven people; many sake breweries in Japan currently suffer from staff shortages, and at the same time, in efforts to increase efficiency, businesses are tending to reduce their staff numbers and promote mechanization. Things are surprisingly different at Mimurosugi. When I ask him whether human resources costs reduce profits, Masayuki answers: "We have no sales personnel and we don't do any advertising. Most of our spending goes on raw materials, wages, and investments in our production facilities. Even if we're not actively recruiting, people come to us from all over Japan after falling in love with our Mimurosugi sake, wanting to participate in its production." More than a decade after Masayuki Imanishi became the kuramoto of his family brewery near the sacred Mount Miwa, he has now opened up a new chapter in the centuries-old tradition of Nara sake. —

# KEY INGREDIENTS AND FERMENTATION

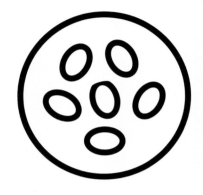

**The production of sake** requires a whole series of precisely coordinated elements and factors. This starts with the basic ingredients of water and rice, which have huge influences on the end result. To these are added two important kinds of microorganisms: koji mold and yeast culture. In total, the sake production process involves eight steps, and a production cycle for premium sake lasts between 60 and 90 days.

When people started brewing sake, they would use the same rice they cooked with. Now, special types of sake rice are available, most of them crossbred and adapted to the climatic conditions of relevant farming regions. For sake production, part of the rice is initially enriched with koji mold spores. This mold produces an enzyme that changes the rice's starch to sugar and protein to amino acids. Later on, to prepare the starter mash, the koji rice is mixed with steamed rice (kakemai), water, and yeast.

But how much rice is required to brew sake? For premium sakes, steamed rice, koji rice, and water are mixed in a ratio of 80:20:130. Following fermentation, the mash is pressed and its liquid part (sake) is separated from the kasu (lees). How much rice used to produce 1 liter of sake depends on its quality class, its level of polishing, and the production method. The production of high-quality junmai daiginjo requires around 1 kilogram of rice per liter; for the simpler futsushu, around 300 grams per liter are used.

The quality of the water is just as important in brewing sake as the quality of the rice. Depending on its hardness and mineral con-tent, it influences the brewing pro-cess and thus also the flavor of the sake. Japanese water tends to be soft, and the most famous brewing waters have come from the regions of Nada and Fushimi (see p. 49).

The brewing yeasts that are used come from a wide range of varieties, from traditional house yeast (kuratsuki) through kyokai yeast, which was developed around the turn of the century, to newly developed flower yeasts (see p. 65).

## A Unique Fermentation System

Sake is brewed following the unique process of multiple paral-lel fermentations. Through this elaborate brewing process, sake can attain an alcohol content of up to 20 percent. Wine, in contrast, is produced through monofermen-tation, since the grapes contain sugar. In the case of sake (just like with beer), the fermentation is a little more complicated, since the grains contain starch instead of sugar.

In order to make alcohol out of a cereal, two processes are required: during the first, starch is broken up into sugar (glucose) by enzymes, and in the second, sugar is fermented using yeast to produce alcohol. With beer, this is described as multiple fermen-tation; here, the starch in the malt is broken up by saccharifica-tion enzymes (amylase) and then undergoes alcoholic fermentation. With sake, both these processes (the saccharification of the starch and the alcoholic fermentation) happen simultaneously inside a mash.

This process is the only one of its kind in the world. The main ingredient of sake, koji rice, con-tains enzymes that break up the starch in the kakemai (steamed rice) into glucose. In multiple parallel fermentation, the glucose concentration is kept lower than in other forms of fermentation, since the saccharification happens in stages and the glucose produced is gradually changed into alcohol through fermentation. This means that the yeast is under less pres-sure from concentrated sugar and allows for a higher production of alcohol.

Sake has the highest alco-hol content of all brewed (i.e. not distilled) products in the world. In most cases, the sake mash is pressed when it reaches an alcohol content of around 17 to 18 percent, so the sake does not just contain alcohol, but also has depth and a full body. —

# ELEMENTS
# OF WATER

**Japan is the land of rice,** but above all of water. All over the country, there are sources and rivers known as "beautiful waters," which are valued and protected by local inhabitants for their daily use. Water is one of the most important commodities for rice farmers, since their harvests depend on its availability. People say that water gods live in rivers, lakes, ponds, springs, and wells; to this day, corresponding divine symbols such as snakes and dragons are paid homage to, and people pray for sufficient water—but also for protection from floods.

In many parts of Europe and North America, groundwater and river water flow over time through calciferous strata, which release mineral elements and "harden" the water. In Japan, the rivers are shorter and their courses tend to be steeper, so fewer elements are dissolved into the water. For this reason, 80 percent of Japanese domestic water is "soft." According to WHO standards, water with a mineral content of over 120 mg/L is hard water; the average value in Japan is around 60 mg/L.

Japan's sake breweries were set up in places where clean water was abundant, hence the saying: "Where there is good water, there is also good sake." Sake consists of 20 percent sugar, alcohol, and amino acids and 80 percent water. The water used to brew sake ("brewing water") has a huge impact on the quality of the final product, since it contains the mineral compounds (calcium, potassium, phosphorus, and magnesium) needed for fermentation and, in addition, ensures the sake will taste good.

Brewing water is used to rinse sake rice, is usually added to rice in the main fermentation tanks, and is then added again to the sake after fermentation in order to reduce its alcohol content. For these reasons, brewing water is subject to more stringent quality standards than tap water in Japan; in particular, its iron and manganese content are strictly regulated, since they can negatively affect the quality and color of sake.

However, it is not just the hardness of the water that is important for the fermentation process in sake brewing—the balance between water's mineral elements is also crucial. A high mineral content promotes fermentation and gives the sake a stronger flavor, while a low mineral content means slow fermentation and a smoother flavor.

## Miyamizu from Nada

The water that has been used to brew sake for centuries in Nada in Kobe is Miyamizu from the Rokko mountain range, originally known as "water from Nishinomiya," then shortened to Miyamizu. This is a medium-hard water (hardness level of 100 mg/L), which does not contain much iron but is rich in the mineral compounds necessary for fermentation. Sakes made with Miyamizu water are dry with clear contours and a high levels of acidity. Due to these properties, Nada sake is also referred to as otoko (men's) sake; it was very popular during the Edo period, since, due to its high alcohol content, it did not tend to spoil even after being transported over long distances.

## Gokosui from Fushimi

The historic sake town of Fushimi in Kyoto is often compared to Nada in terms of the quality of its water. The water that is used in Fushimi to brew sake is called gokosui, and it is considered soft with a hardness level of around 40 mg/L. Its low mineral content enables a slow fermentation, which brings out a mellow, finely-tuned flavor in sake. That is why sake from Kyoto is known as onna (women's) sake.

## Hiroshima

Hiroshima is famous for its soft water, which has an even lower hardness level (10 to 40 mg/L) than that of Fushimi. In the past, water with too low of a hardness level was viewed as detrimental to the production of sake. In the Meiji era (1868–1912), Senzaburo Miura, a sake brewer from Hiroshima, discovered that the taste of sake depended on the quality of the water used to produce it. He developed a new brewing technique, known as the "soft water brewing method," which made it possible to produce high-quality sake even with soft water. Thanks to Miura's new method, Hiroshima became a sake brewing region on a par with Nada and Fushimi.

## Niigata

Most water in Niigata is considered soft with a low mineral content (10 to 50 mg/L). This is what makes the famous Niigata-style sake so light and dry. There is a lot of snowfall in the winter in Niigata, and in the mountain regions, snow stays on the ground even at the height of summer, melting into numerous rivers and rice paddies in the prefecture.

Nowadays, it is theoretically possible to create any desired flavor in sake regardless of the quality of the water used, since brewers can add minerals to the water or use filters to remove iron and other elements. Nevertheless, many breweries value the unique qualities of their region's water, viewing it as part of their identity and drawing on its best qualities when producing sake.

With urbanization leading to the loss of rice paddies and the water retention functions they perform, and with forests no longer being managed as they should be due to a lack of forestry workers, there is concern that the water used for brewing sake could decrease in both quantity and quality. This is why many breweries are striving to preserve the water quality in their regions and to defend the entire cultivated landscape of satoyama (pp. 112–121).

# Tsushima

SHICHIKEN BREWERY
HAKUSHU, YAMANASHI PREFECTURE

HAKUSHU

"Shichiken's terroir is water," says Ryogo fervently. Meanwhile, behind the toji, who looks like an ascetic monk, a waterfall is pouring out into the emerald-green Sengafuchi Gorge. Ryogo Kitahara is in charge of production at the Shichiken Sake Brewery. His older brother Tsushima, a 13th-generation kuramoto, runs the brewery, which was founded in 1750 and is located near the old Daigahara post station in the densely wooded Ojiro Valley in the Hakushu region. Ryogo is usually a calm man, but he becomes extremely passionate when talking about water.

The water from his home region of Hakushu, at the northern point of Yamanashi prefecture, through which one of the five most important trading routes of the empire passed during the Edo period, is considered to be some of the best in Japan. It springs from the mountains of the Southern Japanese Alps and flows down the Kaikomagatake Peak—a sacred mountain not far from Mount Fuji. Over the millennia, granite rocks have filtered this water, which

initially fell as snow before draining away into an underground river; it is now bottled and sold as mineral water, used to make Suntory Hakushu whisky—and, of course, to brew sake.

Ryogo Kitahara studied brewing at university in Tokyo, but he had to find his own way, as far as sake was concerned, once he returned to his family business and its rich tradition. "Right through to the time when my father was managing our brewery, we would hire toji in the winter from other regions as seasonal workers. I worked with them, and each of them had their own style of brewing—but the result was not popular with consumers. When I was named chief brewer at the age of 30 and felt even more pressure, suddenly the words *Hakushu water* came to me like a ray of light in the darkness."

Ryogo gives a discreet smile. "It's thanks to this water that our brewery still exists today and got a new lease of life. At the start, I just had the impression we were simply talking about clean water. But when, back

Kuramoto Tsushima Kitahara receives guests in the noble imperial suite of the brewery

# "

**Suddenly the words *Hakushu water* came to me like a ray of light in the darkness.**

then, as a young toji, I didn't know how to go on, one day I went to this gorge not far from our premises, to listen to the splashing of the water and to think about how I could make my sake imbibe the unique character of Hakushu water. As I reflected on this, it became clear to me that it is not the person who makes the sake, but the water."

Soon afterwards, together with his brother Tsushima, the CEO of the brewery, Ryogo created a new range of products reflecting the image of Hakushu water. This new sake was met with great approval both domestically and outside of Japan—and Ryogo soon came to be viewed as one of the most promising young sake master brewers in Japan.

Keen to take on a new challenge, he spent five years developing sparkling sake. There were already breweries in Japan producing sake by fermenting it in the bottle, like champagne, at the time. The Shichiken brewers, however, did not just want to complete their range with this new product; they intended to become absolute experts in the field, and they wanted their company to become the very best producer of sparkling sake. This was quite a challenge! The sake law does not just prohibit the addition of sugar, as is usual when making champagne. Disgorgement (the process of removing yeast sediment) also requires a high level of skill, due to the different characteristics of sake lees and wine lees. And the unique fermentation process of sake makes it challenging to achieve maturity and depth in sparkling sake. This is why the Kitahara still travel to France every year, in order to compare notes with the best champagne producers. They have also massively invested in their brewery's equipment.

The first Sparkling Dry (Yama no Kasumi) sake produced by Shichiken was slightly cloudy, like a white mist on the mountains, and was characterized by its fine perlage (formation of pearls), a refreshing,

The sugitama ball made of cedar branches is said to give the brewery divine protection.

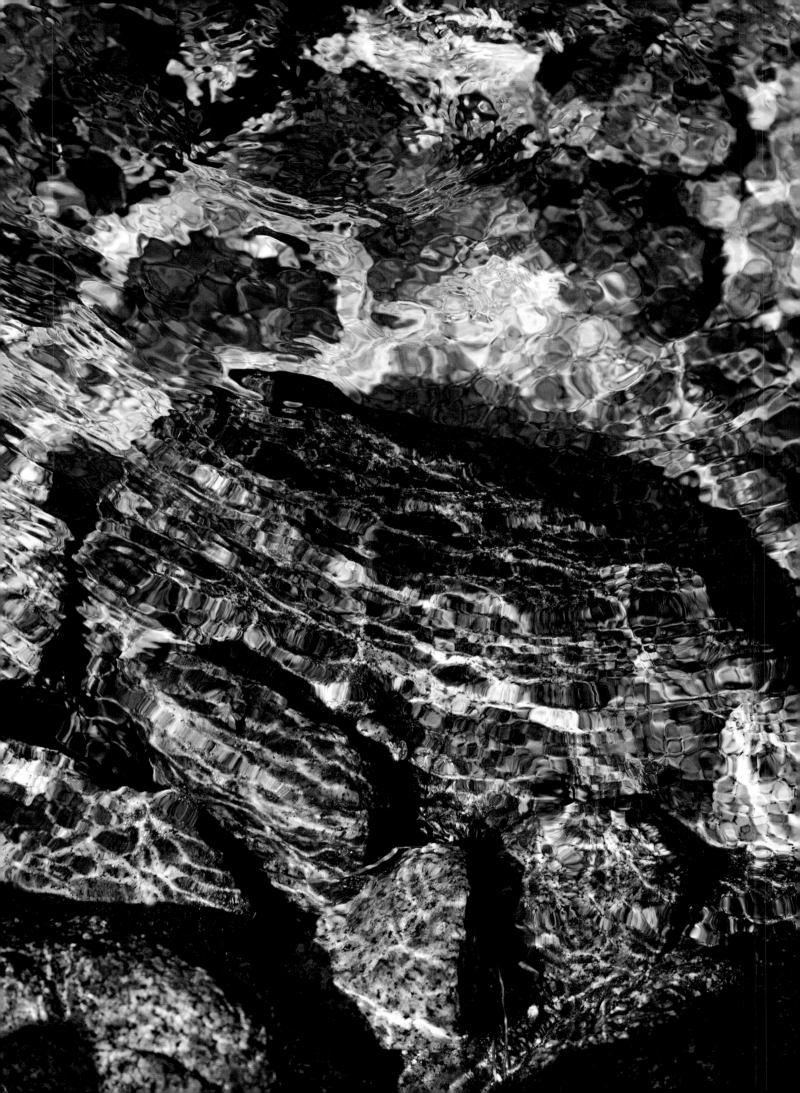

Clear and pure: Hakushu water

Sparkling sake: the fizzy fusion of water and rice

cool aroma, and subtle rice flavor. Soon followed the clear Starlight (Hoshi no Kagayaki), which is disgorged like champagne, and Hakushu (Mori no Kanade), made with sake aged in barrels previously used for Suntory Hakushu whisky. Tsushima Kitahara has taken on the strategic role of commercializing the wonderfully sparkling Shichiken sake; he markets his brother's pride and joy and has initiated cooperations with Michelin-star chef Alain Ducasse and the Ritz Carlton in Kyoto.

The Kitahara brothers have more than just the courage to start a new chapter in the long history of Shichiken sake. They also have—and this is something that up to now has remained rare in Japan—a good instinct for luxury and exclusivity, as well as for international tastes.

Their family were already some of the most prominent inhabitants of Daigahara back in the Edo Period. In fact, in 1880, the family had the honor of hosting Emperor Tenno Meiji for a night. The preparations for this occasion lasted almost a year. "For a long time after the visit, the room our August guest had slept in was no longer entered by anybody, not even by members of our family," says Tsushima. "As children we didn't even know what was in there, and we were even a bit afraid of it." The imperial lodging has however now been opened up and turned into a small museum.

Opening up is an important concept generally for the Kitahara brothers. They take a modern approach to their craftsmanship, occasionally inviting guests to experience the Shichiken production processes close up. "There's a nice story connected to the name of our brand, by the way," Tsushima says, smiling, before we start to taste a Shichiken sparkling sake. "It goes back

to the precious ranma in this room." The family was given these exquisitely carved skylights to mark the completion of the new brewery building around 200 years ago, by the then feudal lord Takato. They recall the legend of Chikurin no Shichiken (the seven sages of the bamboo grove).

It's just the two of us in the old imperial suite when Tsushima opens a bottle of Expression 2020, a flavorful Kijoshu sparkling sake, brewed in 2020 using a 40-year-old daiginjo sake instead of water, fermented for a second time. The kuramoto pours out the effervescent, light gold, shining liquid into my champagne glass with something approaching devotion, kneeling upright at a splendid wooden table as he does so. His fluid movements remind me of those one can observe at a Japanese tea ceremony.

"*Dozo*, here you go!" Tsushima gently places the glass before me. Five bubbles enchant my eye. A light fragrance of melons and white flowers rises into my nose, mixing with mineral, earthy undertones. The Expression 2020 has no champagne-like acidity, but the complexity of its multilayered sweetness and umami create a nuanced aftertaste. The refined, flowery aromas unfold discreetly, and its creamy texture is loosened up by the fine bubbles, each one a reflection of the past 40 years.

My thoughts keep going further back into the past: What kind of sake did Emperor Meiji drink with the Kitahara family back then? He would certainly have been regaled with the highest level of hospitality that could be offered at the time, and would have enjoyed the absolute best the Shichiken Brewery could offer. But could he have imagined that, almost 150 years later, such a fine, lightly sparkling sake would be offered in his little "travel palace" in Daigahara? —

# A YEAR IN THE RICE PADDY

**Rice is an annual plant.** It grows to a size of between 80 and 120 centimeters (31 and 47 inches), and its stalk bears 10 to 20 panicles, each of which can contain up to 300 grains of rice. One single grain of rice, in turn, consists of a hull, germ, silver skin, and endosperm. The latter contains most of the starch in the rice, as well as protein and fat, and the grain is easy for the human body to digest. Plus, it is also a valuable source of energy and important mineral nutrients, such as potassium and phosphorus.

In rainy Japan, rice is farmed using the technique of wet rice cultivation (paddies). Currently, a surface of 1 hectare (2.5 acres) yields around 5,300 kilograms (11,700 pounds) of table rice; in the case of sake rice, such as yamada nishiki, the yield tends to be around 4,000 to 4,500 kilograms per hectare (8,800 to 9,900 pounds per 2.5 acres). The period from sowing to harvest usually lasts around 150 days. Depending on the type of rice and the climate conditions of particular regions, however, there are some variations in corresponding planting and harvest seasons. Traditionally in Japan, rice seeds were taken from the previous year's harvest to be planted for the next one. Today, however, rice farmers buy seeds, and the seedlings are grown by regional cooperatives.

## Preparation of the Paddy Fields (February to April)
The paddy fields are around 30 to 50 centimeters (12 to 20 inches) below street level, and each field is connected to its neighboring ones through levees. So-called "aze paths" serve as separations between fields. To prepare for rice planting, the paddies are plowed and leveled, the heights of the levees are adjusted, and the water is channeled into the paddies.

## From Rice Seed to Seedling (April/May)
Once the fields are prepared, rice seeds are sprouted indoors at nearby nurseries. The rice seeds are soaked in cold water for around two weeks. A germ roughly one millimeter long sprouts out of the grain of rice. The rice seeds are spread out over a layer of soil in a special growing box, then covered with a second, thinner layer of soil; the boxes are placed in a

greenhouse. Over the course of two weeks, the seedlings grow to around 15 to 20 centimeters (6 to 8 inches) tall and are then ready to be planted in the paddy fields.

## Transplanting the Seedlings (May/June)
Until the 1960s, seedlings were transplanted by hand, often by members of the local village. Now, this is a mechanical process. The height of the water level in the paddies is around 10 centimeters (4 inches), so only the tips of the small plants protrude above its surface. Transplanting allows farmers to keep the gaps between the plants regular. The period between transplantation and harvest lasts around 120 days; the exact duration depends on the type of rice. Rice farmers thus calculate backwards from the desired harvest date in order to define when they will carry out the transplantation.

## Growth of the Rice Plant and Water Management (June to September)
During the growing period, water is occasionally drained from the paddies so the rice plants' roots will grow deep into the soil, resulting in stronger stems. After this drying period, the paddies are flooded again.

## Appearance of Rice Ears and Flowers (August/September)
Around two and a half months after planting, the ears, which have been growing inside the stems of the rice plants, slowly start to appear, producing small flowers that only open for around two hours total. As soon as pollination is complete, these flowers close again.

## From Flower to Rice Hull
The pollinated rice flowers need around one and a half months to transform into rice. The rice grains are covered with rice hulls, which store nutrients that help the rice ripen.

## Harvest and Threshing (September/October)
When the ears at the top of the rice plants attain a golden glow and start to give under the weight of the ripened grains, the time has come to harvest the crop. Rice used to be harvested by hand, but today it is harvested mechanically. During threshing, the rice is separated from its stems and leaves so usually only the rice hulls and their grains of rice are left.

## Drying
Freshly harvested rice has a high moisture content (around 25 percent), and storing it in this condition makes it susceptible to rot and mold. That is why, whenever possible, the rice is slowly dried to at least 15 percent moisture within the 24 hours following its harvest. There are two ways of drying rice: the mechanical method (using warm air) and the traditional hazekake (also known as inagikake) method. In the latter drying process, whole rice ears are hung upside down in bunches for around two weeks on haze (upright wooden bars or aluminum tubes set up around the edges of the paddies). An additional benefit of hanging the rice to dry is that it increases the levels of amino acids in the plants and allows nutrients in the stems to enrich the grains of rice.

## Hulling
Once the outer hulls of the dried rice grains are removed, one is

left with amber-colored genmai (brown rice). This hulling of the rice is known as momisuri.

## Atmospheric Exposure

Rice plants are extremely sensitive; a period of overly hot weather can do them considerable damage. If the temperature rises to above 35°C (95°F) during the day and remains at 30°C (86°F) at night, the plants experience heat stress. This means that the plants are losing more water through evaporation and transpiration than they can absorb, leading to wilting and even arresting growth. High temperatures at night increase the rice plants' respiration activity; the starch produced during the day is used up through this respiration, so less of it reaches the ears, leading to lower degrees of maturity and the appearance of milky white, unripe grains. The rice then stays very hard and is difficult to break up, and the sake brewing process has to be adapted accordingly.

# VARIETIES OF RICE

**There are over 100,000 different varieties of rice grown all over the world, most of which are used as foodstuffs (a.k.a. table rice).**

Though sake can be made with any type of table rice, the highest quality brews require very specific varieties. Of the roughly 500 round-grain rice varieties cultivated in Japan, there are currently 125 that are categorized as sake rice varieties (sakamai) because they have qualities that make them particularly well-suited to fermentation and the production of koji (pp. 62–63)—processes which in turn influence the flavor profiles of the sakes they produce.

## Key characteristics of sakamai:

— Large grains (around 25 percent larger than table rice), which do not break during polishing

— Has a white starch core (shinpaku) with a loose, highly porous structure, easy for koji mold to penetrate

— Contains small amounts of protein and fat (both of which have negative effects on the aromas and flavors of the sake)

Rice is divided into different classes in Japan. These classifications are mainly based on the appearance of the rice and are determined by boards of control that are registered with the Ministry of Agriculture, Forestry, and Fisheries. The quality class of a rice crop has an influence on its purchase price.

Sake rice is divided into six quality classes in accordance with regulations governing agricultural standards, as well as the regular size and integrity of the grains. The quality class of sake rice has an impact on the sake that is brewed from it. In order to produce premium sake, brewers can only use sake rice that is classified as third class or higher: tokujo (extra fine), tokuto (fine), itto (1st class), nito (2nd class) and santo (3rd class). The class and information about the origins of any batch of rice are provided on every single sack of grains.

Developing a new variety of rice takes a lot of time. Many prefectures support research, hybridization, and test cultivation in order to better adapt the rice to the local climate. The most successful of these prefectures is

Hyogo, where the most popular sake rice variety, yamada nishiki, was developed through hybridization. However, there are also a few native varieties, such as omachi, kameno-o, and shinriki, whose best grains are selected during the harvest and used as sake rice. Though sake rice can be grown in many different regions of Japan, certain areas and specific farmers are known for producing exceptional harvests. Yamada nishiki rice, for example, is grown in over 30 prefectures, but the best of this variety comes from the Special A district in Hyogo.

In warm regions, such as Hyogo and Okayama on the Seto Inland Sea, rice is planted and harvested relatively late in the year. Typical late harvest varieties (which are planted in June and harvested in October) are yamada nishiki and omachi. Gohyakumangoku from Niigata Prefecture is a well-known early harvest variety of sake rice (planted in May, harvested in September).

In the year 2020, 85,179 tons of sake rice were produced in Japan, most of which was yamada nishiki (33 percent), followed by gohyakumangoku (20 percent). The miyama nishiki variety made up around 7 percent of this total amount, and the remaining 40 percent were varieties of rice that are mainly only cultivated in one single prefecture.

# FAMOUS VARIETIES OF RICE

## Yamada Nishiki

This type of rice, which was registered in 1936 in Hyogo Prefecture, is viewed as the queen of sake rice varieties. It is a hybrid of yamadabo (its pod parent) and tankan wataribune (its pollen parent, and a genetically selected sub-variety of omachi). Yamada nishiki has a large grain, and its shinpaku (starchy core) does not easily break, even when the rice is heavily polished. For a long time, people used to say that you could not win a gold medal at the Annual Japan Sake Awards without yamada nishiki.

Yamada nishiki has the longest history of all hybrid varieties of sake rice, so there is also the largest wealth of experience in how to handle it; it is very popular with toji (master brewers) because it easily produces good quality koji. The main regions in which it is cultivated include Okayama, Yamaguchi, and Fukuoka, as well as Hyogo Prefecture. Sake made with yamada nishiki rice has a deep, rich, full-bodied flavor.

## Gohyakumangoku

This type of rice was developed at the Niigata Agricultural Research Institute and given its name in 1957. It is a hybrid of kikusui (pod parent) and shin no. 200 (pollen parent). Compared to yamada nishiki, this early harvest variety has smaller grains of rice and is not appropriate for heavy polishing, but it is easier to make koji out of it. The rice is a little hard and somewhat difficult to break up. It is mainly cultivated in the Hokuriku Region of Niigata, Toyama, Fukui, and Ishikawa, as well as in 20 prefectures in colder regions. Gohyakumangoku provides the basis for a light, fresh, and clear sake.

## Miyama Nishiki

This is a mutated early harvest variety, which was bred in 1978 in a Nagano Prefecture agricultural laboratory using gamma irradiation of the seeds of takane nishiki sake rice. It is distinguished by its large, round grain and large shinpaku (starchy core). Miyama nishiki is mainly cultivated in cold regions such as Nagano, Akita, Yamagata, Fukushima, and Miyagi. Its grain is hard; it does not easily break up during brewing, and as a result, it usually produces a sake with a pure, light flavor and kire (aftertaste).

## Omachi

Japan's oldest sake rice is a natural variety that was discovered 160 years ago. The plant is so tall (at least 160 centimeters/63 inches) that it falls over easily, and it is also sensitive to the weather and not very resistant to pests. Plus, the grains break easily during processing. These issues account for the fact that, by the 1970s, omachi rice had almost disappeared completely. A kuramoto resurrected the variety around that time in Okayama, and this is where most of it is produced today. Sake made from omachi is defined by a full, round body with lots of umami and earthy notes, a strong acidity and a good kire, and optimal aging qualities.

## Dewa San San

The first variety of sake rice, developed in Yamagata Prefecture as a crossbreed of miyama nishiki and hanafubuki plants. It is exclusively produced in Yamagata and has been the most frequently produced rice in the prefecture since 2020. It is distinguished by its large grains and very pronounced shinpaku (starchy core), which accounts for 85 percent of the grain. In addition, the plant is resistant to the cold and does not fall over very easily. The sake made with this variety of rice has a pure, light, and refreshing flavor with herbal notes. —

# THE SECRET OF KOJI

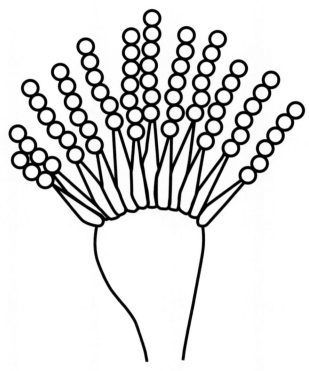

**The microorganism koji** (Aspergillus oryzae) is the most important mold culture in Japan; it is essential not just in the production of sake, but also for producing traditional condiments such as soy sauce and miso. As early as the Muromachi period (1336–1573), a privileged organization known as the Koji Guild was founded, and it is assumed that Kyoto housed numerous koji spore producers from then on. Koji was selected over several thousand years, is safe to eat, is a genuine treasure trove of enzymes—and is the key to umami flavor.

In order to produce alcohol from rice, the glucose chain in the rice starch must be split and turned into pure glucose. Koji does this, thanks to its ability to produce saccharification enzymes (amylase)—thus creating the basis for sake production (pp. 66–81). Koji also plays an important role in the development of the flavor of a sake, since this "national mold," as dubbed by the Brewing Society of Japan, produces proteolytic enzymes (protease) and is responsible for the transformation of rice proteins into amino acids. The latter are what gives sake a full body and umami taste.

## The Type of Koji Determines the Style of Sake

The temperature and atmospheric moisture in the koji room vary depending on the type of koji that needs to be created. Normal sake (such as futsushu or honjozo) and common junmai sake are produced using sohaze koji, in which the mycelium covers the entire surface of the rice and penetrates deep inside it. Sohaze koji has a lot of enzymatic power and can give the rice a sweet, umami-filled flavor. Because the rice in mash that has been produced using sohaze koji is saccharified immediately, its fermentation is intense and fast, producing a strong, acidic, flavorful sake.

In contrast, elegant, aromatic ginjo sake is made with the type of koji known as tsukihaze. In this type, the mycelium only covers

part of the surface of the rice, but it penetrates deeper inside the grain than sohaze. Its enzyme concentration is lower than that of sohaze, and the enzymes only slowly dissolve in the mash. For this reason, fermentation is slow and gentle.

In order to produce tsukihaze koji, the temperature is controlled in such a way that it rises rapidly from 30°C to 43°C (86°F to 109°F) during the last 24 of the 48 hours required to produce koji, so less proteolytic enzymes and more amylolytic enzymes are produced. In addition, creating furrows in the surface of the koji increases said surface, thus promoting the evaporation of the koji's moisture. Because molds tend to grow toward a high degree of moisture, these measures encourage the mycelium to move toward the inside of the moist koji and not toward the surface of the rice. If the mycelium penetrates deep inside the grain, the enzyme concentration is lower and enzymes will dissolve more slowly in the mash, resulting in slower fermentation and eventually in the desired flavor of ginjo sake.

## Three Kinds of Koji Spores and their Producers

There are three main types of koji that are used to brew sake: yellow, black, and white. The most commonly used is yellow koji, but more recently, brewers have also started to use the black and white types when making sake.

There are only four companies in Japan that produce koji spores

for sake. One of them is Hishiroku in Kyoto, which can look back at a history lasting over 300 years. Its young director, Akihiko Sukeno, explains: "We spore producers have a different production method than sake brewers. Our aim is to obtain as many healthy spores as possible. So we create a warm and moist environment, which koji mold likes, but we need 125 hours, so two and a half times the time the breweries take, to produce koji rice."

In the past, koji spores were passed down from one generation to the next; with the development of microbiology around 150 years ago, however, it became possible to isolate the best spores using a microscope.

"Since there is a risk of mutation during the propagation of the spores, we preserve the best lines and monitor them to ensure that they always meet a specific level of quality and have certain characteristics," Akihiko continues: "We have 20 koji products for sake and around 30 for miso and soy sauce. Recently, more and more sake breweries have been using white and black koji to get more fresh citric acid in their sake. Do you know why these types of koji produce acid? Black koji comes from subtropical Okinawa. The mash is protected from contamination in this warm environment by the acid from the koji. So, the koji mold adapted itself to the local climate by mutating. White koji, which is easier to process, is a mutation of black koji." —

# THE POWER
# OF YEAST

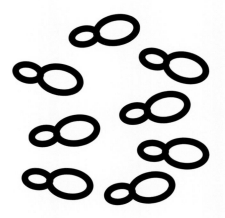

Yeast is a microorganism that is widespread in nature; it grows particularly well on flowers and fruit. Thanks to its ability to change sugar into alcohol, it is an important part of the fermentation process, which is involved in the production of many foodstuffs, from bread and soy sauce to drinks such as wine, beer, and sake.

The alcoholic fermentation of sake is carried out using a unique strain of Saccharomyces cerevisiae, the same type of yeast used for wine and beer, although sake yeast begins fermenting at temperatures between 5° and 10°C (41° and 50°F) and can also actively produce alcohol up to a concentration of 20 percent. Sake yeast has a higher tolerance to alcohol than wine yeasts. It is only when this tolerance is exceeded that the complex system of autolysis begins and the yeast disintegrates. In so doing, it produces unpleasant smells (including the smell of sulfur). For this reason, the mash must be pressed out at this stage in order to separate the yeast from the sake and stop fermentation.

During the fermentation process, yeast also produces various aromas and acids, a combination that influences the flavor of the sake. This is why people sometimes say that yeast has a bigger influence on the flavor of a sake than rice does.

The main components of the aromas that are created by the yeast, above all during the production of ginjo sake, are ethyl caproate, which has a similar smell to apples and pineapples, and isoamyl acetate, which is reminiscent of bananas. The two most frequently produced acids are malic acid and succinic acid. The former gives the drink a refreshing sour taste; it thus perfectly balances out a sweet sake. Succinic acid has more umami than sourness. Traditional sake with a high level of succinic acid thus has a lot of umami, but it can also be perceived as bitter or astringent.

Sake yeasts can roughly be divided into two types: purely cultured ones, such as kyokai yeast, and natural ones, such as kura tsuki yeast. Most breweries use kyokai yeast because it has a stable fermentative power and a characteristic aroma. It is distributed by the Brewing Society of Japan (Nihon Jozo Kyokai).

Kura tsuki yeast, in contrast, lives and grows without human intervention in every brewery. It proliferates there on walls, floors, and barrels, which is why it is also known as "cellar yeast" or "house yeast." It activates late and works unreliably, and, in addition, it is difficult to obtain a stable flavor when using it because it acts spontaneously.

Sake was originally produced using only kura-tsuki yeast. Then, as early as the nineteenth century, the Japanese state started to look for alternatives in the hopes of finding something that would guarantee certain fermentation—and therefore regular tax revenue from sake production. In 1904, the newly formed National Research Institute of Brewing managed to isolate sake yeast from mash collected from all over the country and distribute this to the sake breweries. This essentially marked the start of the age of kyokai yeast.

## Notable Kyokai Yeasts

Kyokai No. 6 was isolated in 1935 from the mash produced by the Aramasa Brewery in Akita. It is characterized by a strong fermentative power and mild, clear aroma.

Kyokai No. 7 was isolated in 1946 from mash produced by the Miyasaka Brewery in Nagano and is characterized by a fine aroma and strong fermentative power. This yeast is used as an industry standard for futsushu, honjozo, and junmai sake. Kyokai No. 9 was isolated in 1953 from mash produced by Kohro Sake Brewing Laboratory in Kumamoto. It is known as the standard yeast for producing ginjo sake, since it is well-suited to slow fermentation at low temperatures. Many gold medal sakes at the Annual Japan Sake Awards used to owe their success to this yeast.

Kyokai No. 1801 was developed by the Brewing Society of Japan by crossing Kyokai No. 1601 and No. 9. It is highly aromatic and is frequently used to produce award-winning sakes.

## Yeast Variants

In addition to the Brewing Society of Japan, every prefecture in Japan has set up research institutes that develop, culture, and market their own strains of yeast. Meanwhile, the Tokyo University of Agriculture has developed the relatively new flower yeast.

Isolated from ten different flowers, among others from Nadeshiko carnations, marigolds, and abelia, this yeast was bred specially for the fermentation of sake. The properties of flower yeasts vary, but many of them produce a spectacular aroma. Flower yeast AK-1 from Akita Prefecture, which was registered as early as 1991, was so successful at the Annual Japan Sake Awards that it was registered as Kyokai No. 1501 by the Brewing Society of Japan. Other varieties include cherry blossom yeast from Himeji Castle in Hyogo and peony yeast from Shimane.

Sake can also be produced using wine yeast. However, though it does produce more malic and acetic acids, this type of yeast produces fewer amino acids and succinic acid than sake yeast. Sake made using wine yeast thus often has a similar acidity and aftertaste to wine itself. —

# How is Sake Made?

*Sakaya banryu*—ten thousand sake makers, ten thousand methods—is the Japanese answer. Whether we are talking about wine made from grapes or its rice-based brother, many roads lead to the end product, but the basic production steps are almost always the same.

Several crucial factors have influenced the production of sake since ancient times. A key element is the choice of basic ingredients: water, rice, and yeast. Then comes their processing: polishing and steaming the rice, producing the koji, creating the starter mash and the main mash. Once fermentation is complete, the rice mash is pressed and pasteurized twice: once at the start of the aging period, then again before being bottled.

So far, so good. But how can you be better than good? How can you turn a simple product into a premium one? How do the location of the brewery, the philosophy of its owner, and the tastes and technical skills of its master brewer influence the character of a sake? What role is played by the production process itself?

Traditionally, sake is only brewed in the winter; industrial plants produce it all year round. Small, traditional breweries only produce 10 batches per season, whereas larger ones can produce about 100. A production cycle for premium sake lasts between 60 and 90 days. Sake brewing is a labor-intensive activity. Large-scale industrial producers automated many steps of the process early on. Smaller, quality-oriented producers, however, continue to use manual methods, since this allows them to have more control over each step in the production process. Here are the basic steps of sake production:

## Polishing the Rice

In order to produce fine, premium sake, the rice must be polished. The external layer of the rice grain contains a lot of protein and fat, which would have detrimental effects on the taste and color of the sake. In addition, the starch inside the grain is important for the rice's required fermentation process. During polishing (seimai), the external layer around this grain is removed to different degrees. The more of it is polished off—the lower the polishing ratio—the more refined, aromatic, and sumptuous the sake will be. The polishing ratio refers to how much of the original volume remains after polishing. For example,

Highly polished rice: the smaller the grains, the finer the sake.

Washing the rice requires large quantities of water.

Magic powder: rice sprinkled with koji spores

a polishing ratio of 70 percent means that 30 percent of the grain has been polished off. Polishing is very time-consuming: a polishing ratio of 50 percent, for daiginjo-quality sake, requires around 50 hours of work, and it takes another day to achieve a polishing ratio of 35 percent. The rice polisher is a computer-controlled centrifuge, inside of which a ceramic stone turning at between 600 and 800 rotations a minute sands down the rice. A medium-size machine can process forty 30-kilogram (88-pound) sacks of rice in one go. Since this process heats up and thus dries out the grains, the rice is usually left to cool down and absorb a little air moisture for around a month after polishing.

## Preparing the Rice

Highly polished rice is extremely delicate, so each further requisite preparation of the polished grains—washing, soaking, steaming, cooling, etc.—requires great care and must follow a strictly controlled schedule. Almost every production hall in a sake brewery has a planning schedule hung up somewhere visible, meticulously detailing the production steps for the day and for the whole week.

After the rice is polished and left to cool, it is divided into batches of between 10 and 15 kilograms (22 and 33 pounds), which are washed in baskets or metal tubs. In order to enable optimal water absorption (around 30 percent of its own weight) for its impending steaming, the rice's soaking time is calculated to the second using a stopwatch.

Once the rice has reached the desired humidity and consistency, it is drained through a mesh cloth, then steamed the next morning. Steaming used to be done in wooden barrels, but now most breweries use large metal tubs called koshiki for this step in the sake-making process. The koshiki is connected to a large steamer, filled with the soaked rice, and covered with a cloth tied tight to the tub with a rope. After about an hour of steaming, the rice grains are soft on the inside but still hard on the outside. The master brewer tests the result by kneading the rice on a board. Rice that has been steamed for too long is too soft; it would disintegrate too fast during fermentation. This would lead to the sake being too acidic and containing undesired components—and thus losing its flavor.

After steaming, the rice is spread out on a piece of white cloth and quickly cooled down to 30°C (86°F) in the unheated production hall.

## Manufacturing Koji Rice

There is no sake without koji. It takes 48 hours to produce, then must sit for 24 hours. In order to manufacture koji rice, steamed and cooled rice is brought into a wood-paneled, dry koji chamber, which is tempered at 30°C (86°F). Next, powdered koji mold spores are scattered over the rice using silk bags. Koji mold produces an important enzyme that transforms the starch in the rice into glucose (sugar) and the protein into amino acids, which are responsible for the umami flavor in sake and other fermented food products.

In order to achieve optimal growth of the mold spores, it is very important to constantly control the temperature and humidity. About 24 hours after the koji mold is sprinkled over the rice, the rice is placed in small crates. During the last 12 hours of the koji fermentation process, the rice is aired out and/or turned every few hours in order to guarantee the desired enzyme structure. The attention and care

The koji rice is cared for round the clock at the brewery.

Sensory properties are key when producing koji.

directed at the fermenting grains is comparable to that of young parents for their newborns: many sake brewers stay close to the koji chamber during the final phase of koji production so they can keep a close eye on their "babies."

The inoculated rice is then taken out of this chamber and brought to a cool drying room, where, spread out onto round pieces of cloth, it will rest for another day to release any excess humidity. Finished koji rice usually smells like roasted chestnuts and tastes sweet.

## Creating the Starter Mash

In order to make the starter mash (moto), koji rice, steamed rice (kakemai—"rice for mixing, rice for pouring"), water, and yeast are mixed together in a small tank in a cool chamber. This enables the healthy yeast culture to best proliferate. In order to protect the mash from being attacked by bacteria, lactic acid is usually added at the start of this process, if using the sokujo method. Controlling the temperature and regularly stirring the mash allows the yeast population to grow within 14 days to a concentration of 200 million cells per milliliter. This process takes around 30 days when using the traditional kimoto method and twice as long when using the sokujo method, which requires a particularly strong yeast culture.

To start the mash, rice, koji rice, and water are mixed in several flat tubs (hangiri oke) in a cool environment. The ingredients are then pounded and ground with wooden rods to stimulate the koji enzymes, which convert the rice starch into sugar. This process (yamaoroshi) is repeated several times a day. In the past, the duration of the grinding was measured using a grinding song. The early stages of the time-consuming yamaoroshi process already see

the proliferation of nitrate-reducing bacteria, followed by highly productive lactobacilli. These kill off most of the harmful bacteria and then disintegrate, so ultimately only the pure yeast is cultured.

A simplified version of the kimoto method, which leaves out the pounding step, is known as the yamahai method. Before cultured yeast was widely used in the production of sake, spontaneous fermentation was the only method available. Kimoto and yamahai sake are distinguished by their general acidity, high levels of umami, and strong, highly-nuanced flavors.

## Creating the Main Fermentation Mash

The main fermentation mash (moromi) is made out of two parts koji rice, eight parts steamed rice, and thirteen parts water. It is created in three stages: On the first day, the starter mash (around 5 to 8 percent of total ingredients), koji rice, rice, and water are mixed together in a large tank (hatsu-zoe). On the second day, the mix is left to rest so the yeast has time to rest (odori). On the third day, double the amount of koji rice, rice and water is added (naka-zoe), and this amount is doubled again for an addition on the fourth day (tome-zoe). Adding these ingredients in several stages avoids putting excessive pressure on the yeast (sandan shikomi).

The fermentation (moromi) days are counted from the day of the last step (tome-zoe); on the third moromi day, a look at the mash will clearly reveal any grains of rice that have not yet disintegrated. In the first one or two days, one can only see how the rice is absorbing water, but in the lower part of the tank, the saccharification enzymes in the koji are slowly beginning to act: The starch in the rice is being transformed into glucose, and the mix becomes increasingly sweet. Thanks to this increase in the sugar content, the yeasts, too, are able to prolifer-

For daiginjo quality sake, the mash is fermented at an extremely low temperature.

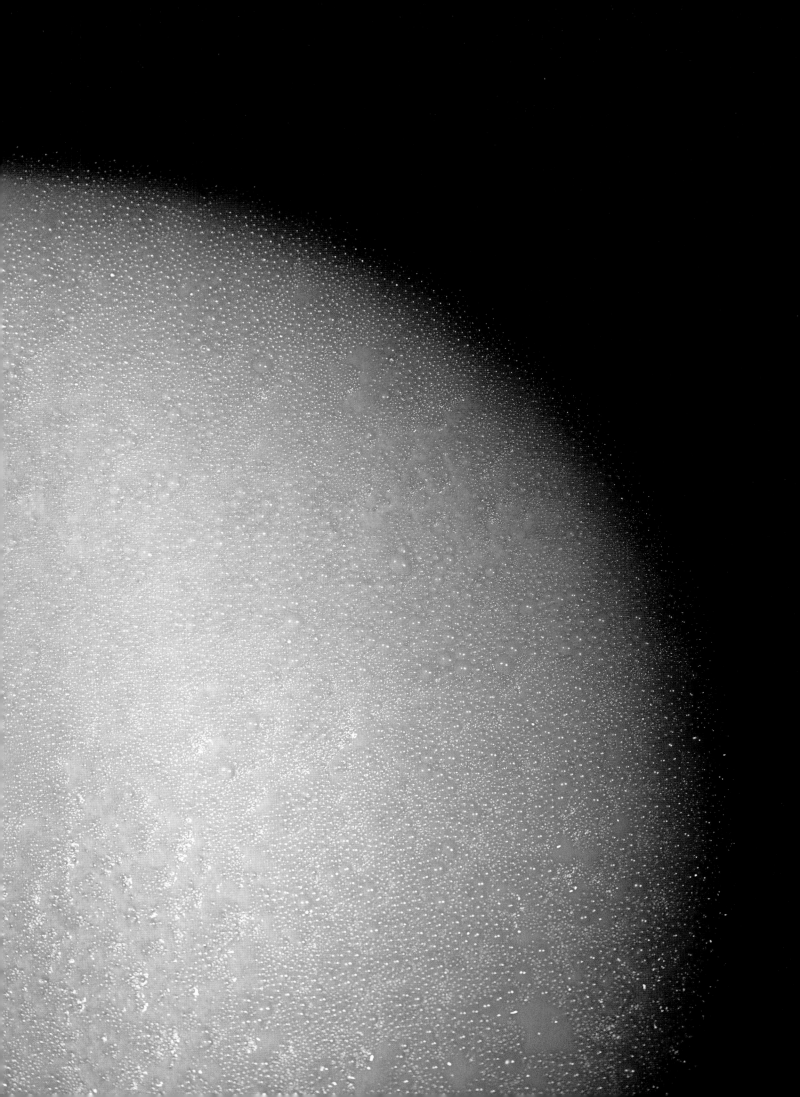

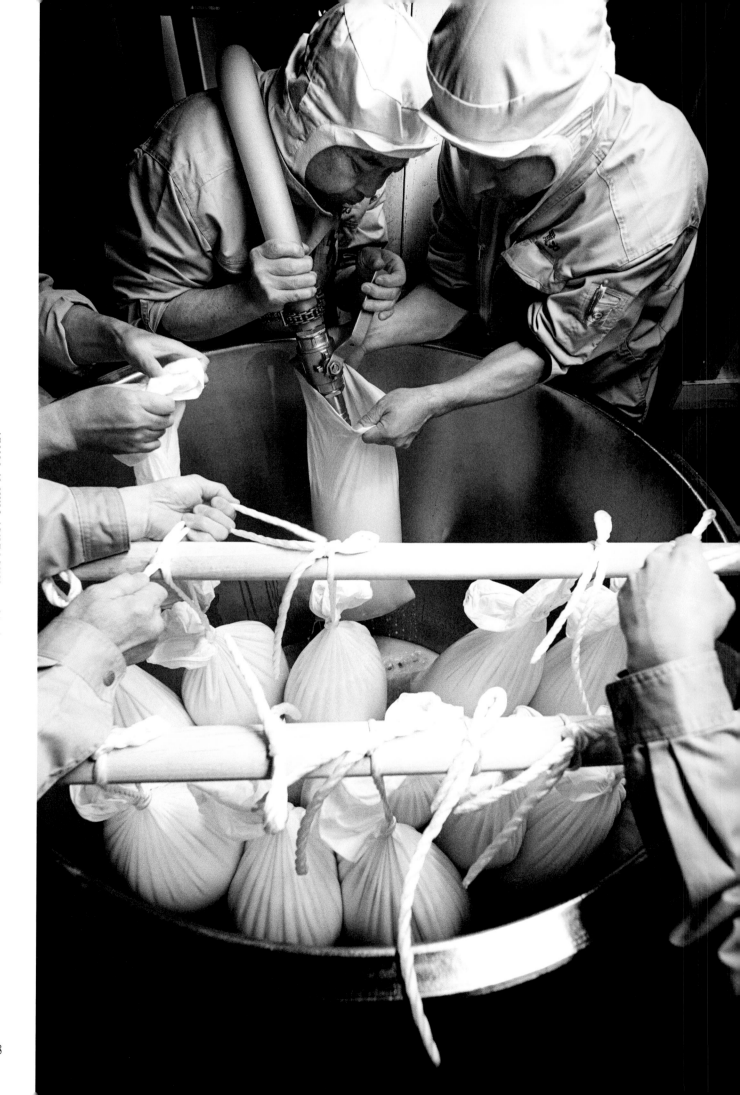

Fukuro-tsuri: getting the best drops out of the mash.

ate and fermentation starts. The proliferation of the yeast causes the formation of bubbles, which reaches its highest point after around 10 days, and the fruity aromas produced by the yeast grow increasingly present. The bubbles then become smaller and finer and fermentation continues gently.

Careful control of the fermentation temperature, which ranges between 5° and 10°C (41° and 50°F) for daiginjo-quality sake allows for the best possible development of the aromas in the finished beverage. The figures for the mash are measured daily, and any required measures are then taken. The progress of the temperature, the alcohol content, and other parameters are saved on a computer and analyzed. In addition to this ongoing analysis, the mash repeatedly undergoes sensory evaluation. Depending on how the temperature is regulated, fermentation lasts between 20 and 40 days. When the toji determines it is time to start pressing the mash, the temperature of the tank is lowered in order to stop fermentation.

## Pressing the Mash

After fermentation is complete, the mash is pressed to separate the sake from its solid residue (kasu). Without this process, the result cannot be classified as sake. In Japanese, the pressing process is known as kosu (straining) or shiboru (pressing). Brewing alcohol is added shortly before pressing (unless junmai types of sake are being produced). This enables the brewer to draw even more aromas out of the mash and also obtain a lighter and drier flavor. There are various methods for pressing the mash. In the tradi-

tional funa shibori process for producing premium sake, the mash is scooped into small bags. These are then carefully stacked inside what is known as a fune press and pressed overnight.

Fukuro tsuri or fukuro shibori is the exclusive pressing method used for the highest-grade sake. Just like with funa shibori, the mash is put in small bags. However, instead of being stacked, the bags are then hung loosely in the tank in order to release the aromatic drops without any pressing power.

In addition, there are now modern pressing machines (assaku ki), often referred to as yabuta after one of their manufacturers. These work using the same principle as a concertina.

After 60 to 90 days, the sake (genshu), the essence of rice, is born! The remaining lees are used to produce kasu shochu (shochu literally means "burned liquor") or sold as a nutritious foodstuff to make pickles or soup.

## Finishing: Microfiltering, Pasteurizing, and Bottling the Sake

After pressing, the sake is sedimented and filtered. Thanks to this, it becomes a clear liquid. Sedimentation refers to the settling of solid matter in a liquid and the subsequent separation of the two (similar to the process of decanting wine). There are also types of sake produced without sedimentation (ori-garami) and without activated charcoal filtration (muroka). In order to remove any microorganisms remaining after sedimentation and filtration, sake is usually pasteurized twice—once after pressing and a sec-

Pasteurization allows sake to keep without any addition of sulfur.

ond time during bottling—at temperatures between 60° and 65°C/140° and 149°F. This allows brewers to ensure their sake is microbiologically stable and fit for storage without them needing to add in any sulfur. Pasteurization methods have hugely evolved in recent years. A one-off bin hiire (pasteurization in the bottle) and immediate cooling is an effective solution. Other options are bain-maries and expensive pasteurizing machines; plate heat exchangers are also popular. In order to produce the desired alcohol content in undiluted sake (genshu), a certain amount of water is usually added during the pasteurization/bottling process. There are also some types of sake that are unpasteurized (nama) or only pasteurized once. These have a fresh flavor.

## Letting the Sake Age

Freshly-pressed sake has a raw flavor. This is why it is usually left to age for 6 to 12 months in a steel tank between two pasteurization processes. This period of aging makes it smoother, and various elements of its aroma and flavor become more harmonious.

However, in recent years, freshness and sparkle have become more desirable than smoothness among Japanese sake consumers, so many types of nama (unpasteurized) sakes are now brought to market right after being pressed or shortly after pasteurization. The type and duration of the aging process determine the flavor of the finished beverage. Some breweries leave their best daiginjo sakes in cool conditions for one to two years, allowing the aromas to develop to their full complexity; typical tobin demijohns for high-quality sake are stored at temperatures below zero for months or years. For koshu (aged sake), the entire production process, right through to aging, is meticulously controlled, meaning that not a single step is left to chance.

## There are two types of aged sake:
### Nojuku (dark and strong)

This sweet, umami-forward junmai sake is produced using rice with a high (70 percent) polishing ratio, brewed following the kimoto/yamahai method, and aged at room temperature. Thanks to its high protein content and residual sugar, the Maillard reaction (a chemical reaction between amino acids and sugars which leads to the liquid becoming darker) is quick to start. This type of sake changes in color from golden yellow to copper, then dark brown as it ages. It also develops aromas of caramel, honey, nuts, and winter spices.

### Tanjuku (light gold and light)

This junmai daiginjo or daiginjo sake is made with highly-polished rice and aged at low temperatures. It is characterized by its silky texture and highly harmonious flavors. However, after five years of aging, the fruity aromas it has at the start are no longer present. —

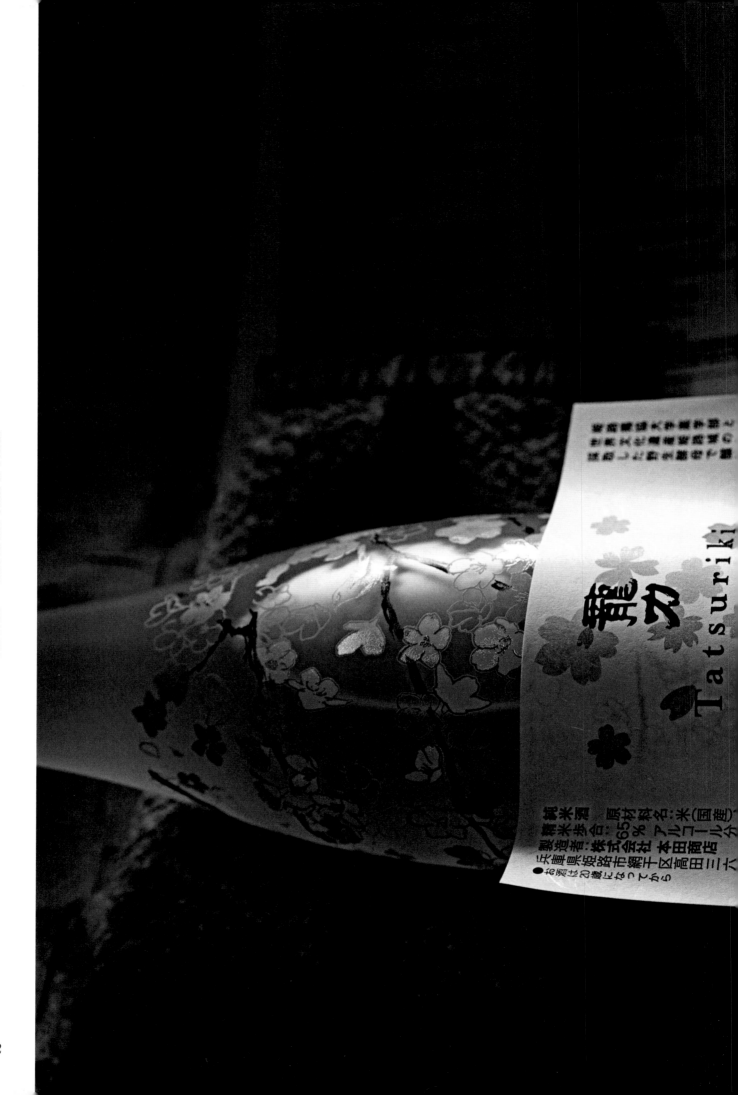

龍力
Tatsuriki

●兵庫製造者：株式会社本田商店
お県姫路市網干区高田商店三六
酒県姫路市網干区高田商店三六
純米酒 精米歩合：原材料名：米（国産）
20歳になってからアルコール分

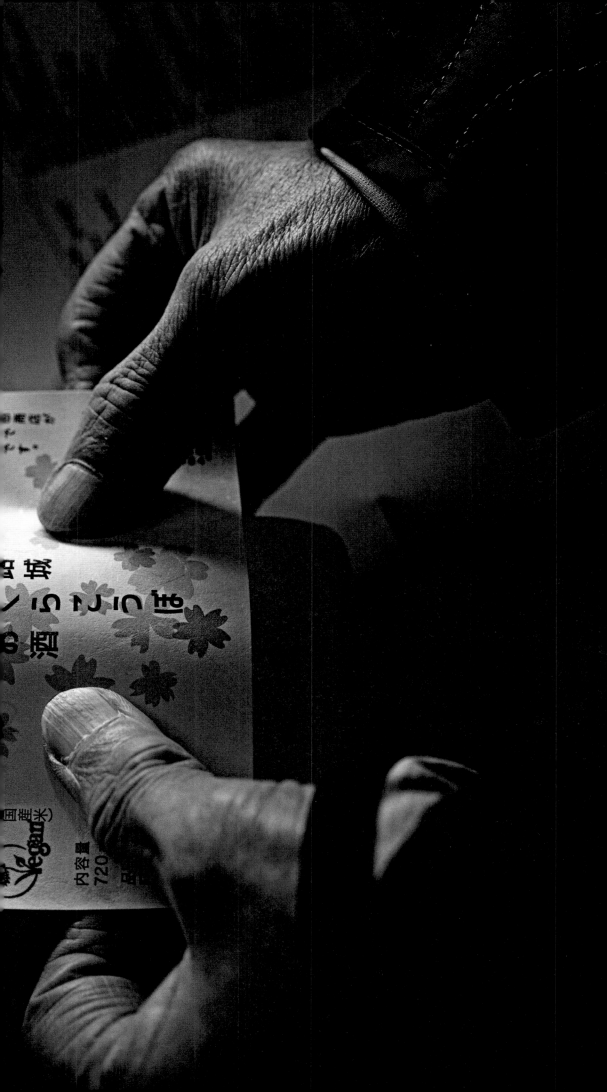

# Yasuyuki

TEDORIGAWA BREWERY
HAKUSAN, ISHIKAWA PREFECTURE

HAKUSAN

The working day starts early in the traditional Tedorigawa Sake Brewery, which was founded back in 1870 in Ishikawa Prefecture. It is seven o'clock on this February morning, still a bit dark outside. In the heated koji chamber on the first floor, Yasuyuki Yoshida and five brewers are monitoring the temperature of the koji rice spread out on a large surface covered with a white cloth. Yasuyuki, the brewery's current kuramoto and a trained toji, looks at the thermometer and says, "I'd like to lower the temperature by another 1.5 degrees, to 31°C (89°F)." Twenty-four hours have passed since the steamed rice, injected with koji spores, was spread out in the koji chamber. Now, it is brought in batches into another heated side room lined with cedar wood, then placed in small wooden crates, each one equipped with a thermostat with a blower to regulate the temperature and air humidity. This way, over the next 24 hours, the koji can continue to develop its mycelium and produce various enzymes—above all amylase—which are essential for brewing sake.

A young man called Koido manages the crucial koji department at Tedorigawa. Once his colleagues have placed the developing koji into a particular crate,

he smooths its surface. Next, he removes the lids of the crates containing the previous day's koji rice, checking the quality of their contents together with Yasuyuki. Both experts take a little of it in their hands and smell it, in order to ascertain whether it has already reached the desired end state.

When we leave the warm koji area, we are surrounded by cold February air. There is no other heating in the brewery. The employees put on their jackets and head over to the raw material processing area in the open production hall. The winter morning light shines in directly through the east-facing window.

The Tedorigawa Sake Brewery is located in a small village on the outskirts of the city of Hakusan, which is surrounded by paddy fields. The stubble from the last autumn harvest still protrudes from the fields as far as the eye can see—a vast, fan-shaped area at the foot of the 2,700-meter/8,900-foot-high holy mountain that gave the region its name and provides the family of brewers with mineral-rich, centuries-old brewing water. We hear the water flow vigorously through the narrow canal in front of the brewery, underneath a clear, winter-blue morning sky.

The young kuramoto Yasuyuki Yoshida

"

We wanted our trademark to be the traditional yamahai style of the Noto toji, and at the same time to create a flavor that would fit with modern eating habits.

The production of koji requires sensitivity and craftsmanship.

Yasuyuki has been responsible for the fortunes of Tedorigawa since 2017, as its owner and master brewer. Even as a child, he would often play in the production hall, and he grew up watching the toji at the time sometimes laughing relaxedly with his many brewers, sometimes strictly instructing them on how to brew the sake. The kuramoto's son so admired him that he hoped he would one day walk in the footsteps of this man from the Noto Peninsula and produce his own sake. This is why Yasuyuki studied fermentation science at the Tokyo University of Agriculture, completed an apprenticeship in a prestigious sake brewery in northern Japan, and ended up working for sake import companies both in the USA and UK. During this period, he got to know a wide range of different types of restaurants, from local Michelin-starred temples to Japanese izakayas and trendy fusion restaurants, and thus discovered new ways of consuming sake.

At the age of 25, Yasuyuki Yoshida returned to his family brewery and immediately became involved in production. By this point, Toji Yamamoto was 66 years old and had more than 50 years of experience in sake production. He had worked for the Yoshidas as a seasonal worker in Yasuyuki's father's day, since in the past it was customary for the brewery owner and his family to not be involved in production, instead hiring a toji and seasonal brewery workers on a contractual basis. Today, however, there is a whole set of kuramoto-toji in Japan, i.e. brewery owners who do not just run the business side of things, but also manage production as master brewers.

When Yasuyuki entered junior high school, Yamamoto took on the position of toji. He viewed the boy as his successor and taught him about his future profession with great passion. The two spent many hours with each other, often from five in the morning until midnight, ate together, and even shared a room. Over time, Yasuyuki adopted his teacher's philosophy: *Wajo ryoshu* ("Harmony between people brews good sake, and good sake brews harmony between people").

Tall, with the taut face of a young samurai and large, beautiful eyes, Yasuyuki radiates willpower and sincerity. He is constantly finding new ways to motivate his 15-person team, bringing everyone together so each brewer is responsible for his part of the sake production process and works purposefully towards producing a unique sake flavor.

It is now twenty past eight: time for the morning conference. Employees from the brewery's various departments assemble in the production hall near the rice cooker, which is still steaming. "Good morning, we'll be dividing our work today as follows . . ." Yasuyuki Yoshida looks at the faces of the brewers responsible for each production step and at the board outlining the day's tasks. In his quiet but tuneful voice, the kuramoto-toji goes through the points that deserve particular attention. His audience also includes Yamamoto, who was the head of sake production until a few years ago but now works as a simple brewer in the young team. His presence gives Yasuyuki and his team a sense of peace and calmness.

Following the 10-minute morning conference, the rice steamer is switched off and opened. Hot steam wafts through the cold production hall. A crane lifts out the first of various layers of rice—there are four of them today—wrapped up in large pieces of cloth, and brings them to the cooler. Other pieces of cloth are ready there; the waiting brewers use them to pick up the rice and carry it on their backs to the koji chamber. Everyone works together during this sweaty process; even Yasuyuki gets involved.

Later on, once the kuramoto-toji has a bit more time, he asks, "We have a new kind of sake. Would you like to try it and compare it with our standard product?" He leads me into the salon. Its ceiling is very high for a Japanese house, and its walls are painted dark red. "This is the color of the Maeda family from the Kaga Clan, which ruled this area during the Edo Period," explains Yasuyuki. "And now it's a tradition here to use Kaga red in rooms that are used to welcome guests. It also perfectly emphasizes the visual appearance of a meal."

The veteran toji Yamamoto upholds harmony within the team.

Yasuyuki recommends I take a place with my back to the wall of the tokonoma, a small, traditional niche. He has filled my wine glass with a Tedorigawa yamahai junmai sake, created by the former toji, Yamamoto. "This is our classic product, our bestselling sake." It smells of freshly cooked rice with a hint of fruity, banana-like aromas. Its flavor has some strong acidity and umami, giving an impression of wildness, but the finish has a wonderful elegance. At its drinking temperature of around 12°C (54°F), fresh out of the refrigerator, this sake feels a little hard, but once you warm it up, it becomes more full-bodied, and the umami is released.

"Up until now, 60 percent of our production was brewed following the sokujo method, which immediately emphasizes the aromatic character of the yeast, and around 40 percent of it according to the yamahai method," explains Yasuyuki Yoshida. "We wanted our trademark to be the traditional yamahai style of the Noto toji, which was also favored by our Mr. Yamamoto, and at the same time to create a flavor that would fit with modern eating habits. This is how we arrived at our current, contemporary yamahai style." Yamahai is a brewing process that uses natural lactobacilli so that, as Yasuyuki puts it, "it is kind to food dishes, people, and nature." He explains further: "The complex balance of acidity and umami in our yamahai sake goes well with seasonal vegetables seasoned simply with olive oil, salt, and pepper, which you would usually pair wine with—as well as with spicy meat dishes seasoned with ginger, pepper, and cumin. Its alcohol content is a low 13 percent by volume."

But Yasuyuki Yoshida is not just working on the development of a new sake style. In order to brew sake in accordance with the principles of holistic sustainability, he is determined to protect the cultured landscape of satoyama (pp. 112–121), which has been shaped by rice cultivation for over 1,000 years. This is why the Tedorigawa Brewery does not just cultivate rice on its own paddy fields; it has also founded the Sake Rice Promotion Association, along with other rice farmers in this Yamashima area who share its vision for the future of agriculture. Together, they strive to reduce the use of pesticides and organic fertilizers in rice production. In addition, the brewery is planning drastic measures to minimize electricity use, striving to produce a sake that does not require any excessive cooling. One of the Yoshida company philosophies is the idea of sampo-yoshi: "good for the seller, good for the buyer, and good for the world." Yasuyuki is determined to manage his business in such a way that ensures all three of these factors are in balance.

It will be lunchtime in half an hour. The sun is shining. I leave the salon and wander through the now mild air of the building containing the yabuta (sake press machine), which looks like a huge accordion. The moromi (mash) is slowly pressed overnight between its metal plates. The former master, Yamamoto, is talking to a young brewer as he removes the lees that remained in the press from its plate. When he still held the position of toji, Yamamoto would always spend the spring and summer occupied with farming rice. During the six months from November to April, once the rice harvest was over, he would live with 10 other brewers in lodgings on the brewery grounds. He only rarely returns to his house, which is a three-hour drive away. "My family felt lonely," admits the old man, "but as soon as I started to make the sake, I couldn't keep my eyes off the production process anymore. I was so preoccupied that I would sometimes go into the dark fermentation hall in the middle of the night to see how the mash was fermenting. Now that Yasuyuki is doing everything right, I feel secure."

The smile on the wrinkled face of this toji of many years is as warm as the winter sun. —

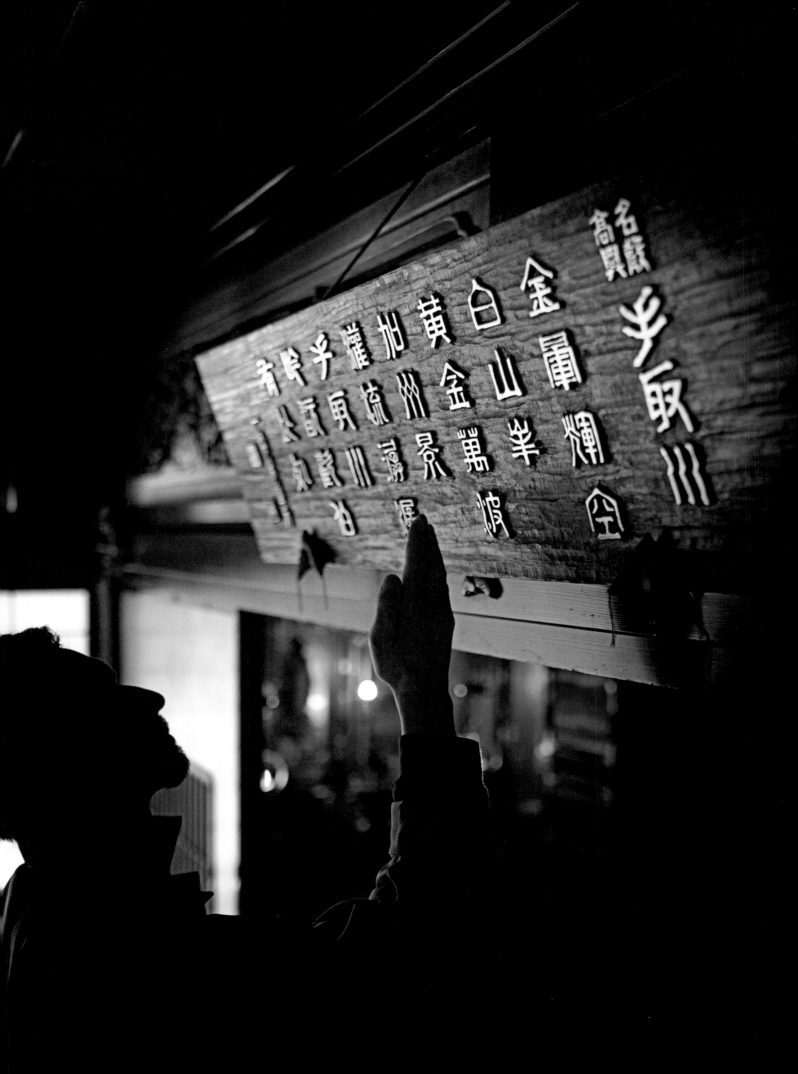

A poem about the Tedorigawa River that has given its name to the brewery

The holy Mount Hakusan provides water for rice and sake.

# Kiichiro

**TOJI OF MASUIZUMI BREWERY**
**IWASE, TOYAMA PREFECTURE**

IWASE

A toji is the person responsible for the sake-making process in a brewery. They supervise all aspects of sake brewing, from the selection of raw materials to production, storage, and quality control. In addition to these tasks, the toji also oversees the brewery's adherence to the alcohol tax and other taxes, the maintenance of equipment, and the mentorship and management of brewery staff, and they negotiate with the owner to take care of all other aspects of the business. Thus, the toji is not just a professional sake brewer, but also the highest-ranked production manager and technical director of the brewery.

The toji system we know today was established during the middle of the Edo period in the eighteenth century, when the Shogunate encouraged people to brew in the cold season so farmers and fishermen, who had no work in the winter, could find off-season employment in sake breweries. Just like the cooks, who were also employed for a season, these workers would start at the breweries after the rice harvest.

As a rule, the toji and brewing staff would spend almost six months, from mid-October to mid-April, on the production of sake, sometimes hundreds of kilometers away from their homes. The toji were well-paid, and people used to say that after three years of successfully brewing sake, you could afford to have your own house built. Though the number of farmers—and also fishermen—who work in this system has recently undergone a steep decline, students who study brewing in college can still find full-time or seasonal employment in Japan. The toji of Masuizumi, Kiichiro Hatanaka, who was born in 1950, is one of the last sake brewers who worked in the seasonal sake-making system. He remembers:

"I didn't become a brewer until I was over 25 years old, so not as early as other people. I started out as an unskilled worker in the prestigious Sogen Brewery on the Noto Peninsula. After I had worked there for around 12 years, Mr. Sanpai, the chair of the Noto Toji Guild and then master brewer of Masuizumi, found a new position for me. I started working as a toji in a brewery in Fukui in 1989. Before I started there, the brewery only produced futsushu in big tanks, following a recipe used by industrial producers. I was asked to improve their range to premium quality and create their own brand. There were only four other brewers apart from me at the time.

In one winter, we would produce around 30 tanks of sake, including the highly aromatic ginjo. The brewers and employees usually have ten days of holi-

A toji oversees all aspects of sake brewing.

day around the end of the year and the New Year, but as toji, I remained in the brewery. I couldn't take a break because of the moromi, the fermenting mass. Aside from the pure ginjo types, we also produced yamahai and kimoto. I worked in this brewery for 18 years as a toji before moving to Masuizumi in 2006. Toji Sanpai had already taken his retirement from them and had become a consultant for the brewery; Toji Domoku took over his position, and I was the koji manager.

At the start I was bewildered, because the production of koji was often carried out in the labor-intensive tsukihaze style (p. 63) to make highly aromatic daiginjo. After Toji Domoku died, Kuramoto Ryuichiro put me forward for the position of toji, but I initially turned down the offer because I thought it would be impossible to manage 15 brewers. It became clear to me that it is the toji who guarantees not just the quality of the sake, but also the harmony between brewery staff members and each individual's motivation, and keeps all of this in balance. Ultimately, I did decide to take on this huge challenge. At the time, the brewery in Fukui would use a new mash every second day, but in Masuizumi it was every day. We have around 40 different kinds of sake here; this year, we are brewing a total of 98 tanks. The production of one single tank requires eight batches of rice: the koji rice and the kakemai rice for the starter mash, and the main mash for the three-step processes of hatsu-zoe, naka-zoe, and tome-zoe. Depending on the batch, we must use different quantities and schedules for the washing and steaming of the rice."

Kiichiro Hatanaka showed me a complicated Excel table spread out across several sheets, which neatly listed the data relevant to each of the eight batches of rice per tank. "This table was developed by our young brewer," he said. "Before, I used to have to write all these lists down by hand and calculate the weight of the rice using an abacus." The venerable toji speaks with a calm, clear voice and smiles. He has done great things in the breweries he has worked for, but he does not boast about them—nor does he speak about the privations he has had to suffer. When I expressed my admiration, he smiled shyly.

"When I go home to the Suzu region in the spring, maybe my wife finds my presence wearing. She's used to managing on her own. But I can't leave the brewery during the brewing season, not even for just a few days, because I worry about the mash. Luckily, my daughter lives in Kanazawa, just a 30-minute drive from the Masuizumi brewery, so I can sometimes meet up with her during the season."

Kiichiro's home, Suzu, is an area at the tip of the Noto Peninsula, known for its high mountains, narrow rice field valleys, and steep coast. The region lives off rice cultivation and fishing and is home to numerous toji. Many families here used to live through the winters without their men, who worked in the breweries of neighboring prefectures such as Ishikawa, Toyama, and Fukui.

There are currently 10 brewers living at Masuizumi. Like Toji Hatanaka, they get up at five in the morning and have breakfast at six. At eight o'clock, when the steamed rice is ready, part of it is brought to the koji room and other parts are sent to fermentation tanks. Kiichiro Hatanaka monitors the temperature sequence of the 20 or so tanks that are fermenting simultaneously, as well as the analysis data from the mash, then gives instructions to the staff. "The period during which futsushu is produced marks the start of the brewing season. Two weeks later, at the end of November, the daiginjo is brewed, and that makes me nervous," said the toji, underscoring the difficulties of this precise brewing process.

I asked him what kind of sake he likes, and his answer made me think that he could still feel the beverage on his tongue: "It doesn't need to have that much aroma, but when you drink it, it should be soft and full-bodied and have a nice kire finish, while at the same time having an enduring aftertaste." This description, very similar to the flavor profile of Masuizumi sake, underscored the toji's strong connection to the brewery and its rich tradition. "I have been brewing sake for almost 50 years already," he said at the end of our interview, "but I still feel like a beginner. This is right, though. Because the rice is different every year." —

# Takeshi

**BARREL MAKER AT FUJII SEIOKESHO WOOD WORK**
SAKAI, OSAKA PREFECTURE

The smell of fresh cedar wood rises to my nose as I step into Takeshi Ueshiba's workshop in Sakai. The workshop was founded in 1916 by his grandfather and now goes by the name of Fujii Seiokesho Wood Work, and it is one of the last traditional barrel making companies in Japan. Five craftsmen work here between stacks of planks and finished or half-finished oke, sake and soy barrels made of Japanese cedar (sugi). They are usually held together solely by bamboo nails, without any glue, and are lashed using taga (woven bamboo cord). One of the men is currently in the process of sawing a barrel cover into shape; two others are balancing on the upper edge of a 30-koku (5,400 liter/1,426-gallon) barrel, which is standing upright in the high-ceilinged shed.

The pair are using ropes to keep hold of a doutsuki, a 2-meter/6.5-foot-long, 100-kilo/220-pound piece of squared timber, and are letting it fall repeatedly onto the bottom of the barrel, while they gradually advance around the edges to the rhythmic call of "Yan-solemo-yansa." Takeshi gives them instructions from inside the barrel: "Bit more to the right," "back a bit," "again." After two rounds, the dull thudding on the doutsuki falls silent. The bottom of the barrel fits perfectly!

"Teamwork is important for manufacturing barrels," says Takeshi. The craftsman, who is in his mid-70s, has just light-footedly climbed up the ladder and into the 2-meter/6.5-foot-high—and equally wide—oke. Now, he is once more standing on the shop floor with a smile on his face, enthusiastically explaining the most important factors in oke production. "You can identify two layers in Japanese cedar wood: it is light on the outside, near the bark, and reddish further in. The area between these two colors is so dense with fiber that no humidity can escape. This precious part of the wood is called koutsuki and is used to make sake barrels. You can only make four planks out of a tree 50 centimeters (20 inches) in diameter, but you need at least 40 planks for one barrel."

We leave the workshop and go to Takeshi's office, which is shaped like an oke! "Wooden barrels have ex-

Takeshi Ueshiba in his office

> ## Wood has countless little pores in which microorganisms, which are the main protagonists of fermentation, live. They create an ecosystem that only exists in each particular brewery.

cellent isolating and heat-storage properties," explains the barrel maker. "Wood has countless little holes in which microorganisms, which are the main protagonists of fermentation, live. They create an ecosystem that only exists in each particular brewery. Over the course of the years, this creates a unique flavor, which can only be produced by that very brewery. Sake brewed in wooden barrels contains many compounds that are not present in other containers, such as those made out of enamel. This is why it has a more complex flavor."

Takeshi Ueshiba is not just an experienced oke-ya, but also a thinker and philosopher who writes articles about the benefits of the sugi-oke, cooperates with academics on research projects, and gives lectures for sake brewer associations and breweries. He was chosen as a sake samurai by the Sake Brewers Association in recognition of his accomplishments.

Before World War II, there were still 50 barrel-making workshops in Sakai; now, only Takeshi's is still active. There used to be around one million wooden sake brewing barrels in the country, but after 1945 almost all of them were replaced with enameled iron or steel tanks. Much of Japan was destroyed during the War, and the price of wood rose sharply in the post-war period, due to the demand for rebuilding houses. On the other hand, there was a surplus of iron, which had previously been in short supply, as it was used to manufacture military goods, and this became the new material for sake brewing containers. Customers complained that the taste of the sake was affected by the new tanks, but during the period of fast economic growth, when cheap sake was consumed in large quantities, the traditional taste of sake fell into oblivion.

"I also thought a barrel maker had no future," says Takeshi, "and so, after studying economics, I lived a life as an office employee. At the age of 28, however, I decided to take over the family business and started an apprenticeship with my father and his

Sugi cedar wood from Yoshino is the best material for oke.

A traditional craft: barrel making has
not substantially changed in 500 years.

four employees." Then the oke-ya tells me a bit more about the oke that have determined the course of his life to this day.

"In the past, sake breweries would make new barrels and use them for around 30 years. Then, they were sold to soy sauce, miso, or vinegar manufacturers. Sugi-oke usually have a life span of 150 years, and they would also be repaired before ultimately ending up as firewood—the ultimate form of recycling. After the war, this cycle broke down; many barrel makers had to give up. Oke are witnesses to history. If you take apart an old cedar wood barrel to repair it and take a close look at the planks, you can identify its date of manufacture, the name of the buyer, and even the price of rice at the time. Many barrel makers would also take note if the buyer was a cheapskate," says Takeshi, laughing.

At the end of the 1990s, a woman named Sarah Cummings saved the oke industry and the last oke-ya, Takeshi. As director of a sake brewery in Nagano, she realized one day, to her surprise, that there were no more breweries in Japan producing sake in wooden barrels. She convinced the toji to revive the traditional method, appealed to all the breweries she knew, founded the nonprofit organization Oke Brewing Preservation Society, and appeared in the media to promote the merits of sake produced in oke.

"We received more orders for new barrels as a result," remembers Takeshi-san. "But I had no successor, so I told people that I would be closing down my workshop in 2020, when I turned 70." However, many

sake and soy sauce producers saw this decision as an existential threat. And so, the owner of Yamaroku Soy Sauce sent his own carpenters to Takeshi's workshop to be trained in the art of oke manufacturing.

"Once they had mastered the technique, they started a project to revive the craft of making oke and simultaneously began to train sake, miso, and soy sauce producers who wanted to make their own sugi-oke," remembers Takeshi-san. "Other people came, too, in order to learn the craft of making oke-ya, and then started to manufacture their own barrels. It's wonderful to see how the circle of barrel makers is getting bigger again."

One problem that still exists, according to Takeshi-san, is the decreasing number of forestry workers. "The woods are not sufficiently managed anymore", he says. Straight, knotless cedar wood that is at least 100 years old keeps getting rarer and more expensive. There are also no workshops left that produce the planes he requires—and only a handful that split and process the bamboo that is used to produce the barrel straps. "So barrel makers have the arduous task of producing all their tools and materials themselves."

More and more breweries, such as Aramasa Shuzo, Ninki Shuzo, and Niida Honke are now striving to produce all of their sake using wooden barrels; many of them have even set up their own systems for building and repairing the oke. But we are only at the start of the steep path toward a revival of the ancient tradition of brewing sake in wooden barrels. —

# SAKE CLASSIFICATION AND VARIETIES

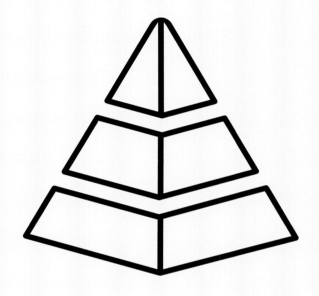

**Not all sakes are the same.** There are hundreds of different types on the market, ranging from cheap futsushu to expensive, premium sake. The classification system that is currently used for premium sake, as defined by Japan's National Tax Agency, includes six classes (eight if you add tokubetsu junmai and tokubetsu honjozo), which differ in terms of their rice polishing ratio (the smaller the finer), the addition (or not) of brewing alcohol, and the temperature at which they are fermented (ginjo method).

# PREMIUM SAKE

## Junmai

A sake with purity at its heart. Junmai means "pure rice," and this type of sake is brewed using only rice and water, without the addition of any brewing alcohol (distilled alcohol, usually produced from sugarcane). There are no requirements regarding the rice polishing ratio for junmai, but the rice is usually polished to under 70 percent of its original weight. Tokubetsu junmai uses rice polished to 60 percent or less or another, special type of rice; or the rice has to undergo a special production process, such as that of nigori sake (p. 108). Junmai has a strong and full-bodied flavor profile. Many sake brewers brew junmai sake using their regional type of rice, so it represents the terroir. This sake can be enjoyed both warm and cold.

**Flavor profile:** full-bodied, umami, rustic

## Honjozo

The addition of brewing alcohol to a level of up to 10 percent of the total weight of rice is authorized for this class. This makes honjozo taste lighter and drier than a comparable junmai brewed under the same conditions. The rice polishing ratio is under 70 percent. Tokubetsu junmai uses rice polished to 60 percent or less or another, special type of rice; or the rice has to undergo a special production process like that of nigori sake (p. 108). Its fine fragrance evaporates slightly when it is heated. Honjozo is a good accompaniment for sashimi and sushi, as well as other light main dishes.

**Flavor profile:** fresh, light, rustic

## Junmai Ginjo

In order to produce this fruity and well-balanced sake, the rice is polished to 60 percent or less of its original weight. Ginjo means "carefully brewed with select ingredients"—in other words, manually and with slow fermentation at a low temperature (8° to 12°C/46° to 54°F). Junmai ginjo tastes milder and more full-bodied than ginjo sake. With its fruity and mild taste, this class of sake is similar to a full-bodied white wine. This is why it can be combined not just with fish, but also with more robust dishes (such as poultry or pork in a dark sauce). Cheese also makes a good partner for junmai ginjo.

**Flavor profile:** fruity, soft, full-bodied

## Ginjo

The requirements and production steps for ginjo sake are the same as for junmai ginjo—except that this style includes brewing alcohol, which is added on the last day of fermentation to bind the aromas from the mash. That is why this kind of sake tastes more aromatic than an equivalent junmai ginjo. The result contains pleasant hints of fresh apples, ripe melons, and bananas.

**Flavor profile:** aromatic, clear, fresh

## Junmai Daiginjo

In order to achieve a harmony of aromas and rice umami, brewers polish the rice for this style to 50 or even 40 percent of its original weight, then brew the sake at an extremely low temperature (around 5° to 10°C/41° to 50°F). The toji master and their employees often endure sleepless nights during the production phase of daiginjo or junmai daiginjo and, just like the rice, lose bodyweight themselves. Junmai daiginjo has a fuller body and more harmonious aromas and flavors than daiginjo sake. Therefore, it is an ideal accompaniment for all kinds of food—from starters to main courses.

**Flavor profile:** aromatic, full-bodied, complex

## Daiginjo

This highly aromatic sake is a genuine jewel of craftsmanship. It shares its position as a top-quality class with junmai daiginjo. Its requirements and production steps are the same as those of junmai daiginjo—except that it contains brewing alcohol. The time at which the addition of brewing alcohol is made, and what amount is added, are chosen with care. This creates a very fine, flavorful sake.

Each brewery can only choose one sake to enter in the Annual Japan Sake Awards and, historically, most used to send their top daiginjos. However, as junmai daiginjo has grown more and more popular, breweries have focused more on the production of this type, and the production share of daiginjo has decreased. Because this type of sake has such a wealth of aromas, it is not that easy to combine it with food: daiginjo is usually enjoyed as an aperitif or an accompaniment to refined main courses such as lobster cooked in clementine butter with cinnamon blossom. Daiginjo sake is also the perfect accompaniment for a meditation.

**Flavor profile:** aromatic, clear, elegant

# NON-PREMIUM SAKE

## Futsushu (Regular Sake), Gosei Seishu

While premium sake can only be brewed using classified polished rice, koji rice, and water, futsushu can be produced using rice bran (a waste product from polishing) and kasu (lees) as well. The addition of brewing alcohol, glucose, acidifiers, glutamate, and other authorized ingredients up to a level of 50 percent of the rice mass used is also permitted. This makes it possible to dilute the sake. There has been a dramatic decrease in the amount of this cheap, boozy sake being produced in recent years, but it still makes up 56 percent of total sake production in Japan. If you are offered hot sake at your local sushi joint or izakaya, it will usually be futsushu. There is also Niigata-style futsushu, for which, just like with ginjo, the rice is polished to 60 percent of its original weight. Gosei seishu, a synthetic sake containing brewing alcohol, can give you something of a hangover the next day. This sake was born of necessity during the war years, when rice was hard to come by.

**Flavor profile:** light, rustic

## OTHER TYPES OF SAKE

Sparkling, made with flower yeast, without any alcohol at all, sherry-colored, nutmeg-flavored—aside from the officially defined classes of sake, there many other fascinating types, some traditional and some inspired by the current zeitgeist.

## Sparkling Sake

This fizzy variant has been enjoying increasing popularity, both in Japan and internationally, for around two decades. Sparkling sake makes a charming aperitif with a fruity, sweet-and-sour taste and between 5 and 7 percent alcohol content: a lovely alternative to champagne. In high-quality products, its fine, natural carbon dioxide bubbles are created by fermentation inside the bottle without any added sugar. There are also sparkling sakes that are produced by being fermented in tanks or with added carbon dioxide. The seasonal product kassei nigori is an unpasteurized, coarsely filtered sparkling sake, whose carbon dioxide and active yeast continue to ferment in the bottle. Due to its active yeasts, which react negatively to warmer environments, sparking sake must be stored in cool conditions, at a temperature of less than 5°C (41°F), and must be consumed very promptly after the bottle is opened. In 2016, a handful of kuramoto founded the Japan Awasake Association in order to ensure the product quality of sparkling sake was continuously improved, and to open up new markets. The association now has 30 members. Their certified awa (sparkling) sake is a disgorged, clear, bottle-fermented version of the classic beverage.

## Kimoto/Yamahai

These sakes owe their names to specific procedures followed during their production. Kimoto is a traditional, time- and labor-intensive method for producing the starter mash; yamahai is a simplified variant of kimoto. Sake produced according to the kimoto or yamahai methods have a lot of umami flavor and natural acidity; for this reason, they go very well with cheese and meat dishes.

## Bodaimoto

This sake takes its name from a sixteenth-century brewing method developed in the Shoryakuji Temple in Nara, during which raw rice is soaked for three to seven days in lukewarm water to promote the production of lactic acid. After soaking, the rice and lactic acidic water (soyashi-mizu) are separated, the rice is steamed, and then the soyashi-mizu is mixed into the steamed rice to create the mash. Bodaimoto sake has a strong and full-bodied taste with pronounced acidity and umami.

## Flower Blossom Sake

New yeast cultures taken from flowers (e.g. begonias, rhododendrons, marigolds, rambler roses, or nadeshiko carnations) give this sake a luscious bouquet, similar to daiginjo. Professor Hisayasu Nakata from the Department of Fermentation Science at the Tokyo University of Agriculture has managed to isolate new sake yeasts from millions of other yeasts in this way. Only 30 sake brewers are allowed to use his precious laboratory-produced yeasts. Now, regional institutes also compete in the development of yeasts from flowers. The flower yeast AK-1 from Akita Prefecture, which was registered in 1991, was so successful at the Annual Japan Sake Awards that it was registered as Kyokai 1501 by the Brewing Society of Japan.

## Aged Sake, Koshu, Jukusei-shu

Generally speaking, it is still assumed today that the taste of sake does not improve with time. Nevertheless, there is an initiative from around 40 sake producers (who have come together to form the Choki Jukusei-shu Association) to revive the tradition of aged sake (koshu). Over time, sake acquires a dark color (ranging from that of sherry and cognac to that of soy

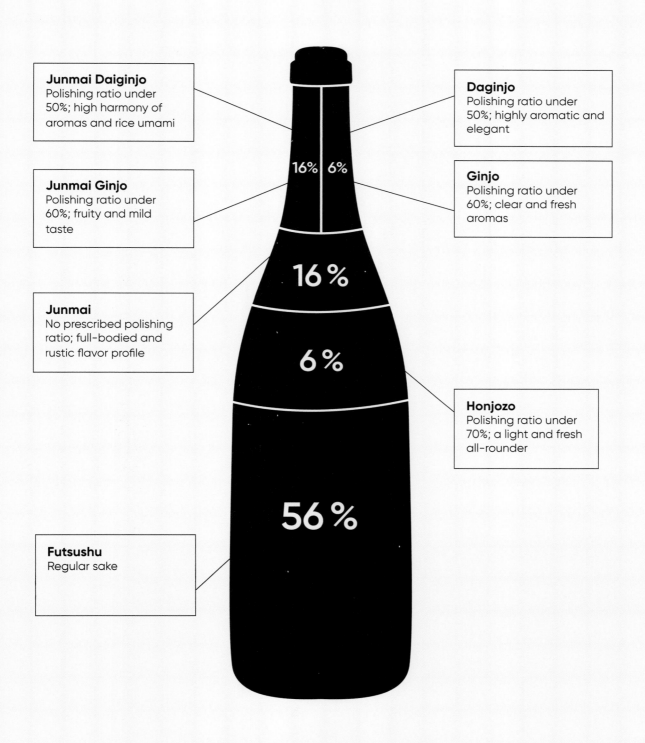

**Junmai Daiginjo**
Polishing ratio under 50%; high harmony of aromas and rice umami

**Daginjo**
Polishing ratio under 50%; highly aromatic and elegant

**Junmai Ginjo**
Polishing ratio under 60%; fruity and mild taste

**Ginjo**
Polishing ratio under 60%; clear and fresh aromas

**Junmai**
No prescribed polishing ratio; full-bodied and rustic flavor profile

**Honjozo**
Polishing ratio under 70%; a light and fresh all-rounder

**Futsushu**
Regular sake

16%  6%

16 %

6 %

56 %

Production share of sake classes in Japan; percentage of total production (Source: National Tax Agency Report, 2021)

sauce) and warm, spicy flavors reminiscent of cocoa, dried fruit, nutmeg, etc. On the other hand, sakes made with minimally polished rice, such as daiginjo and junmai daiginjo, only darken slightly when aged in cold conditions, producing a lighter koshu. In order to guarantee a certain standard of quality, the Toki Sake Association was founded in 2020; it defines the standards for koshu/jukusei-shu and certifies this type of sake.

## Nigori Sake (Nigorizake)
This naturally cloudy sake is the original sake; it was created when fine filtering was not yet possible. According to today's Liquor Tax Act, the mash for sake must be pressed or strained once. However, the method for doing this is not stipulated. The sake acquires a different density depending on how many fragments of rice are left inside it. Fine rice powder definitely gives it a unique texture.

## Nama Sake (Namazake)
Conventional sake is pasteurized twice: before it is aged and when it is bottled. In contrast, nama sake is not pasteurized at all. Because of the active enzymes and yeast that may still be present in this type of sake, its flavor changes quickly, which is why it must be kept in an uninterrupted cold chain. It used to only be possible to buy nama sake directly from the brewer in the winter. Additional varieties are nama-zume, which is only pasteurized once before it is aged, and nama-chozo, which is aged in a cold tank and pasteurized once when the sake is bottled.

## Genshu
This type of sake is not diluted with water after pressing, so it has a high alcohol content (over 17

percent by volume) and an intense flavor. However, in recent years, certain producers have introduced some water during fermentation to reduce the alcohol content to below 15 percent, which also results in a milder flavor.

## Muroka
After pressing and sedimentation, this sake does not undergo fine filtration (usually activated carbon filtration). Muroka sake has a strong and full-bodied flavor."

## Kijoshu, Goshu (Imperial Sake)
Instead of water, finished sake is used to produce kijoshu and goshu sake. In other words, this type is brewed at least twice or as many times as the brewer wishes. In the Middle Ages (Heian era), goshu was produced in the court, exclusively for the emperor. It has a dense and complex spectrum of flavors.

## Ama Sake (Amazake)
This sweet, nutritious, low- or nonalcoholic beverage is produced by adding water to koji rice and letting it rest for 24 hours in a hot environment (around 40°C/104°F). Thanks to its numerous vitamins and amino acids, ama sake was already popular as an energy drink in the Edo period.

## Doburoku
An ancient farmers' sake, brewed and drunk by the people of Japan since they started cultivating rice, doburoku is produced using a similar method to that of sake, but without the pressing and straining. This viscous, sweet-tasting rice beverage has an alcohol content of between 10 and 17 percent by volume. Doburoku used to be produced by many rice farmers for their own consumption, and it was

also made in shrines for religious festivals. Since 1940, though, its production has been forbidden by the Liquor Tax Act, aside from a few exceptions.

## Low-Alcohol Sake
Sake usually has an alcohol content of around 15 percent by volume. In recent years, however, more and more sakes with lower alcohol contents (below 13 percent) have been developed. There are even sakes with alcohol contents between 6 and 10 percent. This low alcohol content is achieved by adding water or interrupting fermentation early in the process. However, it is not easy to produce a sake with low alcohol content and full-bodied taste. Low-alcohol sake has a light, usually sweet-and-sour flavor.

## Craft Sake
Sake produced manually and in small quantities is referred to as craft sake. However, this term, which is commonly used in Japan, does not refer to a type of sake. Rather, craft sake is legally categorized as sonota jozoshu (other brewed alcohol), since various secondary ingredients such as spices, hops, fruits, etc. are added in during fermentation. (Doburoku is also considered sonota jozoshu.) Obtaining a brewing license for craft sake is less strictly regulated than for traditional sake, which is why this type has grown in popularity among young fermentation enthusiasts.

# OTHER JAPANESE ALCOHOLIC BEVERAGES

In Japan, rice is not only one of the essential ingredients for sake of all types and classes, but is also used to make other alcoholic beverages.

## Shochu

This Japanese spirit is most commonly distilled from rice, barley, or sweet potato. Shochu made with added water has an alcohol content of around 25 percent, but select types of shochu can also have alcohol contents of up to 45 percent. There are two classes: scentless and tasteless korui shochu, which is distilled twice or more in order to extract more alcohol from the mash and used mostly in mixed drinks, and premium shochu (known in Japan as oturui shochu or honkaku shochu), which is distilled once at a low temperature in order to preserve the aromas of its ingredients.

## Awamori

Around the year 1500, the technique of distillation was brought from Southeast Asia and China to the Kingdom of Ryukyu, now Okinawa. This is why Okinawa is now known as the birthplace of Japanese spirits. Traditionally, to produce awamori, which has an alcohol content between 25 and 45 percent, people exclusively use long grain rice fermented with black koji mold. Black koji produces citric acid; so, in spite of the subtropical Japanese climate, the mash is protected from other bacteria. While shochu, like sake, has a two-stage fermentation mash, awamori is only fermented in one stage and has a unique ageing system similar to that of sherry wine, during which the beverage matures in clay pots. In traditional Japanese families, awamori is often passed down from generation to generation in such containers.

## Mirin

Though it is well-known as a condiment in Japanese cuisine, the highest-quality mirin (often translated as "sweet sake") is also enjoyed as a liqueur. To produce it, rice shochu or brewing alcohol, mochigome (sweet rice), and koji rice are mixed in a tank. The fermentation does not produce any additional alcohol from the rice, but rather sugar and amino acids (which are responsible for the umami flavor in the condiment and spirit). The alcohol content of mirin is around 14 percent.

# II.
# THE
# COUNTRY
# AND THE
# PEOPLE

Japan is much more than the dozen megacities it includes today: it also has a calm, rural side with landscapes shaped over centuries by the work and lives of its people. In this chapter, we'll reflect on the country's enchanting regional diversity as we meet a rice farmer, two kuramoto from old brewer families, and a former champagne cellar master who now devotes himself to sake brewing.

# Satoyama: The Home of Japanese Gastronomy

Vast fields full of tender, green stalks of young rice, forest-covered mountains, and small villages. If you board a train and leave the cities of Japan, you will see such images almost everywhere in rural areas—sometimes across wide-ranging landscapes, sometimes in smaller ones: the harmonious coexistence of human beings and nature. Satoyama. *Sato* means "village" and *yama* means "hill" or "mountain"; therefore, the term *satoyama* is often translated to "homeland" in English. This rural farming landscape was developed over the centuries in the areas between the foothills and cultivable land, and it has been home to small-scale forestry and rice cultivation for generations.

But Japan's rural landscapes are not just objects of nostalgia—in fact, they fulfill a range of functions. The satoyama ecosystem consists of a complex interrelation among human beings, organisms, and the local environment, which extends across the surrounding arable lands and rivers.

Woods at the edges of villages used to be common property, managed collectively by all the villagers until around 1873, when the Meiji government advanced private land ownership. The community would decide who was allowed to extract what from them, whether this be timber or firewood, foodstuffs such as mushrooms, or even game. Regular logging kept the forests healthy and maintained their functions as water reservoirs. But also, and above all, it is rice cultivation that plays a crucial role in holding the water and thus protecting the landscape and its inhabitants.

It rains a lot in Japan, and the hillsides are steep; these conditions often lead to sediment transport. Every time it rains, the water carves into the mountains, breaking off pieces of them and carrying away sediment in its flow, so that the topography is constantly changing. The presence of rice paddies, however, prevents the run off of sediment: the rice paddies act like a dam that catches the water, but in so doing also catches the sediment and prevents it from flowing downstream.

Rice fields, forests, and farms are characteristic of rural Japan, as here in Maruyama Senmaida in Mie.

Rice farming has shaped Japan and its cuisine.

Minerals that are washed down from the mountains into the sea promote plentiful fish stocks all around Japan.

A new generation: this young Japanese woman champions organic rice farming.

In the Ariake Sea, a large tidal range fosters a unique abundance of fish.

Kaki fruits announce autumn in the countryside.

Previous page: The historic village of Gokayama in Toyama is a World Heritage Site.

Over the course of the centuries, the uplands were eroded and the lowlands filled up with earth, and water channels were exploited in order to transform swathes of land into rice paddies. This created flatlands on which people could settle. It was a long, arduous process, in which both farmers and rulers had a part to play. Nowadays, around 16 percent of the surface of Japan is used for agricultural purposes, and a quarter of this consists of rice paddies.

The splendid landscapes of what we initially thought were flatlands or rivers are known as the land of *Toyoashihara no Mizuho* ("the country in which, according to the will of the gods, rice thrives and is harvested in abundance")—and this is also one of the mythological names for Japan. This is the country that our ancestors have gifted to us by farming rice paddies, and such rice paddies still protect it to this day.

An important factor in Japan's cultured landscape is also revealed by the term *satoumi* ("village of the sea" or "fishing village"). Japan's long, jagged coastline, small islands, and numerous warm and cold currents enable a great variety of fish, seafood, and algae to thrive. But in this area, too, it is not just nature, but also the active contribution of human beings that is responsible for the presence and quality of the fish. Mineral-rich mountain water and organic wastewater from villages and cities feed plankton and algae, which in turn provide food for the fish. Protecting the forest is thus very important for coastal fisheries and fish and algae farming. In addition, rice cultivation and the fisheries, as well as the humid climate, promote the unique diversity of Japan's fermentation culture. These natural cycles and connections are what make Japanese gastronomy so unique.

Japanese people have always lived with the gifts of nature and shaped the land, and many people's hard work helped Japanese cuisine attain its current diversity and globally recognized quality. Healthy and flavorful dishes made with seasonal ingredients and a lot of umami, table culture, aesthetics, gratitude towards nature and human beings, and, last but not least, good sake: all of this is part of Japanese gastronomy. The heart of this, the traditional culinary art of washoku, is now part of the UNESCO Intangible World Heritage list. —

# TOPOGRAPHY, GEOLOGY, AND CLIMATE

Japan is an island nation with four large main islands—Hokkaido, Honshu, Shikoku, and Kyushu—and more than 14,000 smaller ones. The archipelago is shaped like a seahorse and is about 3,500 kilometers long from northeast to southwest, with a spine-like chain of high mountains and mountain ranges in the middle. It is situated between 20 and 45 degrees north, with Tokyo almost at the center.

The country is surrounded by the Sea of Japan in the west, which is connected to the Tsushima Strait in the south, and by the Pacific Ocean (with its warm Kuroshio, or Japan Current) in the east, the Sea of Okhotsk in the north, and the East China Sea in the south.

Its climate is predominantly temperate and can be divided into two main areas, one by the Sea of Japan and the other by the Pacific, with the central mountain range serving as a boundary between the two. Hokkaido, in the northern part of the country, is subarctic, while the Ogasawara Islands to the south of Tokyo and Okinawa are subtropical areas with highly variegated flora.

There are four distinct seasons, a rainy season running from the end of May to the middle of July, and typhoons in the summer and fall. In the summer, the seasonal southeastern wind blows from the Pacific Ocean toward the mountains in the center of the country, which leads to more rainfall on this side of the archipelago and drier air on the side of the Sea of Japan. Conversely, in the winter, the northwestern wind brings with it cold, dry air from Eurasia, which warms up as it crosses the Sea of Japan, absorbing humidity,

and is responsible for considerable amounts of snowfall on this side of the archipelago.

The climate in the central uplands, with the 3,000-meter/9,800-foot-high summits of the Japanese Alps, is less influenced by seasonal winds. From spring to fall, there is little precipitation and wide daily temperature fluctuations, while the winter is cold and snowy. The areas closer to the Seto Inland Sea are warmer and have less precipitation.

Three quarters of the surface of Japan are mountainous and hilly and covered in forests, whose cedars (sugi) and cypresses (hinoki), which make up around 40 percent of the archipelago's tree population, are used as construction materials and to manufacture barrels. There is only a limited amount of flat land where people can live, cultivate foodstuffs, and work. The majority of this population of around 125 million people live in the lowlands. The country's warm and humid climate is perfect for farming rice, so this crop is grown all over Japan. Thanks to its seas and currents, which are rich in plankton at the points where they meet, and to its long coastline, which also includes a rocky estuary, the country is also

very rich in fish—Japan, thus, has some of the most important fishing grounds in the world.

The distances between the mountains and the sea are short in Japan, so its rivers are also short and fast. The Kiso, which rises into the Japanese Alps, has a difference in elevation of 1,000 meters (3,280 feet) between its source and its mouth, and is only 227 kilometers (141 miles) long, whereas the Loire, which has the same difference in elevation, is 1,020 kilometers (634 miles) long, and the Mississippi, with its difference in elevation of 100 meters (328 feet), extends to a length of 5,969 kilometers (3,700 miles). Many of the country's basin regions are surrounded by mountains, and there are alluvial cones around the mouths of the rivers, created by deposits of sediment from the mountains. The most extensive of these areas is the Kanto Plain.

Japan is also characterized by its relatively thin soil strata, even though some soils are composed of weathered basalt and granite, others of weathered volcano ash, and yet others of humus. This is due to the country's high rate of precipitation, which often leads to the topsoil being washed away. —

# TERROIR AND SAKE CULTURES

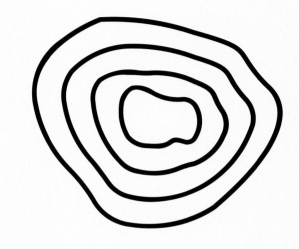

Where exactly in Japan did the art of sake brewing come from? What role is played by the soil the rice plants grow in before they are used to produce this traditional beverage? What impacts do the local climate and water have on sake development? And how do human beings influence all of this? Just like wine, the taste and experience of sake is determined by many different factors, including the environments in which the main ingredients are grown and the beverage is brewed.

The largely mountainous island nation of Japan has comparatively few usable agricultural zones, yet various microclimates have created a diverse and rich terroir. Over the centuries, absolutely unique regional cuisines have developed from the country's coasts to its summits, as have a host of different sake cultures.

## Eastern Sake and Western Sake

Tokyo and the Kanto region in the east are often contrasted with the 1,000-year-old culture of the ancient imperial city of Kyoto and the Kansai region in the west. These regions also differ in terms of their cuisines: dark versus light soy sauce, buckwheat noodles (soba) versus wheat ones (udon), stock made out of katsuo (bonito) flakes versus stock made out of kombu seaweed. And this east-west dichotomy applies to sake, too: In eastern Japan, the drink is clear and lithe, whereas in the west it is smooth and full-bodied.

## Northern Sake and Southern Sake

The climate in the north of Japan and the regions on its western coasts are cold and snowy. Sake ferments slower at cold temperatures but ends up being finer and more aromatic with a clear, dry flavor. In the south, on the other hand, more opulent, full-bodied, and relatively sweet sake tends to be produced and preferred as a beverage.

## Mountain Sake and Coastal Sake

While fresh fish and vegetables are available all year round in the coastal regions of Japan, people in the country's mountainous areas tend to eat food that has been fermented or preserved in salt, especially during winter. As a result, fresh and dry sake is preferred in the coastal regions to go with fish and seafood, while full-bodied and strong sake tends to be favored in mountainous areas to accompany dishes such as sautéed vegetables with miso.

## Men's Sake and Ladies' Sake

In the old sake village of Nada, in Kobe, sake is brewed using the famous Miyamizu water. By Japanese standards, this water is relatively hard and rich in phosphorus and magnesium, which are important to ensure smooth fermentation. Sake made out of hard water is strong and has a clear structure, which is why sake from Nada/Kobe is also known as otoko sake (men's sake). Just 80 kilometers (50 miles) to the east, in the village of Fushimi (Kyoto), however, a mild and sleek onna sake (ladies' sake) is brewed using this area's own distinctive water. —

# Shozo

RICE FARMER AND CATTLE BREEDER
YOKAWA, HYOGO PREFECTURE

YOKAWA

"The yamada nishiki from these paddies is used to produce the Tatsuriki Brewery's junmai daiginjo," proudly explains Shozo Tanaka. We are standing in front of the largest of the 70-year-old's rice paddies, which in total cover 2 hectares (5 acres); laid out in terraces, it is located on a hillside near Yokawa-cho-Yoneda, to the north of Kobe. "This rice paddy only covers 3,000 square meters (¾ acre) and is difficult to access with big machines, so it requires a lot of work," explains Tanaka-san, "but it produces a good rice because the temperature varies a lot between daytime and nighttime."

The two Kanji characters for the district of Yoneda both refer to rice: *yone* means "rice," and *da* means "rice paddies." Rice has been cultivated here since antiquity, and the township was integrated into the Village Rice System at the end of the nineteenth century. Shozo Tanaka is one of the seventh generation of a family of rice farmers; he studied agriculture and has been working in farming since he turned 19. But he does not just tirelessly, and almost single-handedly, devote his time to the noble yamada nishiki, he is also involved in livestock breeding.

It is no wonder, then, that there is a heap of straw mixed with cow dung lying in a corner of his largest rice paddy. "For good rice, you need good soil, so every year towards the end of October, after the harvest, we cover the fields with the rice hulls and straw mixed with cow dung and plough these in, to fertilize them," explains Shozo Tanaka, who also spends the six months before the new seedlings are planted sparing no effort to prepare the ground of his various rice paddies as best as possible.

"The district of Yokawa is Japan's leading production site for yamada nishiki, and the Yoneda paddies were judged to be the best in Yokawa during the 1938 appraisal," the aged but agile rice farmer informs us. "We want to protect the land we inherited from our forefathers and to produce the best sake rice in Japan." However, in recent years, temperatures around the time the ears were growing were very high, sighs Shozo, "so the plants suffered under these disruptions, which caused us a lot of headaches." The grains of rice were much smaller than usual.

"We can't change the weather. Following instructions from the farming cooperative, farmers are implementing measures, such as deferring the time at which they plant the rice, and developing methods to use water and fertilizers. But it's not enough to follow the handbook, since every area the rice paddies are located in has a different topography and microclimate. I walk through the rice paddies every day, even when I don't have any particular work to do, to see what the rice plants look like. Some rice paddies lie in the shadow of the mountains and don't get many hours of sunlight. I check the condition of the rice and change the depth of

Cattle breeding is part of the cycle of rice cultivation: their manure is used as a fertilizer, and rice straw is used as livestock feed.

Shozo Tanaka tends to his rice fields every day.

A well-tended garden is a status symbol for a traditional farming family.

the water if necessary, in order to adjust the temperature. The high temperatures have led to yield losses of up to 30 percent and to drops in quality on other rice paddies, but on my paddies the yield only sank by around 10 percent. I think I really love rice farming. You must know the saying, 'Love is the key to success.' If you're passionate about rice farming, your gaze becomes keener. People do what they can, and then all you can do is pray to the gods."

And indeed, the drive from Shozo Tanaka's rice paddies to Wakamiya Shrine in Inada, which is venerated by the region's rice farmers, barely lasts five minutes. Every year at the beginning of October, this shrine hosts the traditional Yaho-Shinji Festival in honor of the god of harvest. "Our family," explains Tanaka-san, "has been a member of the shrine community for generations already. I also don't just visit Wakamiya Shrine on big life occasions, but also simply to pray to the gods and to thank them." The old man does not limit himself to regularly displaying his reverence to the gods. He ran a committee for the renovation of the Zuishinmon Gate and the roof of the shrine, which were built in 1672 and were threatened with collapse, and collected donations from community members, companies, and the sake breweries that use yamada nishiki rice from Yokawa.

Once we have said a prayer together, we drive to Shozo Tanaka's house. On the front site of the plot stands a small, light wooden barn strewn with rice straw, in which six black Tajima cows are tethered. "Their feed consists of barley, soy, and other types of cereal, but they also eat rice straw," explains their breeder. "The second cow looks particularly good, don't you think? I'm sure she's going to grow up to be a prize-winning Kobe cow."

Next to the cowshed is a beautiful garden with pine trees, rhododendrons, and other plants, which are regularly tended to by a gardener, and at the back of the garden is a splendid traditional wooden house with a black tiled roof. "My father built it. The pine tree is the Tanaka family symbol. My great-grandfather's name already included the Kanji character for pine—just as mine does, too. Perhaps it brings

us luck that there are pinewood carvings on some of our pieces of furniture and walls." Indeed, the pride and prosperity of generations of the Tanaka farming family is evident throughout the house, including its exquisite transom window.

"What are the attributes of good sake rice," I want Shozo Tanaka to tell me. "And what is important for farming it?"

"It's not just about the size and weight of the grains. They also need to be shiny, regular, and pleasing to the eye," answers Shozo. "In good sake rice, the grains are round and have a shinpaku (white heart). In order to achieve this, you have to work at the right place at the right time. My 30 paddies are located in four different areas, so each one has to be worked on individually. It's also important to comply with the basic principles of rice cultivation. You can go to all the effort you like to produce large ears, but if the helms are too thin, they'll topple over during a typhoon and the rice will no longer be of good quality. So, it's important for the helms to be strong and thick. Let out the water at the right moment and let the roots grow deep. When exactly you spread out the fertilizer is important, too," explains Shozo. "It was frustrating when we had a bad harvest because of the high temperatures. Since then, we have concentrated on what's essential and tried to improve the soil in order to increase its stability. And we've been successful! My aim in life is to farm the best sake rice so the brewery can produce the best sake."

As he says these last words, Shozo Tanaka turns with a smile to the young man, Genki Kimura, who is accompanying me. Genki is responsible for buying sake rice for the Tatsuriki Brewery—and has brought along some junmai daiginjo made with Tanaka-san's rice. The latter adds quickly: "Thanks to Tatsuriki, we were able to provide our rice straw for the shimenawa (holy straw rope) at the Omiwa Shrine, which is dedicated to the god of sake. This is a great honor for a rice farmer. I've never been so happy. I thank you." The three of us then drink a toast of Nihon no Sakura (Japanese Cherry Blossom) sake to the connection between the gods, rice farmers, and sake brewers. —

# Ryusuke

TATSURIKI BREWERY
HIMEJI, HYOGO PREFECTURE

HIMEJI

The Tatsuriki master brewer lovingly—if somewhat nervously—observes how sake is trickling out of the spout of a small stainless-steel tub and slowly collecting in the green glass demijohn placed in front of it. Fukuro sibori (droplet sake). It is being produced on this cold winter day for the national new sake contest that is held every spring: the most important contest of all for the sake industry. According to this special, traditional method, the rice pudding-like mash (moromi) is poured into long, narrow cloth bags. These are then hung up loosely over a tub, which collects the liquid dripping out of them. The precious drops of sake shine like diamonds. Unsurprisingly, tension is written all over the face of the Tatsuriki Sake Brewery's toji: will this extract, the result of all his brewing efforts, give his senses satisfaction?

"Last summer was hot and the rice was hard, so it was difficult to dissolve, and it was hard to get the fermentation process started," explains the master brewer. "But our sake still developed a beautiful flavor." As he says these words, he hands us a kikichoko,

a white ceramic cup with blue rings at the base, full of freshly filtered sake. The cool aroma of this elixir, which is reminiscent of green melons, is complemented by a ripe, juicy flavor and the refined sweetness of the rice. This competition sake is produced using the finest yamada nishiki—the king of all rice varieties—fermented for 30 days at an extremely low temperature.

Once I have left the refrigerator-like ginjo chamber, I bump into Ryusuke Honda, the kuramoto of the brewery, which was founded in 1921 under the name Honda Shoten. Ryusuke took the chair of the company on the occasion of its 100th anniversary; he was 40 years old at the time. "We are a young company," says the present company boss, who initially trained in fermentation science at the Tokyo University of Agriculture, then worked as a consultant in brewing management before taking on roles in various departments of his family business. "But our ancestors were at the top of the Banshu Toji Guild for many years. And for generations, our family has been working devotedly with yamada nishiki rice.

Ryusuke Honda, the kuramoto of Tatsuriki Brewery

# "

# We are very proud that 85 percent of our sake is brewed using yamada nishiki cultivated in the Special A district in Harima, one of our grand cru regions.

We are very proud that 85 percent of our sake is brewed using yamada nishiki cultivated in the Special A district in Harima (Banshu), one of our grand cru regions."

As in many parts of Japan, a regional chronicle was recorded at the request of the emperor in the historical province of Harima, as early as around the year 715. It includes, among other things, the oldest known description of sake. "Harima is a fertile region, well-adapted to rice cultivation, the home of yamada nishiki, and all Special A districts are located here," explains Ryusuke. "Sake brewers in the area have a well-known saying: 'When buying sake rice, first look at where it was grown.' My great-uncle Takeyoshi, who was the director of our brewery before my father, wanted to provide scientific proof to support this proposition. Once he had retired, he devoted himself to carrying out a soil analysis

in the regions where yamada nishiki is grown, with the support of Kyoto University. He analyzed how the oils there are composed and how their mineral content influences the taste of sake. He found out, for example, that a higher magnesium content in the rice contributes to a sake's kire (the fast tailing off of a sake's flavor) and to its bitterness. His research was very much admired by sake brewers and rice farmers all over Japan."

As we walk down to the ground floor of the Tatsuriki Brewery, Ryusuke continues to explain: "For over 130 years, we have had a qualification system called Village Rice to define the best farming areas for yamada nishiki. It's a similar classification system to the one used for Bordeaux wine growing areas. Traditionally, farmers and sake brewers would conclude their own sales contracts here in Harima. Nowadays, the large-grained yamada nishiki is

The toji contentedly examines the result of his work.

A soil sample on display: sake is also influenced by its terroir.

viewed as the highest quality of all sake rice varieties, but in the past, not every brewery recognized its value. Our company was one of the few exceptions."

When, in the middle of the 1970s, sales of sake, which until then had been continuously increasing, suddenly plummeted, many breweries could no longer afford their contracts with farmers. "For us, this created an opportunity to take over the best yamada nishiki fields. My great-uncle and my father regularly visited some of the farmers in the Special A district and gradually earned their trust. We were thus able to continuously increase the number of farmers under contract with us and acquire the choicest cuts of the Special A district, such as farmer Tokura-san's plots in Akitsu. Our motto is: 'Brew sake with rice you can look in the face.' We nurture our relationships with farmers and help them during the rice harvest and on many other occasions."

In line with their focus on terroir and rice farming, the Honda family have set up the Tatsuriki Terroir Center in one section of their retail store. The center presents soil samples and other exhibits that provide a detailed insight into the history and characteristics of the yamada nishiki rice paddies of Harima in Hyogo Prefecture, and also offers tastings of sake made from grand cru yamada nishiki.

By this point, I have three different types of sake to compare before me. "These are all junmai sake, brewed under the same conditions using yamada nishiki cultivated in the Special A districts of Yashiro, Tojo, and Yokawa, respectively," explains Ryusuke. An image of glowing green rice paddies immediately appears before my inner eye. That previous summer, Ryusuke had brought me to the Special A districts and showed me the rice paddies under contract with him there. Back then, the young rice plants were swaying in wave-like patters in the wind. The three types of sake now before us were brewed using the grains from their ears.

As Ryusuke pours out one sake after another, he shows me the soil sample corresponding to each one. "The sake in the first glass was brewed using rice from the paddies in Yashiro. The soil there is rich in clay minerals, sandstone, and pyrites, and is well permeable to water, so the rice does not grow such deep roots." The rice used to make the contents of the second glass grew in Tojo District. "There is a clay stratum there known as smectite. Our most exclusive sake, Kome no Sasayaki Akitsu, comes from this district." Finally, Ryusuke pours the last sake in the trio, made from rice grown in Yokawa. "The soil here has a high potassium and magnesium content, as well as a high CEC value (cation-exchange capacity), which makes it very fertile."

Indeed, the three sakes we taste are very different. All of them are smooth with full rice notes and umami. But they differ considerably in terms of their overall characters: Yashiro sake is smooth and light; the one from Tojo has a mineral structure with a slightly bitter note. The sake made from Yokawa rice is aromatic, more voluptuous and full-bodied than the other two, and this is the one I like most. "The three types of soil presumably originate from a period around 25 to 2 million years ago," says Ryusuke, "and back then, they would have been at the bottom of various rivers." Rice may be an annual plant, I think, but it has such deep roots and reflects the force of the land. "Sake made out of rice should taste of rice," confirms Ryusuke, smiling. He, too, has strong roots in the Harima region and is enthusiastically following his family's yamada nishiki tradition. —

# Regional Varieties: 30 Breweries

Japan is currently divided into 47 prefectures, which are regrouped into 8 or 10 districts; this system was derived at the end of the nineteenth century from the 274 feudal districts of the Shogun period. There are now around 1,200 sake breweries distributed all over the surface of the country. The economic and cultural connections among the ancient feudal regions still influence the flavor of regional sakes to this day—to which must be added the influence of each prefecture's research institute. The following pages outline the characteristics of these regional sakes, as well as 30 renowned breweries (see map p. 146).

## Hokkaido and Tohoku

The northern regions of Japan are rich in snow, soft water, rice—and sake brewed with those important ingredients. The large island of Hokkaido borders Russia, and its waters are rich in seafood, fish, and kombu seaweed. In the second half of the nineteenth century, many Japanese people from Honshu moved to Hokkaido and worked there in the coal mining industry, in fisheries, and in farming.

The greater region of Tohoku is made up of six prefectures. In its center is the Ou Mountain Range, which rises up to 2,000 meters (6,562 feet) and separates the snowy western region on the Sea of Japan from the relatively mild eastern region on the Pacific Ocean. Rice is extensively farmed in the multiple deep circular valleys and coastal alluvial cones that lie in between the mountains. The sake master brewers from the famous Nanbu Toji School in Iwate Prefecture are held in high esteem for their fine ginjo style. They mainly work in the Tohoku Region but can be found all over the rest of Japan, too. Their style of sake is clear and lithe, with discreet fruity aromas. The region's cool climate, low bacterial populations, and cold-resistant rice farmed specifically for sake guarantee that brews from Tohoku are of the highest quality. Sake from Hokkaido is clear, light, and fresh.

Looking ahead: tradition also arises out of innovation.

## ① NANBU BIJIN, Iwate

**Brewery:** Nanbu Bijin Shuzo
**Founded:** 1902
**Kuramoto:** Kosuke Kuji (5th generation)
**Toji:** Makoto Tamura
**Annual sake production volume:**
3,000 koku (approx. 5,400 hectoliters /
142,653 gallons)

*Nanbu Bijin* means "beauty of the Nanbu region" and is fitting for this brewery, which produces a beautiful, clear sake in the middle of the mountains. Its brewing method and flavor profile are influenced by the famous Nanbu School. The fifth-generation kuramoto studied fermentation science in Tokyo and has used innovative methods to create a new tradition. These methods have borne fruit, and Nanbu Bijin's "Southern Beauty" won the Champion Sake 2017 award at the International Wine Challenge (IWC).

## ② URAKASUMI, Miyagi

**Brewery:** Saura
**Founded:** 1724
**Kuramoto:** Koichi Saura (13th generation)
**Toji:** Isao Akama, Keiji Takahashi,
Kunio Onodera
**Annual sake production volume:**
8,700 koku (approx. 15,660 hectoliters/
413,693 gallons)

Since its foundation in 1724, Urakasumi has been selling its sake to the faithful, to be given as an offering at the nearby Shiogama Shrine. The name *Urakasumi* comes from a medieval poem and means "sea fog in the spring." The brewery lies on the Sanriku Coast in Miyagi Prefecture, an area renowned for first-class fishing and outstanding rice farming. Urakasumi sake, which is mild and elegant, harmonizes perfectly with tuna fish, oysters, and sushi. Kyokai Yeast No. 12, which used to be sold all over Japan, comes from this brewery.

## ③ KATSUYAMA, Miyagi

**Brewery:** Katsuyama Shuzo
**Founded:** 1688
**Kuramoto:** Heizo Isawa (12th generation)
**Toji:** Mitsuaki Goto
**Annual sake production volume:** 800 koku
(approx. 1,440 hectoliters/38,041 gallons)

Founded in Sendai during the Edo period, Katsuyama is a prestigious brewery with a proud tradition: it used to be the purveyor to the court of the local Date feudal lords. Their sake has a lovely, clear fruitiness and a lot of umami, and it is distinguished by the elegant way it flows down the throat. It is an excellent accompaniment to European dishes. The brewery's signature sake, Katsuyama Ken, was elected Champion Sake (the best sake in the world) at the International Wine Challenge (IWC) in 2019. The company exclusively brews junmai-quality sake, following manual procedures but using the most modern technology. For its best "Diamond" sake, it uses a special centrifuge to press the mash.

## ④ YUKI NO BOSHA, Akita

**Brewery:** Saiya Shuzo
**Founded:** 1902
**Kuramoto:** Kotaro Saito (5th generation)
**Toji:** Toichi Takahashi
**Annual sake production volume:** 4,000 koku
(approx. 7,200 hectoliters/190,204 gallons)

This brewery was built on a hillside in the historic port city of Yurihonjo, in quiet, snowy Akita, and is Japan's first certified organic sake brewery. In order to maintain a balance between the microorganisms in the mash, the latter is not stirred, unlike in most other breweries. The use of house yeast and the resurrection of the yamahai method, under the leadership of the famous toji, Takahashi, underline how the company strives to produce a sake that is high-quality and close to nature. *Yuki No Bosha* means "snowy cabin"—and this sake indeed tastes as clear as melted snow.

## ⑤ HATSUMAGO, Yamagata

**Brewery:** Tohoku Meijo
**Founded:** 1893
**Kuramoto:** Junji Sato (4th generation)
**Toji:** Hideyuki Goto
**Annual sake production volume:**
not published

Hatsumago was distinguished by the IWC as "Brewery of the Year" in 2018, and since then has won the trophy for Best Sake in three categories. This is a great success, since the brewery does not follow any trends but rather brews exclusively following the traditional kimoto method. The quality of its sake is apparent in its fine and deep umami flavor and its typically creamy, dry finish. The brewery is located in the old port city of Sakata, which became very rich thanks to the rice trade and kitamae ships, and the Sato family, which founded it, were also marine wholesalers. *Hatsumago* means "firstborn grandchild."

## ⑥ DEWAZAKURA, Yamagata
**Brewery:** Dewazakura Shuzo
**Founded:** 1892
**Kuramoto:** Masumi Nakano (4th generation)
**Toji:** Yoshiyuki Inoue
**Annual sake production volume:** 7,000 koku (approx. 12,600 hectoliters/332,857 gallons)

The secret of Dewazakura's success is its use of local water, local rice, and the philosophy of its master brewer. Its steady long-term seller, "Cherry Bouquet" (Oka Ginjo), has popularized the term *ginjo* in Japan and throughout the whole world since 1980. In 2008 and 2016, the brewery won the Champion Sake award at IWC. The trade name *Dewazakura* was taken from the cherry blossom of the Dewa Region. Yamagata is renowned for being very snowy, and Dewazakura sake embodies the longing for spring and cherry blossoms.

## ⑦ YAMAGATA MASAMUNE, Yamagata
**Brewery:** Mitobe Shuzo
**Founded in:** 1898
**Kuramoto:** Tomonobu Mitobe (5th generation)
**Toji:** Tomonobu Mitobe
**Annual sake production volume:** 800 koku (approx. 1,440 hectoliters/38,041 gallons)

Founded in snowy Yamagata Prefecture, the Mitobe family brewery uses water with a high mineral content to produce its sake, which is unusual in Japan and gives the drink a clear and distinctive flavor. The company brews exclusively according to the junmai style, meaning without any added alcohol, which emphasizes the full umami flavor of the rice. Since 2004, the brewery has also been involved in rice farming, following the motto that the art of sake brewing starts with tending to your own rice paddies.

## ⑧ NINKI, Fukushima
**Brewery:** Ninki Shuzo
**Founded:** 1897/2007
**Kuramoto:** Yujin Yusa (1st generation)
**Toji:** Yasushi Takahashi
**Annual sake production volume:** 1,150 koku (approx. 2,070 hectoliters/54,684 gallons)

The owner of the Ninki Brewery is Yujin Yusa, who belongs to the 19th generation of an old samurai and brewer family. As the second-born, he took over the neighboring brewery in 2007 and founded a new company, in which he exclusively brews ginjo-quality sake. The trade name *Ninki* means "favorite," referring to the sake brewer's striving for perfection. The snowy region in northern Japan is reflected in the purity of this sake. All this company's sakes are brewed in wooden barrels made out of 100-year-old cedar trees; this gives the sake immense depth and complexity.

## ⑨ NIIDA HONKE, Fukushima
**Brewery:** Niida Honke
**Founded:** 1711
**Kuramoto:** Yasuhiko Niida (18th generation)
**Toji:** Yasuhiko Niida
**Annual sake production volume:** 1,000 koku (approx. 1,800 hectoliters/47,551 gallons)

This brewery's kuramoto—who belongs to the 18th generation of his family—brews his natural (kimoto-style) Shizenshu sake using spontaneous fermentation and rice cultivated without any pesticides or fertilizers. The brewery is surrounded by its own rice paddies and wooded hills covered in sugi cedars. Its aim is to be self-sufficient: to use sake rice from its own farm and large wooden barrels produced in-house out of sugi cedars from the family woods. Nida Honke sake has strong rice notes with a milder umami.

## Kanto and Tokai
Since the sixteenth century, the Kanto district has developed in unison with Tokyo, its largest city. Rice cultivation was promoted on the vast Kanto Plain, and there are many sake breweries lining the rivers and historic roads, such as Tokaido. Sake from Kanto reflects the taste of its townsfolk: refined, fruity, and fresh. Many master brewers from the Echigo Toji School (Ni-

142

igata) and the Nanbu Toji School (Iwate) cherish this flavor profile. In Tokyo, which reports the highest consumption of rice wine, you can find (almost) anything, from classic to trendy types of sake. Breweries in the countryside mostly follow trends from the metropolis, so there is a dynamic exchange between the two. Ibaraki Prefecture boasts the oldest sake brewery in Japan—its foundation goes back to the twelfth century, and it is still producing sake today.

The Tokai region lies on the Pacific Ocean between the major economic areas of Kyoto/Osaka and Tokyo. The humid oceanic climate has enabled the brewing industry to flourish, producing both sake and condiments such as soy sauce, mirin, miso, and vinegar, which season many dishes here. The best accompaniment for such dishes is a full-bodied, occasionally sweet sake that gets its flavor from the region's mild climate, which promotes fermentation. In Shizuoka Prefecture, with its famous fishing port, fresh, fruity sakes are favored as fitting accompaniments to various seafood specialties.

## ⑩ DARUMA MASAMUNE, Gifu

**Brewery:** Shiraki Tsunesuke Shoten
**Founded:** 1835
**Kuramoto:** Shigeri Shiraki (7th generation)
**Toji:** Hitoshi Shiraki
**Annual sake production volume:** 123 koku (approx. 222 hectoliters / 5,865 gallons)

This brewery was founded in 1835 in Gifu, the geographic center of Japan. It is a pioneer for aged sake and has been producing a vintage sake every year since 1975. A married couple, the Shirakis act as dual kuramoto, and they only produce their impressive product in small quantities. Their Daruma sake was named after a legendary Zen monk; its name means "always get up again, overcome all difficulties, don't give up." The brewery was entirely destroyed in 1891 by a severe earthquake, but—faithful to its name—it managed to recover.

## ⑪ OGASAWARA MIRIN, Aichi

**Brewery:** Ogasawara Mirin
**Founded:** 1922
**Kuramoto:** Kazuya Ogasawara
**Toji:** Kazuya Ogasawara
**Annual sake production volume:** not published

Ogasawara Mirin is Japan's smallest mirin brewery, located in the Mikawa Region, in Aichi Prefecture. The region has been the main production site of mirin for over 200 years, thanks to its mild, humid climate, and it is also famous for other fermented products such as vinegar, soy sauce, and sake. This two-person company, which was founded in 1922, is focused on quality and authenticity. Its handmade sweet and mild mirin is a source of fascination for consumers and professional chefs the whole world over.

## Koshinetsu and Hokuriku

The northwest coast on the Sea of Japan and the center of the country, with the Japanese Alps, Hida Mountains, and Tateyama and Hakusan mountain ranges, are famous for their higher-than-average snowfalls. In the winter, short days, low temperatures, and storms (as well as snow) define the climate in Niigata, Toyama, Ishikawa, and Fukui. In spring, melting snow fills the rice paddies in the wetlands—such as the Echigo and Kaga plains—with water. This region is home to the famous sake rice, gohyakumangoku, which is responsible for tanrei karakuchi, the clear, light, dry flavor of sake from these parts. Two famous toji schools uphold the regional flavor: sake in the Echigo Toji style is fine and dry, while sake in the Noto Toji style, brewed according to the yamahai method, is full-bodied and rich in umami. Toyama Bay is famous for its wealth of fish and seafood, such as buri, shrimp, and zuwai crab. Niigata Prefecture, meanwhile, is known as the "Kingdom of Sake" and is proud to boast the country's third-largest production volume and the highest level of sake consumption per adult (8.6 liters per year). Nagano and Yamanashi are situated inland and have mountains rising up to between 2,000 and 3,000 meters (6,562 to 9,842 feet). Their landscapes and climates are favorable for cultivating vines and rice, which require big differences in temperature between day and night, many hours of daylight, and low precipitation rates—though the region is still rich in clear and cold snowmelt water. The land used for farming is situated between 300 and 500 meters (984 and 1,640 feet) above sea level.

## ⑫ SHICHIKEN, Yamanashi

**Brewery:** Yamanashi Meijo
**Founded:** 1750
**Kuramoto:** Tsushima Kitahara
(13th generation)
**Toji:** Ryogo Kitahara
**Annual sake production volume:** 3,800 koku
(approx. 6,840 hectoliters/180,694 gallons)

This brewery is situated in the Hakushu region, surrounded by the majestic Japanese Alps and Mount Fuji. The clear Hakushu water, which comes from one of the best water sources in Japan, is famous for its softness and mineral abundance. Sake from Shichiken reflects the texture and purity of the water and is refreshingly smooth, silky, and soft; the brewery focuses on innovative product development, and its specialization in sparkling sake. Its collaboration with the neighboring Suntory whisky distillery, whose barrels Shichiken and other breweries use to age their sake, is now bearing fruit.

## ⑬ SAWA NO HANA, Nagano

**Brewery:** Tomono Shuzo
**Founded:** 1901
**Kuramoto:** Kenichi Tomono (5th generation)
**Toji:** Takayuki Tomono
**Annual sake production volume:** 680 koku
(approx. 1,224 hectoliters/32,335 gallons)

This brewery was founded in 1901 in Saku. Inspired by the region's splendid nature, which is defined by lush forests and snowy winters, the brewery chose the iris flower as its symbol. The name *Sawa no Hana* refers to the beautiful flowers on the banks of the crystal-clear rivers in Saku, and its sake has a similar flavor: flowery, clear, and refreshing. The master brewer obtains this flavor by exclusively using two local varieties of rice—hitogokochi and miyama nishiki—as well as groundwater from the Japanese Alps.

## ⑭ IMAYO TSUKASA, Niigata

**Brewery:** Imayo Tsukasa Shuzo
**Founded:** 1767
**Kuramoto:** Toru Okada
**Toji:** Satoru Furuta
**Annual sake production volume:**
not published

Niigata, where Imayo Tsukasa was founded in 1767, was a rich port city with many classic ryotei restaurants through to the early Meiji Era (1868–1912). The genteel hospitality culture that was practiced in these restaurants, complete with geishas, encouraged the brewery to produce excellent and elegant sake. *Imayo Tsukasa* means "master of time;" fittingly, the brewery produces a sake that satisfies contemporary tastes. It exclusively brews junmai sake from Niigata rice. The sake is typical for Niigata: light and dry, but still retaining the umami of the rice.

## ⑮ KIRIN, Niigata

**Brewery:** Kaetsu Shuzo
**Founded:** 1880
**Kuramoto:** Shunichi Sato (5th generation)
**Toji:** Hisaaki Hasegawa
**Annual sake production volume:** 1,000 koku (approx. 1,800 hectoliters/47,551 gallons)

This brewery was founded in 1880 in Tsugawa, on the Agano river. Good rice from the renowned local rice farming area and the region's snowy, cold climate in the winter guarantee the purity of its sake's flavor. Kirin sake is named after a mythical creature that is supposed to bring people luck. The current brewery owner, just like his father, used to be an expert sake assessor. The house specialty is aged sake.

## ⑯ MASUIZUMI, Toyama

**Brewery:** Masuda Shuzo
**Founded:** 1893
**Kuramoto:** Ryuichiro Masuda (5th generation)
**Toji:** Kiichiro Hatanaka
**Annual sake production volume:** 1,800 koku (approx. 3,240 hectoliters/85,592 gallons)

This brewery, which was founded in 1893, is located in the trading post city of Iwase on the west coast of Japan. The region, which is surrounded by impressive mountains and clear rivers, offers ideal conditions for rice farming

The very essence of satoyama: Sankyoson in Toyama

**1. Nanbu Bijin**
nanbubijin.co.jp
**2. Urakasumi**
urakasumi.com
**3. Katsuyama**
katsu-yama.com
**4. Yuki No Bosha**
yukinobosha.jp
**5. Hatsumago**
hatsumago.co.jp
**6. Dewazakura**
dewazakura.co.jp
**7. Yamagata Masamune**
mitobesake.com
**8. Ninki**
ninki.co.jp
**9. Niida Honke**
1711.jp
**10. Daruma Masamune**
daruma-masamune.co.jp
**11. Ogasawara Mirin**
ogasawara-mirin.jp
**12. Shichiken**
sake-shichiken.com
**13. Sawa No Hana**
sawanohana.com
**14. Imayo Tsukasa**
imayotsukasa.co.jp
**15. Kirin**
www.sake-kirin.com

**16. Masuizumi**
masuizumi.co.jp
**17. IWA**
iwa-sake.jp
**18. Tedorigawa**
tedorigawa.com
**19. Tengumai**
tengumai.co.jp
**20. Shirayuki**
konishi.co.jp
**21. Fukuju**
enjoyfukuju.com
**22. Tatsuriki**
taturiki.com
**23. Mimurosugi**
imanishisyuzou.com
**24. Kaze No Mori**
yucho-sake.jp/en/
**25. Hanatomoe**
hanatomoe.com
**26. Gokyo**
www.gokyo-sake.co.jp
**27. Dassai**
www.asahishuzo.ne.jp
**28. Bijofu**
bijofu.jp
**29. Ikekame**
ikekame.com
**30. Amabuki**
amabuki.co.jp

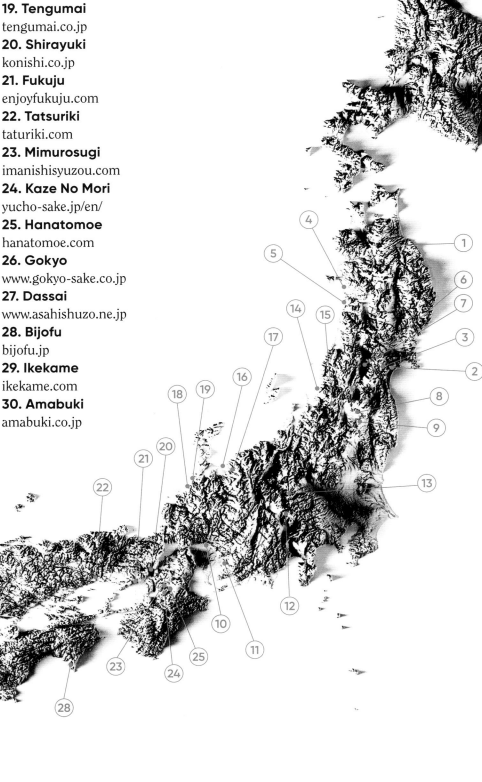

and sake production. Its cuisine centers around fish and seafood dishes; *Masuizumi* sake, which retains the sweetness and umami of the rice and has a mild flavor, is an ideal accompaniment for these. *Masuizumi* means "source of perfect happiness."

## ⑰ IWA, Toyama
**Brewery:** Shiraiwa
**Founded:** 2018
**Kuramoto:** Richard Geoffroy (1st generation)
**Toji:** Masato Yabuta
**Annual sake production volume:**
not published

IWA was founded in 2018 by Richard Geoffroy (the former cellar master of the Dom Pérignon champagne house) and Ryuichiro Masuda (the kuramoto of Masuizumi) in Shiraiwa. The building, a jewel of contemporary brewery architecture designed by Kengo Kuma, is surrounded by majestic mountains, the sea, and rice paddies and embodies the fusion of tradition and modernity. Over 20 different base sakes are now produced at IWA using three varieties of rice, both according to the traditional kimoto method and the modern sokujo procedure. Every year, Richard uses these and the previous year's sake to create a new assemblage.

## ⑱ TEDORIGAWA, Ishikawa
**Brewery:** Yoshida Shuzo
**Founded:** 1870
**Kuramoto:** Yasuyuki Yoshida (7th generation)
**Toji:** Yasuyuki Yoshida
**Annual sake production volume:** 2,800 koku (approx. 5,040 hectoliters / 133,143 gallons)

The inspiration for this brewery's brand name was the Tedorigawa River, which is fed in the spring by meltwater from Mount Hakusan. Its sake, produced using local rice and this clear water, has now been a favorite for 150 years, not just for many locals, but also for sake lovers all across Japan. The documentary film *The Birth of Saké*, which won several prizes in 2015, centers on this brewery and its young kuramoto-toji, Yasuyuki.

## ⑲ TENGUMAI, Ishikawa
**Brewery:** Shata Shuzo
**Founded:** 1823
**Kuramoto:** Kazunari Shata (8th generation)
**Toji:** Joji Okada
**Annual sake production volume:**
not published

This brewery is famous throughout Japan and the whole world for its golden, intensely flavored yamahai sake. It is situated on the Kaga Plain between the Sea of Japan and Mount Hakusan, surrounded by rice paddies. Its brand name, Tengumai, means "dance of the mountain demon." Tengumai sake was developed in 1970 by the legendary Noto-Toji, Saburo Naka. A few years ago, the 8th kuramoto created Gorin, a new brand of sake with a fresh and fruity flavor.

## Kinki/Kansai
The ancient imperial cities of Nara and Kyoto are located in the Kinki region (better known as Kansai), which was a major political, economic, and cultural center through to the Edo period (1603–1867). The landscape and climate in Kinki are variable: the northern part, containing the Hyogo and Kyoto prefectures, has a snowy climate typical for the regions lining the Sea of Japan. In the southern part of the Chugoku Mountains and Tanba plateau, the cities of Kyoto and Nara nestle in deep circular valleys and have hot summers and cold winters. The port cities of Osaka and Kobe are located on the warm Setouchi Bay; during the Edo period, a lot of sake was shipped from here to Edo. Nara is viewed as the birthplace of sake. It is also home to the Omiwa Jinja, the oldest shrine in Japan, where annual sake ceremonies are held, as well as the Shoryakuji Temple, where important brewing techniques were developed in the Middle Ages. Hyogo Prefecture is home to the yamada nishiki variety of rice, which, thanks to its elegant and full-bodied flavor, is essential for producing premium sake. The Tanba Toji School in Hyogo has developed the most important brewing techniques of the past 300 years: kanzukuri and kimoto. The old, renowned sake villages of Fushimi in Kyoto and Nada in Kobe/Hyogo promoted industrialization in the post-war period, and around 50 percent of Japan's sake production comes from there. Small sake breweries in Kinki mass-produced sake for these large breweries through to the end of the 1970s. Nowadays, sake from Kinki is characterized by a rich, broad, and full-bodied flavor with a lot of umami and acidity.

Chasing away evil spirits: a lion dance in a fishing village in Toyama

This Nio guardian has watched over the Todaiji Temple in Nara since 1203.

149

## ⑳ SHIRAYUKI, Hyogo

**Brewery:** Konishi Shuzo
**Founded:** 1550
**Kuramoto:** Shinuemon Konishi
(15th generation)
**Toji:** Hiroyuki Sano
**Annual sake production volume:**
not published

This brewery, which was founded in 1550 in the old sake city of Itami, is the sixth oldest in Japan. The company philosophy is summed up in its motto, *Fueki ryuko* ("The essence of eternity lies in the constant search for novelty and challenges"). The family owns numerous old texts and brews its Edo Genroku no Sake following a 300-year-old recipe. The current kuramoto is committed to preserving traditional Japanese sake brewing techniques using koji.

## ㉑ FUKUJU, Hyogo

**Brewery:** Kobe Shushinkan
**Founded:** 1751
**Kuramoto:** Takenosuke Yasufuku
(13th generation)
**Toji:** Tetsuya Miyamoto
**Annual sake production volume:** 2,500 koku
(approx. 4,500 hectoliters/118,877 gallons)

This brewery, which was founded in 1751, is located in the famous sake village of Nada in Kobe, at the foot of Mount Rokko-Berge, and is blessed with unique local ingredients: mineral-rich spring water (miyamizu) and first-class sake rice (yamada nishiki.) It was rebuilt after the terrible Kobe earthquake in 1995 and now offers innovative products, such as frozen sake and sparkling sake fermented in the bottle. *Fukuju* means "happiness and longevity." The brewery is committed to sustainability, investing in renewable energies so all of its production processes are CO2-free.

## ㉒ TATSURIKI, Hyogo

**Brewery:** Honda Shoten
**Founded:** 1921
**Kuramoto:** Ryusuke Honda (5th generation)
**Toji:** Masayuki Teratani, Shinji Nakamura
**Annual sake production volume:** 2,000 koku (approx. 3,600 hectoliters/95,102 gallons)

The Honda master brewer family founded their company in 1921. It is situated in the midst of the rice production area to the west of Kobe, and it uses the very best quality of the outstanding rice variety, yamada nishiki, which is exclusively grown in the Special A district. Akitsu ("whisper of the rice"), produced from yamada nishiki rice polished to 35 percent, is one of the most expensive sakes in Japan. The brand name *Tatsuriki* means "power of the dragon;" the dragon is venerated as the tutelary god of water.

## ㉓ MIMUROSUGI, Nara

**Brewery:** Imanishi Shuzo
**Founded:** 1660
**Kuramoto:** Masayuki Imanishi
(14th generation)
**Toji:** Eiji Sawada
**Annual sake production volume:**
not published

This brewery was founded in 1660, situated near to the Omiwa Shrine. It embodies the theme of sake as a divine beverage; its slogan is "drink Miwa," and it uses local rice and water from the nearby holy Mount Miwa. Kuramoto Imanishi spares no effort in creating the heavenly flavor. He is resurrecting the bodaimoto brewing method that was developed in the Shoryakuji Temple in the Middle Ages.

## ㉔ KAZE NO MORI, Nara

**Brewery:** Yucho Shuzo
**Founded:** 1779
**Kuramoto:** Chobei Yamamoto
(13th generation)
**Toji:** Yuna Nakagawa
**Annual sake production volume:** 1,500 koku (approx. 2,700 hectoliters/71,326 gallons)

This brewery, which was founded in 1779, has constantly reinvented itself within the long tradition of Nara sake, developing a new style of sake in 1998 that is fresh, sparkling, and without any fine filtering, admixture of water, or pasteurization. The brand name, Kaze no Mori, means "forest of wind" and brings together ideas of unused energy and free spirits. The brewery's new challenge is to produce sake in ceramic containers following ancient recipes from the years 1355 and 1568.

 ## HANATOMOE, Nara
**Brewery:** Miyoshino Jozo
**Founded:** 1912
**Kuramoto:** Teruaki Hashimoto
(4th generation)
**Toji:** Teruaki Hashimoto
**Annual sake production volume:** 400 koku (approx. 720 hectoliter/19,020 gallons)

The Miyoshino Brewery is situated deep in the mountains of Yoshino, where the sugi cedar trees used to produce oke barrels grow. Due to the humid climate in the cedar forest, fermentation culture developed early here; the sake from the brewery is thus produced exclusively using spontaneous fermentation, without the addition of any yeast. This creates a unique product, which displays a pleasant combination of acidity and umami. The brand name, Hanatomoe, means "circle of cherry blossom" and refers to the famous cherry blossom hill of Senbon-Sakura.

## Chugoku

This district is split in two by the Chugoku Mountains. The northern region of San-in (Shimane and Tottori) lies on the Sea of Japan and developed early, both culturally and economically, due to its geographical proximity to China. It is here that the mythological home of Japan is located, and major sacred shrines, such as the Izumo Taisha Shrine, are preserved here. However, this early high culture has now given way to a more rural character. The sake produced close to the Sea of Japan is acidic, full-bodied, and robust, while in the southern Sanyo region on the Seto Inland Sea, people favor a sweet and mild flavor. Okayama Prefecture is home to omachi rice, which is used to brew a sake with rich, full-bodied flavor. People in Hiroshima Prefecture managed to produce ginjo sake using extremely soft water 100 years ago. Nowadays, Hiroshima is home to the National Research Institute of Brewing.

 ## GOKYO, Yamaguchi
**Brewery:** Sakai Shuzo
**Founded:** 1871
**Kuramoto:** Hideki Sakai (6th generation)
**Toji:** Kenichi Morisige
**Annual sake production volume:** 2,700 koku (approx. 4,860 hectoliters/128,388 gallons)

This brewery was founded in 1871 near the Nishiki River, which supplies the soft water used to make mild, aromatic Gokyo sake. All of the company's brewers come from the area, and they produce Yamaguchi sake with a local provenance. The name of the brewery means "five bridges," referring to the five-arched Kintaikyo Bridge, which has spanned the Nishiki in Iwakuni since 1673.

 ## DASSAI, Yamaguchi
**Brewery:** Asahi Shuzo
**Founded:** 1948
**Kuramoto:** Kazuhiro Sakurai (4th generation)
**Toji:** none
**Annual sake production volume:** 32,000 koku (approx. 57,600 hectoliters/1,521,631 gallons)

Under the motto "For joy and delectation," this family-managed brewery in the southwestern region of Japan only produces sake of the highest-quality class, junmai daiginjo, exclusively using yamada nishiki rice. Dassai's sakes have received numerous international distinctions. For Dassai 23, the best yamada nishiki rice is polished to up to 23 percent. The sakes are proudly named according to their polishing ratios, and the name *Dassai* means "otter festival," a poetic nod to the river otters that once roamed the local rivers, fishing and "celebrating" with fish laid out on the banks.

## Shikoku

The large island of Shikoku is located between the Seto Inland Sea and the Pacific Ocean. While people in the western part of the island favor sake with a sweet and smooth flavor, in Kochi Prefecture on the Pacific, dry and fresh sake is preferred. This is due to differences in geology, cultural and historical developments, and each area's drinking culture. The

population of Kochi is renowned for its independent, assertive mentality and requires an easy-to-drink, happy-go-lucky sake.

## 28 BIJOFU, Kochi

**Brewery:** Hamakawa Shoten
**Founded:** 1904
**Kuramoto:** Naoaki Hamakawa (4th generation)
**Toji:** Fumihiro Ohba
**Annual sake production volume:** 1,500 koku (approx. 2,700 hectoliters / 71,326 gallons)

This brewery was founded in 1904 on the southern coast of Shikoku Island in the small town of Tano, and it is surrounded by mountains, the Nahari River, and the Pacific Ocean. Upstream from the river grow dense cedar forests, which make the water soft and pure and the sake smooth. The fourth generation of this brewery developed a quality sake 20 years ago as an answer to the neutral taste that was common in local sakes at this period. The brand name, Bijofu, means "handsome and noble man" and was inspired by Ryoma Sakamoto, a local samurai.

## Kyushu and Okinawa

Kyushu, the third largest island in Japan, is more known for producing shochu (a liquor made from rice, barley, or sweet potato) than sake. But rice is grown in North Kyushu on the vast Chikushi and Saga plains by the Ariake Sea, and the Yoshinogari site, close to the remains of a village from the Yayoi period (fifth century BC to third century AD), is also one of the first places in Japan to have started farming the grain. Sake from Kyushu is generally sweet and full-bodied, a good pairing for local delicacies made out of chicken and pork in strong, sweet sauces. It was barely known outside of the island until 20 years ago. Nevertheless, several producers from this region have managed to develop a new sake style starting from this tradition—and to successfully commercialize it in big cities in Japan and overseas. In Okinawa, famous for its awamori (alcohol made out of black koij, mainly used in cocktails), there is one single brewery that has also been producing a small amount of sake since the 1960s.

## 29 IKEKAME, Fukuoka

**Brewery:** Ikekame Shuzo
**Founded:** 1875
**Kuramoto:** Teruyuki Kamachi (6th generation)
**Toji:** Shunta Sakai
**Annual sake production volume:** not published

This brewery was founded by a famous sword fighting master, who contributed to the development of the local sake industry with his pioneering idea. Its name means "turtle in the pond." The turtle is a symbol of good luck in Japan, connoting longevity. Ikekame Shuzo produces its sake using, among other things, black koji, which normally is only used to produce shochu. Its sakes have fresh acidity and full-bodied umami.

## 30 AMABUKI, Saga

**Brewery:** Amabuki Shuzo
**Founded:** 1688
**Kuramoto:** Sotaro Kinoshita (11th generation)
**Toji:** Ryutaro Inoue, Shinji Hinoshita
**Annual sake production volume:** 1,300 koku (approx. 2,340 hectoliters / 61,816 gallons)

The 300-year-old Amabuki Brewery is situated on the Saga Plain near the Chikugo River. Its sake rice is farmed locally without any chemicals, and its mild brewing water is taken from the Sefuri Mountains. The current kuramoto brought with him new know-how from the renowned Tokyo University of Agriculture. His sake, which is brewed using flower yeast, marks an innovative new moment in a long tradition of sake brewing.

Bird's eye view: three quarters of Japan are mountainous and covered in forests.

A tutelary god at the gate of the Masuizumi Brewery: the dragon symbolizes creativity and the element of water.

# Yasuhiko

NIIDA HONKE BREWERY
KOORIYAMA, FUKUSHIMA PREFECTURE

KOORIYAMA

Golden ears of rice sway under the clear autumn sky on the Niida family's field. Some of the ripe stems have already been cut by the small harvesting machine; the air smells of fresh straw. On the neighboring field, the ears are cut by hand. "We actually wanted to harvest our omachi rice in October, as usual, but it rained so much this year that we had to wait until the plants had dried," says Yasuhiko Niida. He is the 18th kuramoto and also the toji of the Niida Honke Sake Brewery, an agricultural company renowned for its traditional brewing methods—but above all for its commitment to using natural, raw materials and its efforts to become self-sufficient, in terms of these raw materials and its equipment for brewing sake.

The Niida estate, founded in 1711, is close to Tamura-cho Kanezawa in a beautiful landscape of evergreen forests, rice paddies, and small villages. There is a plum grove on the brewery land, as well as its newly renovated historic brewery building, with walls made out of loam and rice straw, a low wooden house in the traditional style, and an ancient wooden gate. I also discover a beehive made out of cedar wood and a stone fountain, burbling with crystal-clear water. Subterranean strata of young and old granite formations make the area around the brewery into one of those unusual places that flow with both hard and soft water. Niida Honke uses this for two different brands of products: Shizen-shu and Odayaka.

The Shizen-shu brand of sakes was developed by Yasuhiko's father, Yasumitsu, back in 1967, at the request of an organization for the promotion of natural foodstuffs: It is brewed using organically farmed rice, house yeast, and natural—hard—spring water, without the added alcohol and preservatives that were typical at the time. His additive-free sake was well-received; Niida Honke's production increased more than sixfold. The Odayaka brand, in contrast, which is brewed with soft water, owes its present quality to Yasuhiko, who took over the management of his family brewery at the age of 28, when his father fell seriously ill.

At first, the young kuramoto found it difficult to match his father's success. But Yasuhiko found his own way when he met the woman who would later become his wife, Maki—a jazz pianist. "When I dove into the world of jazz, in which the musicians vary the arrangements at whim, it became clear to me that the flavor of sake can change if the rice it is made with is different every year. So, I freed myself from the idea that I always have to produce the same sake."

Yasuhiko's natural approach and sake methods are unique in the sector. "The rice and the world of microorganisms in my cellar change every year—that goes without saying," he says. "But from time to time there are unexpected incidents. This year, our sake turned out to have a high acidic content, and we thought we wouldn't be able to sell it. However, a sake

Yasuhiko Niida, the kuramoto-toji of the Niida Honke Brewery

Sake rice from the brewery's own fields

The brewery workers' nameplates hang above the entrance to the toji chamber.

The cedar wood for the sake barrels comes
from the kuramoto family's own forest.

dealer in Tokyo found it very original, and so he absolutely wanted to have it." The kuramoto-toji jokes: "Other sake breweries worry about how close they have come to the quality of sake they are aiming for. We worry about whether we'll even be able to sell the sake our mash produces."

But Yasuhiko does not just think about his sake turning out alright. "We are always thinking about how we can use what our ancestors left behind, and what we can add to it in order to improve it for the next 100 years. For the blessings of nature cannot be taken for granted here—rather, they are the result of our forefathers sticking their hands into the ground for generations to protect it."

Yasuhiko's grandfather, for example, would regularly replant sugi trees (known in English as Japanese cedars) in order to support the ecological balance of the region. Yasuhiko keeps this small family forest healthy, and every year he has some of its trees cut down, using these to produce one large and one small sake barrel. One of the few remaining barrel makers in Japan transmitted his knowledge to the Niida employees in order to keep this tradition alive. "Our aim is to replace all our enameled brewing tanks with our own wooden barrels," explains the kuramoto-toji as we wander through the brewery premises, which were largely built with wood taken from the family forest. "In the wooden barrels, we only brew using the yeast that lives in the brewery. I thought that brewing in these barrels would suit our sake better, so as to create a flavor that you can only obtain in this brewery."

It was the catastrophe of Fukushima that led Yasuhiko to focus entirely on the issues of nature and self-sufficiency—even though the brewery was only slightly damaged by the seaquake back then, and was not affected by the radioactivity either, thanks to its topography and the wind direction. A good decade later, Yasuhiko says, "We want to be a model of a sake brewery that is also self-sufficient in terms of energy. But in order to provide for ourselves, we have to improve the environment around us. Our task is thus not just to ensure all the circa 60 hectares (148 acres) of rice paddies here are managed naturally, and that the farmers can live from their farming. We also want our electricity in the future to no longer come from energy providers around us, but rather from our own sources."

Many things have changed already under the management of the 18th generation of Niidas. There is even now a grand piano in the brewery's fermentation hall. Maki plays it from time to time; during client events, the hall changes into a concert venue. But the kuramoto-toji's wife does not just provide music at Niida Honke; she also plays several important roles in the new direction the brewery is taking. For example, she has encouraged the development of fermented foodstuffs, such as narazuke vegetables, and sugar-free sweets made using koji, and she initiated the production of ama sake, alcohol-free sake. In addition, she heads up the young branding team, whose ideas have increased the brewery's notoriety among new generations of sake drinkers. Maki also created the School in the Rice Paddies, in which volunteers organize activities for children and take part in planting and harvesting rice.

As my visit comes to an end, Yasuhiko Niida hands me a glass of shizen-shu made from 80-percent polished rice. It has a full aroma of koji and steamed rice, with a hint of white peaches. Its gentle acidity, sweetness, and umami are well-balanced. Then, I try a hyakunen kijoshu, which first went into production in 2011. Its aroma is reminiscent of raisins, dried plums, figs, and nuts, with notes of caramel and brandy; its flavor includes a complex sweetness and umami. This sake is produced according to a process in which, every year, finished sake from the previous year is added to the new mash instead of water. When the company celebrates its 400 years of existence, this will be a kijoshu that will have been brewed hundreds of times. How will that sake taste, I wonder? —

# Richard

**IWA BREWERY**
SHIRAIWA, TOYAMA PREFECTURE

SHIRAIWA

A wintery silence—the landscape stretches out completely white before you. Behind the snow-covered rice paddies on the edge of Tateyama Mountain, a large modern building with a glass façade and low, black roof stretches up toward the sky: Shiraiwa, the brewery responsible for IWA sake. Richard Geoffroy founded the company in 2018, after working for over a quarter of a century as the cellar master of the champagne house Dom Pérignon—in which capacity he frequently travelled to Japan.

"I was born in the Champagne region of France, and after studying medicine, I spent a large part of my life devoting myself to the production and commercialization of champagne," explains Richard. "In order to promote the sale of our products, I travelled to many parts of the world, but the culture, the people, and the sake in Japan particularly fascinated me. I was successful on the wine market, I had a great team, but gradually I started to feel the desire to leave my comfort zone, to take on some new challenges and do something for my beloved Japanese sake."

The Frenchman set off with just a suitcase and his great respect for Japan's over-1,200-year-old fermentation culture, and, having arrived in his new adopted home, made extensive visits to a range of sake breweries. "But it wasn't until my friend of many years, the architect Kengo Kuma, who had worked far beyond the borders of Japan, introduced me to the kuramoto Ryuichiro Masuda from Iwase and told me that he had felt the same energy between the two of us, that the decisive moment came to bring IWA into the world."

Kengo Kuma created an appropriate home for the new brewery in Tateyama-machi Shiraiwa, a beautiful village 30 minutes away from Toyama City, toward the holy mountain of Tateyama. He drew inspiration for it from the region's traditional farmhouses, which offered a living space, a workshop, and also room for animals underneath their overhanging roofs.

The Shiraiwa kura (brewing facility) also conceals a variegated inner life under its slanted cedar poles; as soon as they enter the impressive building, visitors find themselves in the 10-meter/33-foot-high atrium of the central tasting room. A large table placed in a recess and surrounded by benches is meant to be reminiscent of an irori, the fireplace in traditional Japanese houses. Another impressive aspect of the room is a concrete wall stretching up to the ceiling, covered in 10,000 leaves of washi, paper manufactured in the UNESCO Word Heritage Village of Gokayama, made out of rice hulls and straw from the fields surrounding the Shiraiwa Brewery.

Tastings and internal conferences are carried out in this setting, and clients from the gastronomy sector are often treated to multiple-course menus created by renowned chefs from Toyama, paired with different variations of IWA sake. The brewers also relax here between tasks. In the future, the doma, as this atrium area is referred to, and from which it is possible to

The shape and contents of the IWA bottles epitomize the philosophy of the brewery.

Architect Kengo Kuma has combined tradition and modernity in this building.

In Japan, the doma is the typical central space in a building for meeting and spending time with others.

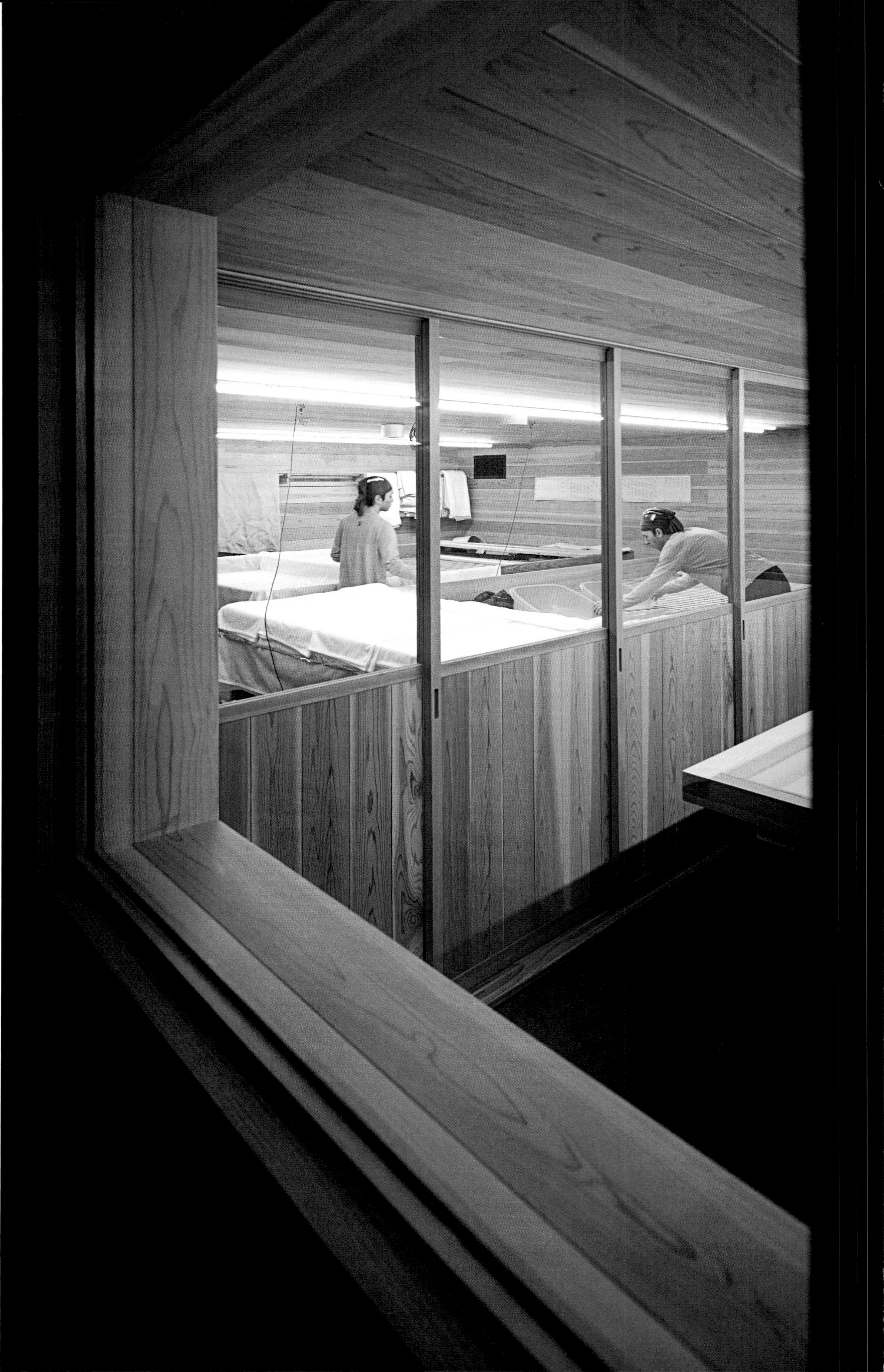

In a brewery, both human beings and microorganisms work together on the same product.

see into the brewing chamber with its stainless-steel tanks, thanks to a wide glass wall, is intended to promote exchanges between the brewery and the inhabitants of Shiraiwa.

"The concept of the IWA Brewery is welcome here," says Richard, who initially started out in the Masuda Brewery, producing various types of sake together with Kuramoto Ryuichiro and Toji Masato Yabuta from the Tanba Guild, who was versed in traditional brewing techniques. "But then we came to the decision that assemblage, a method used in champagne production in France, would be the best way to unlock the potential of sake." Using three varieties of rice polished to 35 percent—yamada nishiki from Hyogo, omachi from Okayama, and gohyakumangoku from Toyama—and five different types of yeast, Richard Geoffroy and his brewery workers now produce over 20 different base sakes following the traditional kimoto method and the modern sokujo process. Each May, Richard uses these and the sake from previous years to create a new assemblage.

"The clear, abundant spring water from the Japanese Alps has a beautiful minerality," enthuses the Frenchman. "But the real terroir of sake comes from the brewery. Unlike wine, which is influenced by the climate of a particular year and the quality of the grapes, the taste of sake is not just determined by its raw materials—rice and water—but also by the character of the brewery and, to a large extent, by its complex brewing process. The environment of the kura and the temperature and air humidity in the koji chamber are also important factors, comparable to the microclimate of a vineyard. This is the most exciting part for me as a winemaker. Compared to wines, which must comply with the A.O.C. system and are heavily limited by further formalities, sake is, in my view, surprisingly free. Unfortunately, the Japanese are barely aware of this and have not taken advantage of this freedom, for example, to use the technique of

assemblage, up until now. At IWA, we have an assemblage of over 20 different base sakes, which are then aged in the bottle for 15 months." The brewery's famous IWA 5 sake, as this experienced champagne man explains to us, "does not however have a finished recipe, but instead further develops every year through experimentation. The number five symbolizes balance, harmony, and essence."

By this point, we are each holding a wine glass with the current junmai daiginjo in our hand, ready to be tasted. For this type of sake, its aroma is astonishingly restrained, dignified, and pure, with herbal as well as mineral notes. After a while, it grows more complex with spicy notes of aniseed and white pepper. This sake floats lightly on the palate, while still feeling strong and full-bodied. Its structure is concise, profound, and has an exquisite finish.

"Complexity and drinkability are not contradictory concepts." Richard Geoffroy is convinced of this, just as he is convinced that sake has the potential to compete with champagne. "But it needs to spread more globally and lay a claim to being on the same level as wine, because sake is more in its element when it is not enjoyed on its own, but rather combined with food." Richard even has an example ready: "When recently I combined a series of spicy Chinese dishes with different sake variations, our slightly warm IWA 5 sake revealed a wonderful harmony. Neither a Burgundy wine nor an aromatic junmai daiginjo from a renowned Japanese brewery would have been able to compete."

Richard Geoffroy is connected to some of the world's best chefs, such as Massimo Bottura and Alain Ducasse, as well as Japanese kaiseki chefs Murata-san and Tokuoka-san, and he wants to "bring sake culture to the world," as he says full of near-youthful passion, his eyes blazing. In some renowned restaurants in Singapore and New York, IWA 5 is already part of the menu. —

# III.
# A FEAST
# FOR ALL
# THE SENSES

How does sake smell and taste? What vessel do you drink it from? With which foods does it go best? Sake means variety. In this chapter, meet a kuramoto and the gourmet destination he helped create, as well as a brewery owner dedicated to aged sake. Insights into the endless possibilities of sake pairing and tasting tours of Tokyo and Japan round out this culinary journey.

# Ryuichiro

MASUIZUMI BREWERY
IWASE, TOYAMA PREFECTURE

It is early afternoon in Iwase. Just a few steps away from the dock, Ryuichiro Masuda is waiting for us outside his family's centuries-old brewery.

"I want to show you our neighborhood first, though," he says. And so starts our excursion through the ages.

From the middle of the eighteenth century through to the end of the nineteenth century, Iwase, which lies on the mouth of the Jinzu River, where it flows into the Sea of Japan, was the home of the leading merchant navy wholesaler in Japan. Its historical businesses, living and storage premises along the canal, are a testament to the wealth they accumulated through trade between Hokkaido, Kyushu, and Osaka. Their kitamae-bune schooners, which once upon a time gave their name to the entire northern shipping route of the island nation, transported rice, sake, and cotton—among other things—out of Iwase and brought dried herring and kelp on the return journey.

Ryuichiro Masuda embodies the fifth generation of the Masuizumi sake brewery family. The first generation had already started trading rice wine at the end of the nineteenth century, but their son and his wife left Iwase for Hokkaido and went to Asahikawa to build a brewery there. However, following a possibly record-breaking cold period, these successful pioneers returned to their hometown in 1903, in order to continue exercising their brewing trade.

"Initially, they called their sake Iwaizumi," says Ryuichiro. "In order to ensure that the geishas in the ports could also enjoy their product, they founded a new brand, Masuizumi, which gets its name from our family. *Masuizumi* means 'source of perfect happiness'—and this sake did indeed immediately become a great hit."

When the rail network expanded and modern means of communication were developed at the end of the nineteenth century, shipping agents moved into banking and real estate and their sons left Iwase to set up new companies in Kansai and Tokyo or take on important government posts. Once resplendent commercial premises fell into ruin, and Iwase's heyday, during which paper and medicinal glass manufacturing had also long flourished, seemed to be over.

Ryuichiro Masuda, the kuramoto of the Masuizumi Brewery

A FEAST FOR ALL SENSES — AROMA. FLAVOR. DIVERSITY.

Sushi master Gejo prepares his fish of the day.

A FEAST FOR ALL SENSES — AROMA. FLAVOR. DIVERSITY.

Glass artist Taizo Yasuda has set up his workshop in an old storehouse.

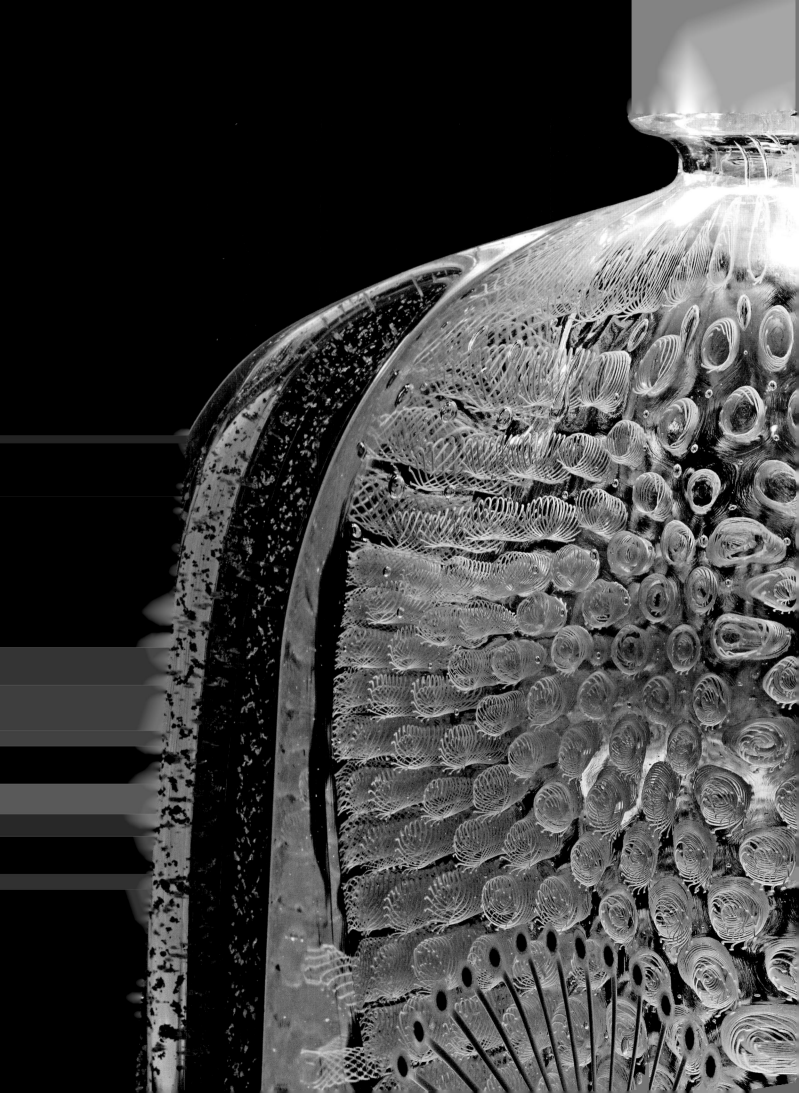

However, Ryuichiro Masuda refused to simply accept this. He bought up the empty buildings and started to restore them, one after the other.

"After studying in Europe and seeing medieval towns that were pulsating with life, in which people still felt comfortable and did business today, and which were becoming—just like Michelin-starred restaurants—the heart of the new development of small provincial towns, I decided to revive the historic streetscape of Iwase and to turn my city into an attraction for gourmets from the whole world over. I also remembered the wine cellars I had visited during my time in Europe and thought, if we have good sake, good food, and good culture here, then that will also attract people."

As Ryuichiro speaks, the tall kuramoto opens a sliding door on one of the former commercial buildings, from which hangs a modest sign reading "Kuchiwa" and walks in as briskly as if it were his own. "Good morning, how are you?" Under the high, black beamed ceiling, the first thing one notices is a table with a diameter of maybe two meters, made out of a halved tree trunk and supported by an iron frame. The presence of the wood is overwhelming. From the back of the house, Mr. Kuchiwa now comes to greet us. He used to run a soba restaurant in Toyama City, but when Ryuichiro invited him to do so, he moved his business to Iwase, which has now become a gourmet destination. Ryuichiro exchanges a few words with the restaurant owner, takes his leave with the promise that he will be back the next day, and quickly goes outside.

We too leave the premises and now turn into an alley next to a large sake shop, where we arrive at the Mori family's old warehouse complex. The building used to belong to one of the five most important shipping agents in Iwase. It is about 50 meters (164 feet) deep, located at the back end of the canal with a whole series of side doors. "This place is quiet now, but there must have been a lot of activity going on during the kitamae-bune era, when the ships were receiving or unloading their cargoes?" I ask Ryuichiro. By this point, we are standing in front of the front entrance to the complex. It leads into Cave Yunoki, a Michelin-starred French restaurant. Just like at Mr. Kuchiwa's, at the heart of Cave Yunoki is a large, massive wooden table. Ten people can sit down here.

Ryuichiro lovingly places his hands on the wood rings. He has a weakness for ancient wood, and when he hears about a good opportunity, he will travel around the world to buy it and have it turned into a table for one of the new shops, galleries or restaurants in one of the historic trading houses he has brought back to life.

The neighboring storehouse, which we enter now, is now used as a studio by the glass artist Taizo Yasuda. Inside, there is an iron table, a glass-blowing rod leaning on the wall, and a fire flickering inside a brick oven. On the table are glass artworks in various shades of color. I pick up a drinking glass with a delicate, diagonal pattern at the top. Its creator explains: "I make glass rods with various patterns, like spirals and lattices, and then I put them side by side and blow them thin." But it's not only hand-sized objects that are created here. There is also a large glass object hanging on the wall, which, as I learn, is worth several million yen.

Next to the glass art workshop is Gaku Shakunaga's studio. His ceramics are now used in Michelin-starred restaurants all over Japan. The potter tells me about how he became acquainted with Ryuichiro and how the kuramoto asked him, "You enjoy drinking sake—can't you make a cup that would be particularly good at expressing its qualities?" Ryuichiro then brought wonderful sake from his brewery every day, even junmai daiginjo. "While we drank the sake," adds the potter, "I would think about how I could do what he had asked of me. I think I've learned a lot from Ryuichiro and his sake."

Gaku Shakunaga now turns again to the Masuizumi kuramoto. The latter smiles discreetly, turns around, leaves the studio, and guides his steps to a side alley leading to what used to be a small canal, though it has now been filled in. "Shall we go and get a quick beer?" I hurry after Ryuichiro. Just 20 meters (65 feet) later, he stops in front of what used to be the rice store of the Baba wholesaler family. It is now a beautiful beer tavern with shiny brass tanks, run by a Czech master brewer and his Japanese wife. Once we have slaked our thirst with a glass of amber nectar, we stroll for a few minutes down the Omachi Shinkawa-cho Dori and enjoy the many historic wooden houses with sliding bamboo doors—an architectural style unique to this region. Our destination is the

A FEAST FOR ALL SENSES — AROMA. FLAVOR. DIVERSITY.

The taste of ikejime fish is unique.

Koshiki-daoshi: at the end of the brewing season, the brewers celebrate with their sake.

Giving and taking: the ritual of serving sake

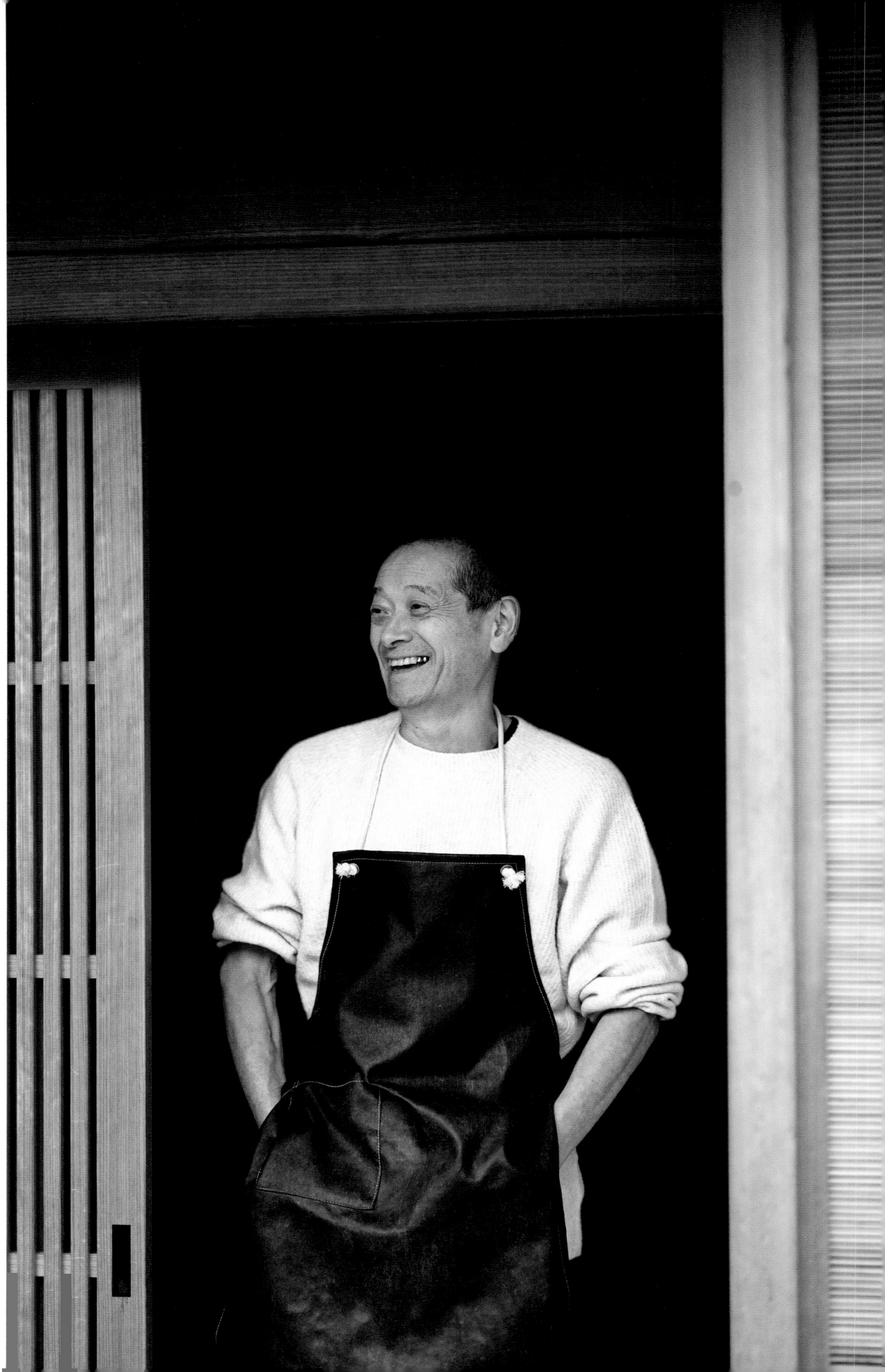

Chefs travel from as far as Tokyo to meet ikejime master Miura.

Saseki sake bar, which belongs to the Masuizumi Brewery. "This is where my grandmother used to live," explains Ryuichiro. Now, this old trading house contains a small wooden tasting cellar where you can try out around 100 different types of sake, all lined up in four glass-doored fridges. Here, too, there is a table made out of centuries-old wood, around which chatting customers enjoy their sake.

Next to Saseki, there is a two-Michelin-starred restaurant called Fujii. On the other side of the street is Gejo, Japan's most innovative sushi restaurant, just next to Nenjiri-tei, which frequently receives visits from Tokyo chefs, who come to observe how Master Miura keeps his fish fresh using the ikejime method (a method of killing fish very quickly by spiking their brains). Seven or eight types of perfectly matured white fish with wonderful textures are served here as sashimi. Masuizumi sake is served with the food everywhere. But Ryuichiro also enjoys drinking sake selected by the owner from other producers.

When we finally enter the Masuizumi Brewery, I am astonished to see dozens of junmai daiginjo bottles from the past 30 years lined up in Ryuichiro's private cellar. However, there are only a few bottles left from the year when this special sake was served for the wedding of the oldest Masuda son. At the back of the building complex is a storehouse that was built 150 years ago with thick, fire-proof plastered walls. A door with a carving of a dragon—a divinity that protects against fire—leads into a room full of bottles of further sake vintages and boxes of fine French and German wines. Ryuichiro has close friendships with a several top European winemakers, and the wines stored here, just like the various sakes, reflect his personal taste and contacts.

"This evening, we're celebrating koshiki-daoshi," announces Ryuichiro at the end of our walk. "You're welcome to join us!"

Excited anticipation at "tipping over the rice steamer" is written all over the face of the dynamic brewery owner. "We are a traditional brewery, and so we have a celebratory dinner on the night during which the last rice in the brewing process is steamed, to which we invite the toji and all other brewers and administrative employees." Indeed, as the day ends, around 50 Masuda guests find themselves sitting together on tatami mats in the large room of a traditional ryotei restaurant. Ryuichiro, who has taken his place in the middle of the room, makes a toast to the toji, thanking him for his work this year. Then, the toji gives his impressions of this year's production.

The festive ceremony is followed by an actual party. Ryuichiro and his wife, as well as his parents, pour out sake for the brewery workers and employees. During the first round, Ryuichiro chats and drinks with the guests. His family does the same. Even when, later on, the guests begin to mingle and pour sake for each other out of a tokkuri (carafe), those who are still sitting hold up their o-choko cup to the person serving with both hands. Once their cup has been filled, they bow their head in thanks before drinking. The dishes are then brought in one after the other, from sashimi to grilled fish and pickled shrimps. Just as I am trying to remove the cover from a bowl containing fish soup, the brewer in front of me takes the lid, hands it back to me, upside-down and pours sake into it. I am reminded of Ryuichiro's words: "Only someone who eats well can make good sake"—and I quietly enjoy my slightly warm Masuizumi junmai. —

# AROMAS, APPEARANCE, AND FLAVOR

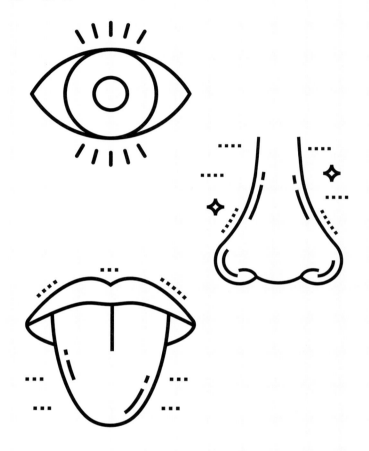

Sake is meant to be enjoyed with all the senses. The rice wine is viewed as the drink of the gods in Japan—and, just like there are a wide variety of Japanese gods, sake comes in a wide variety of aromas and flavors. Thanks to expert hands and modern brewing techniques, up to 500 different nuances can be created, each one aimed at bewitching the trio of eyes, nose, and tongue, as well as giving us indications about the origin and properties of a sake, the processing of its ingredients, its fermentation and storage.

Sake is enjoyed in a similar way to wine—as an aperitif, an accompaniment to food, and a digestif—and it is best enjoyed in small sips. Compared to its grape-based brother, the rice wine opens up an entirely different world to our senses: discreet aromas, low acidity, and a lot of umami all at once. Around 80 percent of a wine's character is communicated through the nose, around 20 percent through its flavor. This ratio is different with sake, which appeals more to one's perception of flavor. The following pages will introduce you to the typical aroma and flavor components of sake.

## Tasting Sake

Sake has many aroma and flavor components. In official professional tastings, people often use a white ceramic (180-milliliter/6-ounce) cup with straight, smooth sides and two blue circles painted on the inside bottom, which helps experts assess the clarity of the sake. In international sake tastings, this classic cup is replaced by wine tasting glasses so the aromas can be released by swirling the glass. The color, aroma, and flavor of a sake give many indications as to how its ingredients were processed, the fermentation method used to make it, and the way in which it was stored.

## APPEARANCE

Most sakes are clear and transparent. Sakes that are rich in extracts and have not undergone fine filtration (muroka) have a high level of viscosity, a slightly cloudy appearance, and often a discreet yellowness tending towards green. In many types, a reflective sheen can also appear.

Naturally cloudy sake (nigori) is coarsely filtered and contains fine rice particles. Red sake can be produced by using an ancient, black-purple variety of rice, or by fermenting the beverage with yeast that produces a red color (sekishoku-kobo). Aging can make the color of a sake change to dark brown, a result of the gradual binding of sugars and amino acids (Maillard reaction). This reaction is particularly encouraged when the sake being aged was made with less polished rice (meaning that it has a high protein content) and/or if it was not put through any fine filtering after being pressed. Uncontrolled aging through bright light and high temperatures (from room temperature) will also make a sake darken in color—but these factors have negative influences on the flavor and quality of the sake.

## AROMAS

The aromas of sake are discreet in the nose (uwadachi-ka) and on the tongue (fukumi-ka). In the case of premium ginjo sake and aged varieties, drinkers can enjoy an enduring aftertaste. Here are the most common aromas detected in various types of sake.

## Fruit, Flowers

Premium sake (ginjo) has a rich spectrum of aromas that can be reminiscent of fruit, such as apple, pear, banana, melon, peach, strawberry, citrus, muscat grape, pineapple, lychee, and quince. Added to these are floral components, such as white blossom, cherry and lime blossom, rose, lily, acacia, violet, lilac, and peony. These ginjo aromas are produced by chemical reactions during the fermentation process. For an impactful ginjo aroma, it

is essential to use highly polished rice and precisely control the very low fermentation temperature (5–11°C / 41–52°F).

## Grass, Wood, Minerals

Many sakes have fresh, green notes of grass, mint, bamboo, green tea, bay leaf, cherry leaf, oak leaf, hinoki (false cypress), cedar, pine needles, fennel, chervil, lemongrass, radish, chicory, or asparagus. Other notes include wet rock, moss, limestone, chalk, iron, or mountain water. Taruzake stored in cedar wood barrels has an aroma of freshly-split wood.

## Cereals, Cooked Vegetables

Classic junmai sake has aromas of cereal, steamed rice, rice flour, cookies, hay, bread, muesli, or cooked root vegetables such as carrot, radish, ginseng, and black salsify. These aromas come from the rice.

## Mushrooms, Koji, Yeast

The most important ingredient of sake, koji (fermented rice), has an aroma similar to that of mushrooms (e.g. button mushrooms) and sweet chestnuts. Additionally, many sakes (especially unpasteurized ones) have intense notes of bread. Aged nama sake or moroka sake can also sometimes have intense mushroom notes.

## Dairy Products

As a result of the way in which they are fermented, many types of sake develop aromas such as milk, butter, sour cream, yogurt, or aged cheese. Kimoto and yamahai sakes often have aromas reminiscent of yogurt. These are created by lactobacilli in the starter mash (moto).

# THE SAKE AROMA AND FLAVOR WHEEL

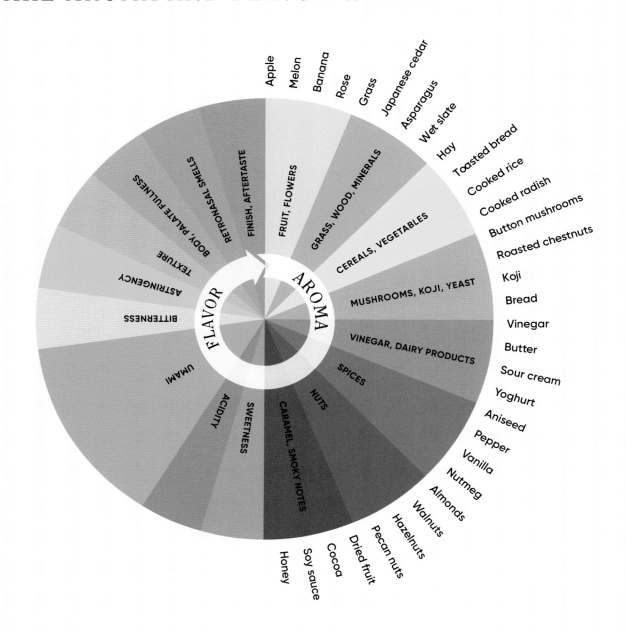

## Spices

Many ginjo sakes have notes of aniseed, tonka beans, or licorice. Sake that has been aged for a long time can develop aromas reminiscent of vanilla, pepper, clove, cinnamon, and nutmeg.

## Nuts

The aromas of aged sake are sometimes reminiscent of walnuts or roasted almonds. Some types of unpasteurized sake (nama sake) have hazelnut aromas.

## Caramel, Smoky Notes, Dried Fruit

Over time, many sakes with high residual sugar and amino acid content develop aromas of honey, chocolate, cocoa, brown sugar, coffee, black tea, raisins, or soy sauce.

## Faults

Storing sake in poor conditions (for example, in a bright shop window or on an uncooled rack) and contamination by bacteria can cause the development of undesired odors (stale, musty, animal). These include, for example, onion, vinegar, sulfur, and natto (isovaleric acid). The spoiled flavor unpasteurized sake can sometimes develop is referred to in Japanese as namahine.

## FLAVOR AND MOUTHFEEL

When drinking sake, one initially senses sweetness and sourness, then umami and bitterness, since the gustative nerves that detect bitterness are located at the back of the tongue. Astringency and texture are also detected in the mouth and mucous membranes. The retronasal smell, finish, and aftertaste are also important elements when enjoying sake.

## Sweetness (Amami)

During alcoholic fermentation, the yeast breaks up the sugar contained in the mash into alcohol and carbon dioxide; the sugar that cannot completely be broken up at this stage gives the sake its sweetness. This is not a strong sweetness, rather a gentle one, and it is reminiscent, when it diffuses in the mouth, of that of chestnuts and sweet potatoes. The ratio of sweetness to acidity determines whether a sake will be perceived as dry or sweet. The higher its acidity, the drier the sake will seem. Alcohol and sweet aromas can also contribute to a sweet impression if their perception can be intensified by umami. In the 1980s and 1990s, people used to favor dry sakes, such as Niigata-style sake; in more recent years, however, slightly sweet sakes with balanced umami are growing increasingly popular. *Amakuchi* means sweet, and *karakuchi* means dry.

## Acidity (Sanmi)

Sake has low amounts of acidity, which comes solely from its fermentation and gives the beverage its structure. The average acid content of sake corresponds to around one-fifth to one-tenth of that of wine made from grapes. Around 73 percent of the organic acids in sake are produced by the yeast in the mash, around 17 percent come from the starter mash, and the remaining 10 percent come from the steamed rice and koji. Sake contains lactic and malic acids, citric and acetic acids, and succinic acid. In classic sake, the lactic and succinic acid content is considerably high, endures in the mouth, and comes across even more strongly when the sake is warmed up. Malic and citric acids give the sake freshness, but this disappears quite quickly from the mouth. Some sake brewers now use black or white koji to produce fresh, acidic sake; low-alcohol sake and sparkling sake contain relatively high proportions of sugar and require high levels of acidity to balance out their flavors. The composition of the organic acids in a sake can be very different depending on the type of yeast used.

## Umami

This meaty, savory, and pleasant type of flavor was discovered 100 years ago by a Japanese man, Kikunae Ikeda. During koji production, a minute amount of protein in the rice turns into amino acids (glutamic acid, alanine, aspartic acid, and arginine). These, however, do not contribute only to umami, but also to sweetness, bitterness, and acidity. The less umami a sake contains, the lighter, clearer, and airier it will seem. If the proportion of umami is higher, the sake's flavor profile will be full-bodied, earthy, and complex; with too much umami, however, a sake will seem coarse and heavy. Cheap sake (futsushu) can have artificial umami (monosodium glutamate), acidifiers, and glucose added to it.

## Bitterness (Nigami)

A bitter taste is not desired in most types of sake. Bitterness is created by alcohol and other substances that arise during aging, such as amino acids, succinic acid, and peptides. A hint of these, however, gives an aged sake depth and complexity. Sake with a sweet or sour taste can be palatable at first, but quickly becomes boring. If, however, a slight bitterness is added to sweet or sour sensations, the taste buds are stimulated and the overall flavor intensifies.

## Astringency (Shibumi)

Sake does not contain any tannins, but it still has an astringent effect on the tongue. This adds complexity to its flavor.

## Texture (Kime)

A mild, "round" texture is particularly valued in sake. Young sake has a coarse texture. It is normally pasteurized after production and usually aged for half a year, which makes it smoother.

## Body (Kosa), Palate Fullness, and Koku

Koku is the overall impression created by all the flavors, aromas, and textures of a sake—a phenomenon determined by the complexity of the stimuli, as well as their spatial dimensions and durations. Sugar and acidity have big roles to play here. Sake with a high sugar and acid content is rich, full-bodied, and dense. The levels of amino acids (umami), peptides, and alcohol also contribute considerably to a sake's body, which is often referred to in Japan using one of two terms: tanrei (light and clear) and nojun (thick and full).

## Retronasal Smells (Fukumi-ka)

Aromas are not just perceived through the nose, but also through the oral cavity while drinking. The aromas that volatilize in the mouth and arrive in the nose through the airways are referred to as retronasal smells. Discreet aromas in sake can be detected with far more breadth and complexity when the beverage is warmed up on the tongue. The retronasal smell is thus an important key to harmonizing sake with food.

## Finish (Kire), Aftertaste (Yoin)

Many traditional Japanese sake aficionados value a clear and dry finish (kire) without any aftertaste, since the contrast between a full-bodied sensation on the tongue and a dry finish tempts you to take the next sip. However, a long and opulent aftertaste is valued in aged sake and in modern, premium sake.

## Harmony, Overall Impression

Balance and harmony are important to Japanese people in all circumstances—including, of course, when they are drinking sake. All good elements of taste are useless if they are not in harmony with each other. If a highly aromatic daiginjo sake does not have a corresponding body, it cannot provide an enduring taste experience. In 1964, Professor Kinichiro Sakaguchi wrote these words about the flavor of good sake: "Which sake is the best is difficult to say, since, being a luxury beverage, it can have a range of properties. Nevertheless, a fine harmony between the different elements of taste is an essential characteristic of a good sake."

## PARAMETER

### SMV (Sake Meter Value, Nihonshu-do)

An SMV measurement is a simple way of evaluating how sweet or dry a sake may be. This is done using a special hydrometer. If, at a temperature of 15°C (27°F), the sake weighs the same amount as 4°C (7°F) water, then the SMV is zero. If a sake contains more sugar and is heavier than water, the hydrometer will display a minus sign; a dry, light sake will show a plus sign. The sake's density will change according to its alcohol content, and sweetness is overpowered by acidity on the tongue—so a sweet sake with a high degree of acidity will taste dry.

# STYLES OF SAKE AND FLAVOR PROFILES

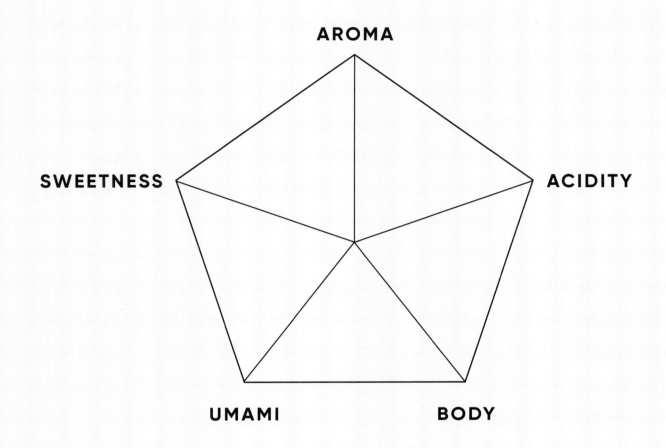

In Japan, sake is thought to be the highest form that rice can take. But the world of sake is huge. How does one navigate it? What opportunities are there to evaluate a particular sake? Depending on its combination of aromas and flavor components, a sake will conjure up different impressions and emotions. What criteria should you apply when you are trying to find your own favorite variety of this beverage? The following pages will give you an overview of the best sakes in Japan, complete with detailed descriptions of their flavor profiles, ranging from traditional to modern.

### The Five-Element Model

Is a sake light or full-bodied? This depends a lot on the interplay or composition of its individual elements. The five-element model (see template on p. 187 and following diagrams) is meant to show how your senses would perceive different sakes. The intensities of the five most important sensory elements (aroma, sweetness, acidity, umami, and body) are broken down here into six levels, from Level 1 (low) to Level 6 (high). Therefore, each style of sake takes on a different shape within this model: While the shape of a slender sake is small and compact, a rich, robust sake will inspire a much wider shape.

## STYLE A:
## Sparkling

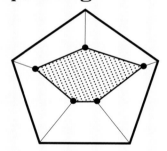

**Category:** Sparkling
**Characteristics:** Sake for those moments that make you tingle. A naturally cloudy, sweet, and sour creation with 6 to 8 percent alcohol content. Very accessible. You can also have a clear, dry, and complex sparkling sake with 12 percent alcohol content in a champagne bottle. A good option for an aperitif or to go with light starters. Enjoy this sake chilled (5–7°C/9–13°F).
**Aromas:** Peach, citrus fruit, gooseberry, lychee, chicory, rose petals
**Evaluation:** Aroma 3–4, Sweetness 3–5, Acidity 4–5, Umami 2–3, Body 2–3

## STYLE B:
## Light & Fresh

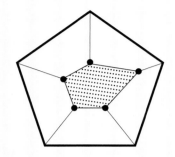

**Category:** Honjozo, ginjo, any sake with a high level of acidity and a low alcohol content
**Characteristics:** Light, fresh sake with discreet aromas of green fruit and herbs. Goes well with light dishes and starters, including fish carpaccio, sashimi, and sushi, as well as deep-fried dishes such as tempura. Enjoy this sake chilled (7–10°C/13–18°F).
**Aromas:** Grapefruit, green apple, nashi pear, chervil, pine needles, chalk
**Evaluation:** Aroma 2–3, Sweetness 2–3, Acidity 2–4, Umami 2–3, Body 2–3

## STYLE C:
## Fruity & Mild

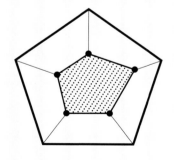

**Category:** Junmai ginjo, tokubetsu junmai, junmai
**Characteristics:** Well balanced, fruity aromas and mild rice flavor. Not brash, but rather harmoniously mild. An ideal accompaniment for food, pairing well with dishes such as fish or vegetables with butter or cream. Enjoy this sake chilled (10–15°C/18–27°F).
**Aromas:** Peach, apple, pear, banana, acacia, steamed rice, almond milk
**Evaluation:** Aroma 3–4, Sweetness 2–3, Acidity 3–4, Umami 3, Body 3

## STYLE D:
## Aromatic & Expressive

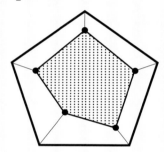

**Category:** Junmai daiginjo, daiginjo, junmai ginjo, nama
**Characteristics:** A highly aromatic and expressive sake with numerous fruity and flowery nuances and a strong flavor. Wakes up all the senses. Pairs well with fatty, well-seasoned dishes such as teriyaki salmon, lobster, steak, and game. Enjoy this sake chilled (10–15°C/18–27°F).
**Aromas:** Melon, red apple, pineapple, pear, lily, Muscat grape, fennel, aniseed
**Evaluation:** Aroma 4–5, Sweetness 3–4, Acidity 3–4, Umami 3–4, Body 3–4

# STYLE E:
## Complex & Refined

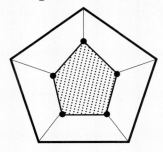

**Category:** Daiginjo, kimoto junmai daiginjo

**Characteristics:** A sake for bon vivants and connoisseurs. It has multilayered aromas, silky texture, and a complex range of flavors with a unique aftertaste. Pairs well with caviar and oysters, but also with wagyu beef. Enjoy this sake chilled to 10–15°C/18–27°F; kimoto sake can also be warmed to 35–45°C/63–81°F.

**Aromas:** Melon, jasmine, acacia, satsuma, golden delicious apple, lychee, violet, sherry, cream

**Evaluation:** Aroma 3–4, Sweetness 2–3, Acidity 2–4, Umami 2–4, Body 3–4

# STYLE F:
## Traditional & Umami

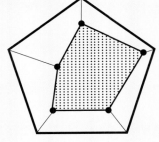

**Category:** Junmai, kimoto, yamahai, bodaimoto, genshu, spontaneous fermentation

**Characteristics:** Rich and full-bodied with clear rice notes and well-integrated acidity and umami. Depending on the season, it is enjoyed at temperatures between 10° and 55°C/18° and 99°F. This sake develops different nuances of flavor and pairs just as well with sashimi as it does with well-seasoned dishes.

**Aromas:** Steamed rice, bread, banana, butter, yoghurt, cocoa, hazelnut

**Evaluation:** Aroma 3–5, Sweetness 2–4, Acidity 4–5, Umami 4–5, Body 3–5

# STYLE G:
## Aged

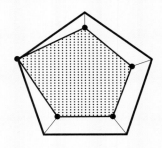

**Category:** Aged junmai with kimoto/yamahai, genshu, aged in the barrel

**Characteristics:** Golden-brown, heavy sake with complex aromas and an equally complex flavor, both developed over time. Notes of caramel, honey, winter spices and chocolate. Complex sweetness and umami. Can be enjoyed on its own or with foie gras, nuts, chocolate, dessert, or a cheeseboard at temperatures ranging between 10° and 45°C/18° and 81°F).

**Aromas:** Forest honey, caramel, chocolate, soy sauce, walnut, raisin, dried apricot, nutmeg, cloves

**Evaluation:** Aroma 5–6, Sweetness 2–6, Acidity 5–6, Umami 4–6, Body 4–6

# STYLE H:
## Sweet & Aromatized

**Category:** Sweet junmai, kijoshu, premium mirin, sake liqueur

**Characteristics:** Sake or liqueur for a relaxed end to a meal or day. Viscous, with high residual sugar content and complex umami. Has notes of fruit, honey, and caramel and pairs well with foie gras, cheese, chocolate, and dessert. Enjoy this sake chilled (5–15°C/9–27°F).

**Aromas:** Ripe melon, banana, steamed rice, caramel, honey, fruitcake, milk chocolate (in the case of mirin and kijoshu); aromas of the fruit used (in the case of sake liqueur)

**Evaluation:** Aroma 4–6, Sweetness 5–6, Acidity 3–6, Umami 4–6, Body 4–5

# KANKI
A MOMENT OF INDULGENCE

Kanpai! Clinking champagne flutes, a good-humored hustle and bustle, the sharing of smiles and joy in good company. Bubbly pleasure.

## NINKI
### Sparkling J-Ginjo

**Category:** Junmai ginjo, sparkling
**Rice:** Chiyo Nishiki, 60% pol.
**Alcohol:** 7%, **SMV:** -70
**Characteristics:** This light, sparkling sake has a well-balanced sweet and sour flavor and is very accessible for people who are just beginning to discover sake. Thanks to its low alcohol content, it makes the perfect start for a hot summer evening. The fine perlage from the bottle fermentation underscores its freshness. It is very rare to have a sparkling sake in the junmai ginjo category.
**Impression:** Naturally cloudy; aromatic, with fruity notes of banana, pear, and melon; fresh on the palate and stimulating with its juicy acidity
**Pairings:** As an aperitif, together with a fresh goat's cheese or fruity desserts

Aroma: ●●●○○○
Sweetness: ●●●●●○
Acidity: ●●●●●○
Umami: ●●○○○○
Body: ●●○○○○

## SHICHIKEN
### Sparkling Hakushu

**Category:** Junmai, sparkling
**Rice:** Sake rice
**Alcohol:** 12%, **SMV:** -13
**Characteristics:** The base sake for this exclusive sparkling variety is aged in Suntory Hakushu whisky barrels, which results in its distinctive aromas, complexity, and density. The bottle-fermentation produces a fine, refreshing perlage.
**Impression:** Clear with a golden sheen; aromas of brioche, vanilla, apple must, and maple syrup; incredibly dense and complex on the palate with a stimulating acidity
**Pairings:** As an aperitif, with goose liver pâté, oysters with pumpernickel bread and cheddar

Aroma: ●●●●○○
Sweetness: ●●●○○○
Acidity: ●●●●●○
Umami: ●●●○○○
Body: ●●●○○○

## KAZE NO MORI
### Akitsuho 657

**Category:** Junmai
**Rice:** Akitsuho, 65% pol.
**Alcohol:** 16 %, **SMV:** n.a.
**Characteristics:** Kaze no Mori specializes in sparkling nama sake. The brewery puts the greatest efforts into producing the tangy, fresh flavor of this freshly pressed, unpasteurized sake, which was viewed as avant-garde when it was introduced in 1998.
**Impression:** Aromas of lychee, peach, steamed rice, almond cake, tonka beans; slight prickle on the palate, combined with fresh acidity and full-bodied umami
**Pairings:** Teriyaki salmon, grilled chicken with herbes de Provence

Aroma: ●●●●○○
Sweetness: ●●●○○○
Acidity: ●●●●○○
Umami: ●●●●○○
Body: ●●●●○○

## SHICHIKEN
### Sparkling Blue Sky

**Category:** Junmai, sparkling
**Rice:** Sake rice
**Alcohol:** 12%, **SMV:** -1
**Characteristics:** Like a rainbow in the sky, the combination of modern and traditional sake techniques in this junmai creates a variegated spectrum of aromas. This emphasizes the freshness and complexity of this light-bodied sake. Modeled on champagne, this sake gets its natural perlage from its bottle fermentation and is disgorged.
**Impression:** Clear; aromas of yellow apple, chervil, and lemon sherbet; fresh and light on the palate with stimulating bubbles
**Pairings:** Oysters with tart apples, grilled scampi with lime shavings, scallop carpaccio with grapefruit salad

Aroma: ●●○○○○
Sweetness: ●●●○○○
Acidity: ●●●●○○
Umami: ●●○○○○
Body: ●●○○○○

## FUKUJU
### Awasaki Sparkling

**Category:** Junmai, sparkling
**Rice:** Sake rice, 70% pol.
**Alcohol:** 6%, **SMV:** -60
**Characteristics:** A sparkling sake with a light perlage, perfect as an aperitif. Its slight cloudiness is due to the fact that it is not filtered again after having been fermented in the bottle. With its low alcohol content, this light, sweet, and sour sake is reminiscent of a Moscato d'Asti.
**Impression:** Milky, slightly sparkling; aromas of lychees, rose petals, and raspberry yogurt; light on the palate, stimulating balance between sweetness and sourness
**Pairings:** As an aperitif or with sweet woodruff rice with fresh berries; with a soft-ripened triple-cream cheese, such as a Brillat-Savarin

Aroma: ●●●○○○
Sweetness: ●●●●○○
Acidity: ●●●●●○
Umami: ●●○○○○
Body: ●●○○○○

# SEICHO
## A MOMENT OF FRESHNESS

Blue sky, birdsong, and a breeze blowing over a fresh, green landscape. Cool water bubbles out of moss-covered cliff-faces. A summer morning by the lakeside.

## IMAYO TSUKASA
### IMA for Oyster

**Category:** Junmai
**Rice:** Gohyakumangoku, 65% pol.
**Alcohol:** 12%, **SMV:** -11
**Characteristics:** This sake was specially created to be paired with oysters, whose umami is emphasized by its interplay between sweet and sour. Its incisively acidic flavor profile is quite atypical for the usually light, tangy, and dry Niigata-style sake.
**Impression:** Aromas of green apple, steamed rice, and wet wood in the nose; very juicy on the palate with its invigorating acidity and fine umami
**Pairings:** Oysters with lemon, tuna fish sashimi with ponzu vinaigrette

Aroma: ●●●○○○
Sweetness: ●●●○○○
Acidity: ●●●●○○
Umami: ●●●○○○
Body: ●●●○○○

## BIJOFU
### Honjozo

**Category:** Tokubetsu honjozo
**Rice:** Matsuyama Mii, 60% pol.
**Alcohol:** 14%, **SMV:** +6
**Characteristics:** A sake for every occasion. When it is served cool, you will enjoy its freshness and lightness; when warmed up, it releases a full-bodied, rich flavor.
**Impression:** It is discreet in the nose with aromas of grapes and steamed rice; smooth and dry on the palate, with mild flavor and a round finish
**Pairings:** Grilled cod with yuzu juice, green salad with olives

Aroma: ●●○○○○
Sweetness: ●●○○○○
Acidity: ●●●○○○
Umami: ●●○○○○
Body: ●●○○○○

## NANBU BIJIN
### Ginjo

**Category:** Ginjo
**Rice:** Miyama Nishiki, 60% pol.
**Alcohol:** 14%, **SMV:** +4
**Characteristics:** Its mild freshness with lovely fruity notes is typical of the Nanbu Toji School. Spring water from the Basenkyou Gorge gives this sake its softness and mild aroma. Trophy winner at the International Wine Challenge 2016.
**Impression:** Aromas of fennel bread, green tea, and pears are underscored by a juicy, soft mouthfeel.
**Pairings:** Fish carpaccio, sashimi, and yakitori

Aroma: ●●●○○○
Sweetness: ●●●○○○
Acidity: ●●●○○○
Umami: ●●○○○○
Body: ●●○○○○

## NINKI
### Junmai Genshu 11

**Category:** Junmai daiginjo, genshu
**Rice:** Sake rice, 50% pol.
**Alcohol:** 11%, **SMV:** -18
**Characteristics:** With its well-balanced, fruity sweetness and invigorating, fresh acidity, this sake feels almost like a wine. It is brewed in cedar wood barrels, so the genshu has a full-bodied umami flavor in spite of its low alcohol content.
**Impression:** Fruity aromas of muscat grapes, ripe apple, and quince; similar to an off-dry wine
**Pairings:** Sea bass ceviche, lemon chicken, roasted chicory, tom yam khum, tofu with snow crabs and goose liver, pumpkin soup

Aroma: ●●●○○○
Sweetness: ●●●●○○
Acidity: ●●●●○○
Umami: ●●○○○○
Body: ●●○○○○

## MASUIZUMI
### Karakuchi

**Category:** Futushu
**Rice:** Yamada Nishiki, 60% pol.
**Alcohol:** 15%, **SMV:** n.a.
**Characteristics:** A dry all-rounder sake with a clear profile, an uncomplicated accompaniment to everyday dishes. Karakuchi means dry; warming this sake enriches its umami and depth and emphasizes its dry finish.
**Impression:** Discreet aromas of steamed rice, nuts, and hint of apple; a slight sweetness from the alcohol and an elegant umami on the palate
**Pairings:** Sashimi, sushi, steamed kohlrabi, Waldorf salad, shrimp cocktail, raw fish, and seafood

Aroma: ●●○○○○
Sweetness: ●●○○○○
Acidity: ●●○○○○
Umami: ●●○○○○
Body: ●●●○○○

# YUUBI
A MOMENT OF GENTLENESS

Like a breath of wind over a sea of cherry blossoms. Fine, elegant, balanced. A gentle embrace. Johann Sebastian Bach's "The Well-Tempered Clavier." A quiet rejoicing in the here and now.

## GOKYO
### Junmai Ginjo

**Category:** Junmai ginjo
**Rice:** Saito no Shizuku etc., 55% pol.
**Alcohol:** 15%, **SMV:** +1
**Characteristics:** This sake is full of distinctive aromas but still makes a mild impression, thanks to the soft water from the Nishiki River. Produced using sake rice from the region, this junmai ginjo comes across as melting and juicy and has a clear, pure finish.
**Impression:** Aromas of pear, steamed rice, jasmine, and tarragon in the nose; very mellow on the palate with a juicy acidity and elegant umami
**Pairings:** Steamed sea bass with beurre blanc, spinach quiche

**Aroma:** ●●●○○○
**Sweetness:** ●●●○○○
**Acidity:** ●●●●○○
**Umami:** ●●●○○○
**Body:** ●●●○○○

## TEDORIGAWA
### Shukon Junmai Ginjo

**Category:** Junmai ginjo
**Rice:** Gohyakumangoku, 50-60% pol.
**Alcohol:** 15%, **SMV:** 0
**Characteristics:** This sake has a silky texture and mild, fruity notes and is gently brewed with water from the holy Mount Hakusan. The Kanazawa yeast gives it aromas of yellow fruit. Its well-integrated fresh acidity and elegant umami make it a versatile accompaniment to food.
**Impression:** Aromas of bananas, green apple, fennel, boiled celeriac, and kaki; unusually harmonious, with a light umami and a dry finish
**Pairings:** Tuna fish tataki, scallops au gratin, roasted black salsify with sherry vinegar vinaigrette and black truffle

**Aroma:** ●●●○○○
**Sweetness:** ●●○○○○
**Acidity:** ●●●●○○
**Umami:** ●●●○○○
**Body:** ●●●○○○

## YUKI NO BOSHA
### Snow Cristal

**Category:** Junmai ginjo
**Rice:** Akita Sake Komachi, 55% pol.
**Alcohol:** 16%, **SMV:** +2
**Characteristics:** The clarity and coolness of this junmai ginjo are reminiscent of pure, white snow. Its clear fruitiness and silky texture give it a fresh and aromatic finish, and this impression is enhanced by its only being pasteurized once.
**Impression:** Aromas of melon, pear, grapefruit, and white flowers in the nose; lithe and elegant; very clear and smooth on the palate
**Pairings:** Sea bream and scallop sashimi, herb salad, tuna fish ceviche with yuzu, beef tartare

**Aroma:** ●●●●○○
**Sweetness:** ●●○○○○
**Acidity:** ●●●●○○
**Umami:** ●●○○○○
**Body:** ●●●○○○

## URAKASUMI
### Junmai

**Category:** Junmai
**Rice:** Manamusume, 65% pol.
**Alcohol:** 15%, **SMV:** +1
**Characteristics:** This sake is an ideal type of junmai from northeastern Japan. Slightly fruity with a balanced umami flavor and aesthetic—everything, in short, that defines the Nanbu Toji style. It makes an ideal accompaniment to many dishes without losing its character.
**Impression:** Discreet in the nose and clear, with aromas of pear, unripe plum, and wet wood; soft on the palate with tender, sweet notes from the rice
**Pairings:** Oysters with lemon, roasted sea bass glazed with miso, shabu shabu, sea bream carpaccio

**Aroma:** ●●●○○○
**Sweetness:** ●●●○○○
**Acidity:** ●●●○○○
**Umami:** ●●●○○○
**Body:** ●●●○○○

## NANBU BIJIN
### Southern Beauty

**Category:** Tokubetsu junmai
**Rice:** Ginotome, 55% pol.
**Alcohol:** 15%, **SMV:** 0
**Characteristics:** Discreet, but beautifully balanced fruity notes, a gentle sweetness from the rice, and an elegant umami create a typical flavor profile from the Nanbu Toji School. This sake, produced from a variety of rice developed in Iwate, was Champion Sake at the International Wine Challenge in 2017.
**Impression:** Aromas of peach, juicy apple, steamed rice, white sesame, and buttermilk completed by an umami and full body
**Pairings:** Chicken fricassee, ratatouille, roasted sea bream with boiled potatoes garnished with parsley

**Aroma:** ●●●○○○
**Sweetness:** ●●○○○○
**Acidity:** ●●●●○○
**Umami:** ●●●○○○
**Body:** ●●●●○○

# KAREI
## A MOMENT OF AROMA

A rain of gold from the sky, rising sun, firework of aromas, a bouquet of 100 roses, Beethoven's 9th Symphony. Overwhelming. A pleasure for all the senses.

## DEWAZAKURA
### Ichiro

**Category:** Junmai daiginjo
**Rice:** Yamada Nishiki, pol. 45%
**Alcohol:** 15%, **SMV:** +4
**Characteristics:** Champion Sake at the International Wine Challenge in 2008. Its opulent and clear aromas of fruit and blossom are very elegant and communicate a longing for spring. This sake is brewed at the coldest time of year, then aged at temperatures below freezing. It melts in the mouth and has a long aftertaste.
**Impression:** Intense aromas of cherry and melon, acacia blossom and raspberry, and tonka beans; very complex flavor with an upmarket sweetness and fine acidity; its lush juiciness is also reflected in its fruity aroma
**Pairings:** Salmon fillet with yuzu butter, langoustine with shellfish foam, braised pumpkin with ginger and orange juice

Aroma: ●●●●●○
Sweetness: ●●●○○○
Acidity: ●●●○○○
Umami: ●●●○○○
Body: ●●●○○○

## AMABUKI
### Strawberry Blossom

**Category:** Junmai ginjo, nama
**Rice:** Omachi, 55% pol.
**Alcohol:** 16%, **SMV:** 0
**Characteristics:** This sake is brewed with strawberry blossom yeast and will give you a spring feeling at any time of year. A successful mix of charming sweetness and crisp acidity make it juicy and lively; leaving it unpasteurized accentuates this impression.
**Impression:** Aromas of almond blossom and mango in the nose are completed by strawberry jam on the palate; invigorating acidity
**Pairings:** Pizza with smoked ham and arugula, crêpe with whipped cream, roast pork with dark beer sauce and caraway, quiche

Aroma: ●●●●●○
Sweetness: ●●●○○○
Acidity: ●●●●○○
Umami: ●●●●○○
Body: ●●●●○○

## SAWA NO HANA
### Pure White

**Category:** Junmai daiginjo
**Rice:** Miyama Nishiki, 40% pol.
**Alcohol:** 16%, **SMV:** n.a.
**Characteristics:** A clear and aromatic premium sake with elegant drinkability, it embodies the purity of snow and is reminiscent of a Sauvignon Blanc. This sake is fermented at extremely low temperatures in the typically snowbound region where it is produced.
**Impression:** Aromas such as elderflower, acacia, melon, white peach, and muscat grape; very clear, elegant, and complex on the palate; beautiful balance of sweet and sour
**Pairings:** Asparagus with hollandaise sauce, scallop carpaccio with herbs and olive oil

Aroma: ●●●●○○
Sweetness: ●●●○○○
Acidity: ●●●●○○
Umami: ●●●○○○
Body: ●●●●○○

## IKEKAME
### Turtle Red

**Category:** Junmai daiginjo
**Rice:** Yamada Nishiki, 50% pol.
**Alcohol:** 15%, **SMV:** -2
**Characteristics:** This aromatic sake with incisive, fresh acidity is produced using black koji, which is very rare in sake production. The resulting citric acid makes this sake very accessible to European taste buds.
**Impression:** Strawberry, red apple, cherry, and exotic aromas of coconut and pineapple; juicy on the palate, thanks to its invigorating acidity—very accessible, similar to wine
**Pairings:** Spaghetti with hard clams, roast meat with rosemary, okonomiyaki (savory pancakes)

Aroma: ●●●●○○
Sweetness: ●●●●○○
Acidity: ●●●●○○
Umami: ●●●●○○
Body: ●●●○○○

## KATSUYAMA
### Ken

**Category:** Junmai ginjo
**Rice:** Yamada Nishiki, 50% pol.
**Alcohol:** 16%, **SMV:** +2
**Characteristics:** World-class sake with numerous options for pairing. Thanks to meticulous handicraft, it has very intense aromas and deliciously melts in the mouth. Champion Sake at the International Wine Challenge in 2019.
**Impression:** Very expressive with aromas of ripe apricot, melon, and fennel blossom; well-balanced flavor and juicy, viscous mouthfeel
**Pairings:** Hassun (a selection of starters in kaiseki cuisine), paella with seafood, bouillabaisse

Aroma: ●●●●○○
Sweetness: ●●●●○○
Acidity: ●●●○○○
Umami: ●●●●○○
Body: ●●●●○○

# TENKEI
A MOMENT OF HEAVEN

Noble elegance. Pure brilliance of diamonds. Golden rays of light through the clouds. Music of the spheres. Unique encounter (ichigo-ichie). Pathway to eternity. Devotion, philosophy, craftsmanship.

## IWA 5
## Assemblage 3

**Category:** Junmai daiginjo, kimoto
**Rice:** Yamada Nishiki, Gohyakumangoku, Omachi, 35% pol.
**Alcohol:** 15%, **SMV:** n.a.
**Characteristics:** The former cellar master of Dom Pérignon creates this perfect, harmonious sake out of an assemblage of 20 different base sakes. Its intricacy and complexity are striking, whether you drink it cold, warm, or at room temperature.
**Impression:** Fruity aromas of apricots and figs, as well as white pepper; very similar to wine on the palate; complex and elegant with an invigorating acidity and rich umami
**Pairings:** Steak with rosemary jus, Peking duck, calf's head terrine, French onion soup, pasta with sea urchin and bottarga (mullet roe)

Aroma: ●●●●○○
Sweetness: ●●●○○○
Acidity: ●●●●○○
Umami: ●●●●○○
Body: ●●●●○○

## AMABUKI
## Rhododendron

**Category:** Junmai daiginjo, kimoto
**Rice:** Omachi, 40% pol.
**Alcohol:** 16%, **SMV:** +3
**Characteristics:** This quiet yet complex sake is brewed using rare rhododendron yeast. The traditional kimoto method gives the sake a round and enduring acidity and elegant umami aromas, which brilliantly bring out the flavor of food dishes.
**Impression:** Aromas of yellow peach, pear, white blossoms, bananas, freshly baked bread, and cream; full-bodied and powerful on the palate with a creamy texture
**Pairings:** Grilled langoustine, smoked duck breast, roasted venison with blueberry sauce

Aroma: ●●●○○○
Sweetness: ●●○○○○
Acidity: ●●●●○○
Umami: ●●●●○○
Body: ●●●●○○

## DASSAI
## Beyond

**Category:** Junmai daiginjo
**Rice:** Yamada Nishiki
**Alcohol:** 16%, **SMV:** n.a.
**Characteristics:** This sake comes from the best-known junmai daiginjo expert in the world. Striving to achieve the lowest polishing ratio is virtually his trademark, as his bestseller Dassei 23 recently showed. The Beyond is the answer to this, but with other qualities—an original style with elegance and complexity.
**Impression:** Cool aromas of green tea, unripe kiwi, and rose; very clear and elegant on the palate with a magnificent balance of sweetness, sourness, and umami
**Pairings:** Lobster with truffle butter, oysters, caviar with sour cream and blinis, fugu-sashi (puffer fish sashimi)

Aroma: ●●●●○○
Sweetness: ●●●○○○
Acidity: ●●●○○○
Umami: ●●○○○○
Body: ●●●○○○

## TATSURIKI
## Dragon Blue

**Category:** Daiginjo
**Rice:** Yamada Nishiki, 50% pol.
**Alcohol:** 16%, **SMV:** n.a.
**Characteristics:** The ideal type of daiginjo, made using the highest quality yamada nishiki rice. This sake's complex, fruity notes are released particularly elegantly in a wine glass. It is slowly fermented at a very low temperature, using classic ginjo yeast, which gives it beautiful aromas and a silky drinkability.
**Impression:** Aromas of melons, pear, star fruit, chervil, and cream; slightly sweet on the palate at first; silky and harmonious; clear, fruity aftertaste
**Pairings:** Sole sashimi with ponzu sauce, Bresse chicken with lemon and thyme oil, Peking duck with orange sauce, sea bass cooked sous vide with truffle beurre blanc

Aroma: ●●●●○○
Sweetness: ●●○○○○
Acidity: ●●●○○○
Umami: ●●○○○○
Body: ●●●○○○

## FUKUJU
## Shizuku Jewelry

**Category:** Daiginjo
**Rice:** Yamada Nishiki, 35% pol.
**Alcohol:** 17%, **SMV:** +4
**Characteristics:** This buttery sake best releases its sumptuous aromas in a crystal glass. It gets its complexity and melting viscosity from the exclusive drip process, during which the daiginjo mash is hung in cloth bags and the sake is collected in drops without pressing. Only 100 bottles are produced each production run.
**Impression:** Aromas of water lily, violet, jasmine, melon, and green tea; creamy and elegant sweetness on the palate; light umami flavor
**Pairings:** Guinea fowl with orange and rosemary jus, bouillabaisse, lobster Thermidor, wagyu beef tartare

Aroma: ●●●●○○
Sweetness: ●●●○○○
Acidity: ●●○○○○
Umami: ●●○○○○
Body: ●●●○○○

# DAIGO
A MOMENT OF EARTHINESS

Back to basics, Mother Earth energy, the natural cycle. Rice paddies shining gold in the fall, origin of sake, authenticity.

## YAMAGATA MASAMUNE
### Junmai Dry

**Category:** Junmai
**Rice:** Dewa San San, 60% pol.
**Alcohol:** 16%, **SMV:** n.a.
**Characteristics:** This sake is brewed using rice from the brewery's own paddies and water with a particularly high mineral content, which is very rare in Japan. This result in a fresh, direct, and elegant junmai.
**Impression:** Fruity aromas of wild peach, lychee, and unripe pear; dry and elegant on the palate with a fine umami flavor
**Pairings:** Grilled mackerel, udon noodles with egg yolk and truffle miso butter, chestnut soup

Aroma: ●●●○○○
Sweetness: ●●○○○○
Acidity: ●●●●○○
Umami: ●●●●○○
Body: ●●●●○○

## TENGUMAI
### Yamahai Junmai

**Category:** Junmai, yamahai
**Rice:** Gohyakumangoku, 60% pol.
**Alkohol:** 16%, **SMV:** +4
**Characteristics:** This golden, aged junmai represents the yamahai style of the Noto toji. The use of gohyakumangoku rice gives this full-bodied yamahai sake a certain coolness and elegance.
**Impression:** Intense aromas of dashi, miso, lovage, yogurt, caramel, and tobacco; dry flavor on the palate, with additional aromas of Parmesan rind and Arolla pine wood
**Pairings:** Eggplant with miso honey mayonnaise, truffle fries, tonkatsu (deep-fried pork), roasted root vegetables

Aroma: ●●●○○
Sweetness: ●●○○○○
Acidity: ●●●●●○
Umami: ●●●●○○
Body: ●●●●○○

## HANATOMOE
### 100

**Category:** Junmai, yamahai
**Rice:** Local rice, 70% pol.
**Alcohol:** 19%, **SMV:** +3
**Characteristics:** This strong yamahai sake is brewed using spontaneous fermentation in cedar wood barrels that are over 100 years old, which allows it to develop its unmistakable character and very pronounced acidity. It has a beautiful gold color, suggestive of its plentiful levels of rice and umami.
**Impression:** Intense aromas of chocolate, licorice, and caramel; its full body is supported by a powerful acidity and plenty of umami
**Pairings:** Unagi (eel), ossobuco with gremolata, gyoza, mushroom risotto, pork roast with spicy miso sauce, teriyaki chicken

Aroma: ●●●○○
Sweetness: ●●○○○○
Acidity: ●●●●●○
Umami: ●●●●○○
Body: ●●●●●○

## MIMUROSUGI
### Bodaimoto

**Category:** Junmai, bodaimoto
**Rice:** Yamada Nishiki
**Alcohol:** 14%, **SMV:** n.a.
**Characteristics:** This traditional sake is brewed in cedar wood barrels according to the medieval bodaimoto method. Despite its being fermented spontaneously, it has a clear flavor profile with depth, a complex acidity, and umami. It is crafted with skillful know-how and modern finesse.
**Impression:** Aromas of freshly cut wood, banana, quince, orange peel, steamed rice; lively and complex on the palate; round, persistent acidity; wide range of umami; long aftertaste
**Pairings:** Snails with herb butter, paté de campagne, grilled lamb chops

Aroma: ●●●●●○
Sweetness: ●●●●○○
Acidity: ●●●●●○
Umami: ●●●●●○
Body: ●●●●○○

## HATSUMAGO
### Kimoto Tradition

**Category:** Honjozo, kimoto
**Rice:** Haenuki, 70% pol.
**Alcohol:** 15%, **SMV:** -2
**Characteristics:** This kimoto sake is very accessible and perfect for a daily banshaku (evening meal with drink). Its full-bodied, hearty flavor is achieved by using a larger share of koji rice than usual for the mash. Awarded the trophy of best honjozo at the International Wine Challenge in 2018.
**Impression:** Distinctive aromas of granola, cocoa, salty caramel, and apricot; balanced on the palate with a clear interplay between sweet and sour; plenty of umami
**Pairings:** Yakitori, gyoza filled with pork belly and mushrooms, Parmesan cheese, South Tyrolean speck, Caesar salad

Aroma: ●●●○○
Sweetness: ●●●●○○
Acidity: ●●●●●○
Umami: ●●●●○○
Body: ●●●○○○

# JUKUWA

A MOMENT OF ETERNITY

A gift of time, great harmony, exciting developments. A journey through the years. Intimations of Paradise, depth, complexity, longevity.

## NIIDA HONKE
### 100 Year Kijoshu 2023

**Category:** Kijoshu
**Rice:** Kamenoo etc., 85% pol.
**Alcohol:** 16%, **SMV:** n.a.
**Characteristics:** A very luxurious and extravagant kijoshu sake, which is brewed 12 times. Since 2011, which marked the 300th anniversary of its foundation, the brewery has started producing a new kijoshu out of the previous year's kijoshu every year. Thus, by the year 2111, this tradition will culminate in a 100-year kijoshu. This shining gold sake is something like a witness to the passage of time.
**Impression:** Fruity in the nose with aromas of passion fruit, peach, candied orange; on the palate, aromas of cheesecake, roast apple, and acacia; rich, profound flavor with a multi-layered, velvety sweetness and acidity
**Pairings:** Tarte tatin, foie gras, cheese selections, roasted nuts

Aroma: ●●●●●○
Sweetness: ●●●●●○
Acidity: ●●●●●○
Umami: ●●●●●○
Body: ●●●●●○

## KIRIN
### Vintage 2022

**Category:** Junmai, yamahai, koshu
**Rice:** Koshitanrei, 70% pol.
**Alcohol:** 17%, **SMV:** -19
**Characteristics:** A sake that is full of extracts and with great aging potential, but which can also be enjoyed young. It is brewed following the yamahai method, and its koji rice content is over 99 percent, which produces not only its characteristic aroma, but also its typical acidity.
**Impression:** Reminiscent of sherry, with aromas of honey, nut, chocolate, and dried fruit; on the palate, sweetness supports its full body; pronounced acidity counterbalances sweetness
**Pairings:** Saltimbocca, wild boar goulash, quiche with roquefort and pear, roast beef with fried onions

Aroma: ●●●●●○
Sweetness: ●●●●●○
Acidity: ●●●●●●
Umami: ●●●●●○
Body: ●●●●●○

## SHIRAYUKI
### Edo Genroku Sake

**Category:** Junmai, genshu, koshu
**Rice:** Yamada Nishiki, 88% pol.
**Alcohol:** 17,5%, **SMV:** -35
**Characteristics:** This sake is brewed according to a house recipe dating back to the end of the Genroku Era (seventeenth century). At the time, it was not possible to polish rice to less than 88 percent; and in addition, only half the amount of brewing water was used, compared to modern recipes. These unique qualities give the sake a very rich flavor.
**Impression:** Amber colored; intense ripe notes in the nose with aromas of dried fruit, caramel, hazelnuts, honey, and acacia; very full body on the palate with a complex sweetness and umami
**Pairings:** Mezzelune pasta with smoked speck, brie cheese with nut bread and apricot chutney

Aroma: ●●●●●●
Sweetness: ●●●●●●
Acidity: ●●●●●○
Umami: ●●●●●●
Body: ●●●●●●

## DARUMA MASAMUNE
### 1979

**Category:** Junmai, koshu
**Rice:** Nihonbare, 70% pol.
**Alcohol:** 17%, **SMV:** -48
**Characteristics:** This brewery specializes in aged sake, and this variety, which is over 45 years old, tastes a little like the highest quality tawny port. This particular vintage has won numerous prizes and is available only in limited supply.
**Impression:** Spicy aromas of caramel, nuts, dried fruit, winter spices, and pumpernickel, emphasized on the palate by a strong sweetness, acidity, and intense umami flavor
**Pairings:** Chocolate cake with walnut, hard cheese such as Parmesan, English Christmas pudding

Aroma: ●●●●●
Sweetness: ●●●●●●
Acidity: ●●●●●○
Umami: ●●●●●●
Body: ●●●●●○

## MASUIZUMI
### Junmai Daiginjo Special 2018

**Category:** Junmai daiginjo, koshu
**Rice:** Yamada Nishiki, unter 50% pol.
**Alcohol:** 16%, **SMV:** n.a.
**Characteristics:** This complex vintage sake is aged for over six months in used French wooden barrels, giving it its characteristic aromas, full body, and complexity. A perfect alternative to Burgundy wine.
**Impression:** Golden reflexes; intensive aromas of honey, salty caramel, and vanilla; creamy on the palate; pronounced, juicy acidity enhances its full body and distinctive umami flavor
**Pairings:** Truffled chicken, grilled octopus, smoked duck breast, pheasant with morels, poached halibut with mushroom ragout, pan-seared foie gras

Aroma: ●●●●●○
Sweetness: ●●○○○○
Acidity: ●●●●●○
Umami: ●●●●○○
Body: ●●●●○○

A FEAST FOR ALL SENSES — AROMA. FLAVOR. DIVERSITY.

203

## Style H: Sweet & Aromatic

# KANRO

A MOMENT OF SWEETNESS

Delight and a feeling of security, moments of happiness. Morning dew and honeydew. Letting yourself be pampered. Sweet dreams, childhood memories, candy floss at a Christmas market.

## NANBU BIJIN
### All Koji 2022

**Category:** Junmai
**Rice:** Toyonishiki, 65% pol.
**Alcohol:** 15%, **SMV:** -20
**Characteristics:** This vintage sake is made exclusively out of koji rice, which gives it high levels of acidity and umami, resulting in a very juicy and full-bodied mouthfeel, as well as hearty and sweet flavors. It ages well, and its color grows increasingly darker with time.
**Impression:** Intense aromas of candied ginger, honey, and walnuts in the nose; powerful on the palate, thanks to its complex sweetness, which is counterbalanced by a pronounced acidity and perfectly rounded off by plenty of umami
**Pairings:** Spicy grilled pork ribs, vanilla ice cream, seared duck liver with apricot chutney, vanilla almond biscuits, apple strudel, Munster cheese with nut bread

**Aroma:** ●●●●●○
**Sweetness:** ●●●●●●○
**Acidity:** ●●●●○○
**Umami:** ●●●●○○
**Body:** ●●●●○○

## KATSUYAMA
### Lei

**Category:** Junmai ginjo
**Rice:** Hitomebore, 55% pol.
**Alcohol:** 12%, **SMV:** -23
**Characteristics:** This aromatic, sweet, low-alcohol sake is very popular in European Michelin-starred restaurants. With its elegant umami and fruity aromas, it makes a good alternative to sweet white wine. It is very versatile and can be paired with many dishes.
**Impression:** Pronounced fruity aromas of melons, lychee, and peach yogurt; gentle and juicy on the palate with plenty of umami and a clear sweetness
**Pairings:** Goose liver terrine, Parma ham with honeydew melon, papaya salad, gorgonzola dolce, custard

**Aroma:** ●●●●●○
**Sweetness:** ●●●●●○
**Acidity:** ●●●●○○
**Umami:** ●●●●○○
**Body:** ●●●●○○

## OGASAWARA
### Mirin Isshi soden

**Category:** Mirin
**Ingredients:** Sweet rice, koji rice, shochu
**Alcohol:** 14%, **SMV:** n.a.
**Characteristics:** A particularly high-quality, flavorful mirin, which is very balanced, thanks to being aged for four years, and can be enjoyed as a liqueur. It is produced by hand using glutinous rice, koji rice, and rice shochu.
**Impression:** Aromas of caramel and treacle; a very intense, charming sweetness, which melts on the tongue like a floating cloud; distinctive umami flavor
**Pairings:** Can be enjoyed on its own as an aromatic liqueur or paired with goose liver, chocolate, or (vanilla) desserts

**Aroma:** ●●●○○
**Sweetness:** ●●●●●●
**Acidity:** ●●●○○○
**Umami:** ●●●●●●
**Body:** ●●●●●○

## MASUIZUMI
### Kijoshu

**Category:** Kijoshu
**Rice:** Yamada Nishiki etc.
**Alcohol:** 15%, **SMV:** n.a.
**Characteristics:** This high-class sake with a slightly golden color and complex sweetness is brewed twice, according to the kijoshu method. Its characteristic aromas are reminiscent of sweet wine, and it is very viscous. It ages well in its beautiful bottle.
**Impression:** Intense aromas of lychee, coconut, almond, white nougat, honey, and candy floss; multilayered sweetness on the palate, balanced by luscious acidity
**Pairings:** Duck liver terrine, veal fillet with gorgonzola sauce, honey-glazed pineapple, peach Melba

**Aroma:** ●●●●○○
**Sweetness:** ●●●●●●
**Acidity:** ●●●○○
**Umami:** ●●●●●○
**Body:** ●●●○○

## URAKASUMI
### Umeshu

**Category:** Sake liqueur
**Ingredients:** Sake, ume plums, sugar
**Alcohol:** 12%, **SMV:** n.a.
**Characteristics:** The invigorating interplay between sweet and sour and the broad umami flavor of junmai genshu make this umeshu unique. Aromatic, hand-picked ume plums from Miyagi are infused for several hours with the warmed-up sake.
**Impression:** Intense aromas of ume plums, cherry, and marzipan in the nose; on the palate, the sweetness is balanced out by a strong but juicy acidity
**Pairings:** Plum cake, almond cake, vanilla ice cream, or as an aperitif with prosecco

**Aroma:** ●●●●●●
**Sweetness:** ●●●●●○
**Acidity:** ●●●●●●
**Umami:** ●●●●○○
**Body:** ●●●●●○

# Shigeri

## DARUMA MASAMUNE BREWERY
## KADOYAKADO, GIFU PREFECTURE

KADOYAKADO

Intensely focused, the figure lifts its shinai (long bamboo sword) over its head. It pauses and stays completely still for a moment before slicing through the air with equal measures of strength and skill. The figure is a woman: Shigeri Shiraki. She represents the seventh generation to manage Daruma Masamune Brewery, which brought back to life the ancient Japanese tradition of koshu (aged sake).

Bottles containing the various koshu are lined up in neat rows on the shelves of the small direct sales room. Their contents gleam amber, gold, or almost black with a reddish shimmer. In contrast, the bright red daruma puppet in front of the traditional residential and production buildings, in the midst of the Nobi plain rice paddies, is already visible from far away. Shigeri's ancestors chose this symbol of happiness and constancy as a hallmark for the rebirth of their brewery after they had lost everything in the devastating 1891 earthquake.

This would not, however, be the only setback this family business would have to face. "During the Japanese boom cycle in the 1960s, small sake breweries like ours were pushed out of the market by the big breweries in Nada and Fushimi, and my father, who had a wife and three children to look after, was very distraught," explains Shigeri.

Perhaps it was the daruma's power that led Yoshiji Shiraki to find, back then, in a corner of his production facility, a bottle of sake whose contents had gone brown. When he tasted it, he was beguiled by aromas of honey and winter spices. The brewer was simultaneously struck by a flash of inspiration: in the future, he, Yoshiji Shiraki, would only sell aged sake—that specialty that was savored by aristocrats and samurai in the Middle Ages but disappeared from the market around 1871.

Shigeri's father puzzled over his idea of bringing koshu back into the world for almost 20 years—years full of setbacks and the scorn of his colleagues—leaving a large part of his production to age and adapting his production methods. Various vintage sakes and cuvées came into being during this period, including the Daruma Masamune Vintage 1979. Dark-brown with a hint of red, it delights the nose with aromas of raisins, dried figs, toffee, forest honey, and salted caramel; it feels creamy on the tongue and full of a complex sweetness, reminiscent of dark chocolate, caramelized walnuts, and dried fruit.

Yoshiji Shiraki promoted his novel sake with tastings and seminars, tailored to consumers, colleagues, and brewing institutes. Little by little, buyers for department stores in Tokyo and other beverage experts began to notice his koshu. Even Shinya Tasaki, the Japanese world champion sommelier 1995 and former president of the global union of sommelier associations ASI, praised Shiraki's pioneering innovation and

Treasure chest: Shigeri Shiraki is proud of her vintage sake.

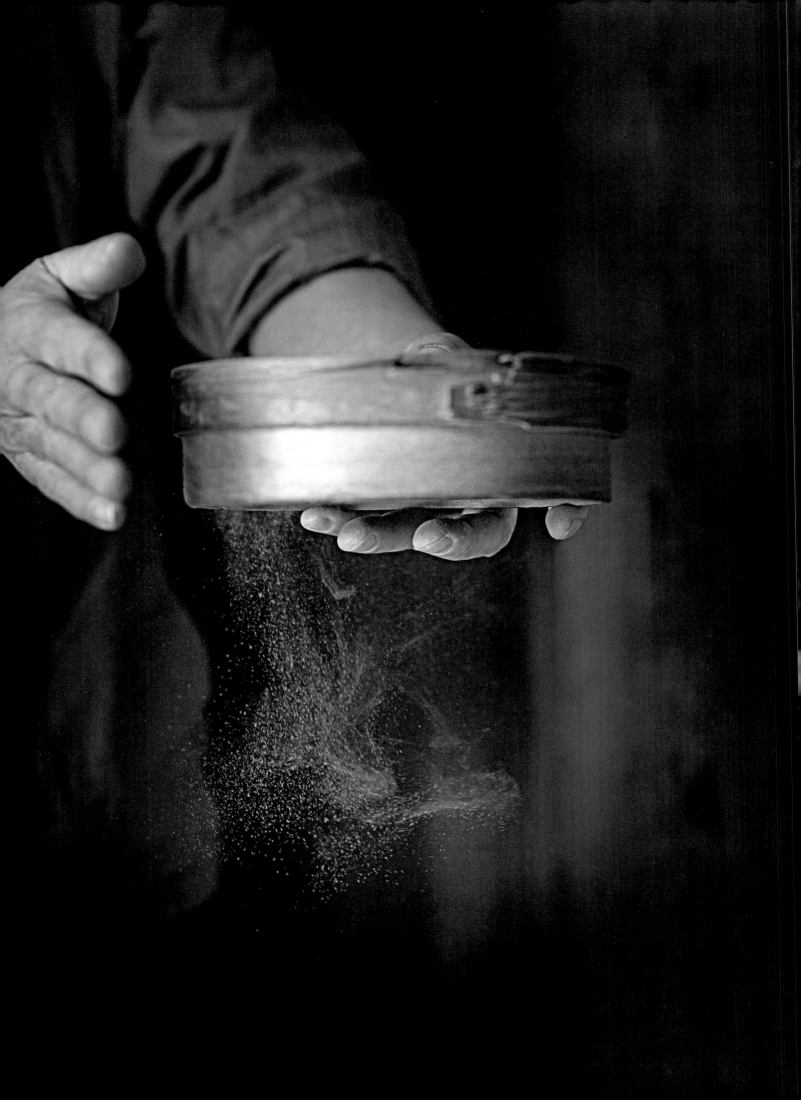

Koji spores are sprinkled over steamed rice.

Shigeri's husband, Hisashi, is the toji of this family business.

persistence and actively took part in presenting the aged sake from Daruma Masamune to other countries.

It's late afternoon, and all is quiet in the brewery. The early morning rice steaming and koji production ended long ago. Shigeri takes me to one of the two storehouses, which are each over 100 years old. It contains neat rows of dark green, two-meter/7-foot-high enamel tanks. "We use some of them to ferment the mash," explains Shigeri. "But most of them are used to store the various sake vintages." The thick loam walls of the historic buildings ensure that the air humidity and temperature remain constant, and "this creates ideal conditions for aging."

By the green tanks, we bump into Shigeri's husband, Hisashi. He is the master brewer of the family business and is just in the process of writing something in chalk on one of the green containers. He seems like a modest and well-considered master craftsman, a good complement to the spontaneous, open Shigeri, who is responsible for sales and marketing at the Shiraki Brewery. She is the second of three sisters, but when the eldest, who was supposed to take on her father's succession, left the house after she married, the younger one took a spur-of-the-moment decision: "Then I'll take over the brewery." So, Shigeri studied fermentation science at the Tokyo University of Agriculture for two years—and soon also met Hisashi, who at the time was working in a brewery in his hometown of Akita.

"We had a very bumpy start," remembers Shigeri. Business went well at first, but in 2009 the company's revenue plummeted dramatically. "I didn't know what we should do anymore. I was on the train to a sales event in Tokyo, and I suddenly burst into tears and couldn't stop crying." Shortly before she arrived, however, the Shiraki kuramoto was struck by a flash of inspiration: "We're going to make a sake that has never existed before. A sake that will be by people's sides in good times and in bad." As soon as she returned, Shigeri consulted her trusted master brewer and brought koshu for ice cream onto the market. "Many people criticized the product. They said it was a waste

of precious old sake and predicted that nobody would buy such a thing."

However, Shigeri's creation was seized upon by the press and television and found a great success. Since then, Shigeri Shiraki has launched further innovative sake products. Sake aged under water, for example, and sake intended to be a gift to newborns, which will not be opened until they reach their maturity, giving the sake many years to continue to age.

The kuramoto tries to communicate the diverse nature of old sake in an easily accessible way, using hand-printed flyers inserted into local newspapers, as well as posts on social media. For example, she often shares videos of her private dinners and invites people to take part in virtual visits of the brewery. This has earned her many fans and considerable recognition for the Daruma Masamune product range, throughout Japan, overseas, and particularly in Europe, where the topic of aging has a long tradition with beverages such as wine, sherry, and whisky. For all this international reach, though, Shigeri remains intimately connected to her home region. Among other things, it is the nihonbare rice farmed in the neighborhood that gives Daruma Masamune its unique taste, which combines umami with sweetness and acidity.

If you walk up a narrow wooden staircase in the Shiraki premises to the upper floor, where the steamed rice is left to cool before it is brought into the koji chamber, there is a thick, square beam spanning over the door. On it is written *Shiraki Tsunesuke*. "Tsunesuke was my great-grandfather," smiles Shigeri. "I think he would be quite proud of our kura, which was newly built after the big earthquake as a symbol of the resurrection of our business." He would doubtless also be proud of his energetic great-granddaughter, who knows not only how to wield her bamboo sword with skill and concentration, but also how to manage the family brewery her forefathers founded in 1835. What, I wonder, will the sake that Shigeri and Hisashi have already brewed to celebrate their 200th anniversary taste like? —

# DRINKING VESSELS AND DINING CULTURE

**Which sake out of what?** Another important aspect of Japan's dining culture is its precious, varied tableware, which has often been accumulated over generations and is tailored to each particular occasion: what season of the year it is, what kind of food is being eaten, what a particular guest desires. The same applies to savoring sake. The shape, size, and material of the drinking vessels are just as important in ensuring an optimal taste experience with high-quality rice wine as they are for wine made out of grapes. Japanese restaurants sometimes offer a choice of sake glasses or cups. However, a real sake lover will always bring their own cup with them.

## Porcelain and Ceramic

Japanese ceramics and Japanese porcelain are some of the most famous traditional earthenware or clay items of table culture in the world. These creations—which are as decorative as they are useful—have been exported to Europe since at least the eighteenth century. There are several ceramics schools in Japan, each one defined by the quality of the local clay, its history, and the culinary culture of its region. Famous schools include Kutani (Ishikawa Prefecture) and Karatsu and Imari (Saga), which all teach the manufacture of porcelain, and Hagi (Yamaguchi), Bizen (Okayama), Shigaraki (Shiga), Seto (Aichi), and Mino (Gifu) which focus on ceramics.

Sake cups have different names depending on their shape: sakazuki (a flat cup), o-choko (a small cup), and guinomi (a large cup). Incidentally, when selecting a cup, Japanese people do not just pay attention to its aesthetics, but also to what it feels like to hold it.

As a general rule, sake drunk out of a ceramic cup feels milder and more mellow. The same sake will taste stronger if drunk out of a hefty cylindrical cup, rather than a delicate, flat cup. On the other hand, it is also a real pleasure to drink a strong junmai sake out of a clay cup the size of the palm of one's hand. When drinking out of a flat cup, you can feel the umami in the sake directly on your tongue, and its aromas and flavor will be brought out far more clearly if savored out of delicate porcelain.

Japanese cups are usually very small, measuring between 10 and 50 milliliters (.3 and 1.7 ounces). When celebrating or entertaining, Japanese people pour the sake for each other, since one should not fill one's cup oneself. When someone says, "Kanpai! (cheers!)," you are expected to empty your cup immediately; this is why the vessels are so small. In Japanese, a sake carafe is called a tokkuri.

**Appropriate styles of sake:**
Light and fresh, traditional and umami

## Glass

There is a reason why wine glass manufacturers have developed specific designs for Riesling, Bordeaux, Burgundy, Sherry, etc. The appropriate glass ensures that the flavors in each wine can best be released. The same applies to sake. Sake glasses come in all shapes and sizes, but most of them have no foot and are relatively small. Wine glasses are better adapted for aromatic and high-quality types of sake, since the aromas can be released more easily by, for example, swirling the sake around in a thin wine glass rather than drinking it out of a small cylindrical glass or a traditional small porcelain cup. The diameter and curve of a glass' bowl will bring different flavors to the fore. For example, at the end of the 1990s, together with numerous sake producers and connoisseurs, following an elaborate selection process, the Austrian glass manufacturer Riedel developed a special daiginjo glass and, in 2018, a junmai glass. The latter has a markedly wider diameter, which gives the junmai sake plenty of room to breathe.

**Appropriate styles of sake:**
White wine glass: sparkling, light and fresh, fruity and mild, aromatic and expressive, complex and refined. Burgundy glass: traditional and umami. Brandy glass: aged. Liquor glass: sweet

## Wood

Wooden cups (masu) made out of Japanese sugi (cedar) and hinoki (white cedar) pinewoods were originally used as measuring cups. They have a 180-milliliter (6-ounce) volume, which corresponds to the Japanese measuring unit ichi-go (ichi = one, go = 180 milliliters). Originally, people used to buy sake by the cup, and would go to the shop with a large ceramic carafe (o-dokurri). It was not until the late nineteenth century that people started putting sake into bottles.

People like to serve sake in round or square wooden cups at weddings and other festivities. Guests are given cups inscribed with the names of the bridal couple, which they can take home as keepsakes. Wooden cups act like instant barriques and overpower the aroma, so they should not be used for the most expensive brands of sake.

**Appropriate styles of sake:**
Light and fresh, traditional and umami

## Tin

Tin has a high heat conductivity, antibacterial properties, and the ability to make sake milder and more flavorful. Because it is very soft, it is often combined with other metals, e.g. with lead. In Japan, tin is a very popular material for sake (and tea) cups. The company Nosaku produces sake cups entirely made out of tin. These cups are malleable and easy to reshape as one likes. Their soft surface feels very pleasant.

**Appropriate styles of sake:**
Light and fresh, traditional and umami

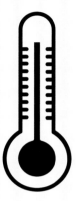

## TEMPERATURE

Many people in the West believe that sake should be enjoyed hot—but this is wrong!

Sake can in fact be enjoyed at different temperatures: slightly cool (10° to 15°C/50° to 59°F), at room temperature, and warm. Japanese people like to give their sake beautiful names, such as hana-hie (blossom-cold, meaning around 10°C/50°F), since there are often cold snaps during the cherry blossom season, but the appropriate temperature really depends on the type of sake.

In the past, people did drink sake hot in Japan, and there were many reasons for this: heating up a rough young sake was supposed to make it smoother, warming cheap industrial sake was supposed to make it more palatable, and people wanted to get drunk more quickly. Today, though, Japanese people tend to drink sake cool, since the beverage is increasingly offered at a modern, more sophisticated level of quality. An aromatic sake (ginjo or daiginjo) will usually be served cool, whereas a strong and full-bodied sake can be served cool or warm. The appropriate temperature will open up the variegated aromas and flavors of a good sake.

Warm sake tastes rounder and more full-bodied than cool or cold sake; the alcohol tastes drier and evaporates more easily and the aroma is more open, broader, and less fresh, which allows its sweetness to fully emerge. As far as acidity, bitterness, and astringency are concerned, a warm sake thus tastes more harmonious with more and longer-lasting umami. Cool sake, on the other hand, offers a more streamlined, firm impression; the alcohol feels heavier and tastes sweeter, and the aromas stay locked up at temperatures under 7°C (45°F), only fully unfolding at 10° to 15°C (50° to 59°F). Cool sake has a dry sweetness, more pronounced acidity, bitterness, and astringency, and less umami.

## The best way to heat sake

If you want to warm up your sake, start by preparing a bain-marie (hot water bath). Bring water to a boil in a saucepan, take it off the stove, and let it cool down for a few minutes to around 80°C (176°F). Then, transfer the sake to a tokkuri (sake carafe) and place this in the hot bain-marie for around one to two minutes. The water should reach up to the shoulder of the carafe. It is important to warm the beverage in this gentle manner, since too much heat will cause the sake's wonderful aroma to evaporate. The recommended drinking temperature for warm sake is between 35° and 45°C (95° and 113°F). —

# 8

# TIPS FOR ENJOYING SAKE

## 1. Start with premium sake

Your first encounter with sake is very important. Sakes sold off the shelf in a supermarket or an Asian grocery shop for a price of 10 euros/dollars are not worthy ambassadors of Japan's 2,000-year-old brewing culture. Nor should you expect much from a sake served in a cheap sushi restaurant; those are usually industrially produced outside of Japan. Non-premium sake is often mixed with a lot of brewing alcohol and water and can contain additives. If you want to discover the world of sake, you must absolutely start with the right kind.

## 2. Go to a restaurant with a good sake menu

Employees in Japanese restaurants often find it difficult to explain the properties of a sake and give recommendations because they cannot easily communicate with foreign patrons. This is why many restaurant owners have now drawn up sake menus with short descriptions in the relevant language. Nowadays, high-end Japanese restaurants and other haute cuisine establishments all over the world are beginning to offer a wider range of premium sakes, along with recommendations by sommeliers and well-trained staff.

## 3. Buy your sake from a trusted retailer

Do not purchase a bottle of sake that's been sitting in a sunny shop window or has gathered dust at the back of a shelf with a bottling date over two years in the past. These are obvious signs that the sake has not been properly handled. Sake can also suffer from being transported in non-temperature-controlled containers on its way from Japan; if you have any doubts, you should ask a trusted retailer. Now, online shops allow you to order sake right from their temperature-controlled storage facilities, and many of them have customer service representatives who can answer questions and give advice.

## 4. Pay attention to labels

The front labels on sake bottles are fascinating! Japanese characters will win you over aesthetically, but they won't tell you much about the origin and quality of the product. The back of the bottle, on the other hand, will provide you with required information about the sake's ingredients and alcohol content, as well as the address of the importer or retailer. It is not mandatory to include production and bottling dates of the sake, characteristics of its flavor, and information about its producer on the label, but, when available, these details can also be helpful in making your selection.

## 5. Drink it young

Though some types of sake can age well when stored in temperature-controlled environments, this traditional beverage is generally meant to be enjoyed soon after it is made and bottled. However, should you find a sake in your cellar that was given to you 20 years ago by a Japanese business partner, just try it! It may have a light brown color and a mature note reminiscent of sherry. It will definitely have lost its initial freshness and original aroma, but this sake may instead have gained a smoother flavor. If it doesn't convince you, just use it for cooking!

## 6. Give it a go — together with food

Not sure about sake? Try it with food. In addition to floral, fruity, and earthy notes, premium sakes also have distinct umami flavors, which make them excellent accompaniments to many different dishes. (For more about sake pairing, see pp. 218–221)

## 7. Store it correctly

Sake is sensitive to light and temperature variations. It is thus important for the most premium types of sake to be transported in refrigerated containers or by air freight. Once purchased, it should be stored in your fridge or cellar. The storage life of sake depends on its type and how long it was aged before bottling. A bottle that has been opened can be kept for about a month in the fridge.

## 8. Do your research

There is now a lot of information about sake online; many sake breweries and associations have English-language websites, and sake fans also exchange information on social media. The Japan Sake & Shochu Makers Association's website is definitely worth visiting. Plus, there are various courses available for anyone who wants to dive deeper in a more structured way into the world of sake. For example, the Wine & Spirit Education Trust, the world's largest school for wine and spirits, offers WSET sake courses from Level 1 (a one-day course) to Level 3 (three to four days). The most challenging course is the Japan Sommelier Association's J.S.A. Sake Diploma International. (For other course providers in Japan and all over the world, see pp. 292–294)

# ENJOYING SAKE ALL YEAR ROUND

Whether you are surrounded by cherry blossoms in spring, enjoying a warm, sunny summer day, attending an autumn moon festival, or welcoming the new year's god in winter, there is a fitting sake to help you best experience the season. Sake is best enjoyed with other people and at a temperature that fits your environment (and, of course, the specific variety you are drinking). Try it well tempered, straight out of a picnic basket, served with ice on the shore of a lake or sea, warm as part of a harvest festival, or aromatized with herbs while you watch the snow fall.

## Spring: Hanami Sake

In March and April, the pink of cherry blossoms (sakura) colors vast swathes of Japan. Together with family, friends, and colleagues, Japanese people take position under these blossoming branches armed with bento boxes and sake brewed during the winter to celebrate the end of the cold season. On this occasion, people prefer to drink freshly pressed nama sake or other sakes with fruity, mild aromas. This tradition goes all the way back to the Nara and Heian eras (eighth to twelfth centuries). Back then, when there was not much entertainment available, Hanami, the cherry blossom festival, was the biggest event of the year for the common people. The most famous and largest Hanami in history was held by the warlord Toyotomi Hideyoshi in March 1598 in the Daigoji Temple in Kyoto. Hideyoshi had around 700 ornamental cherry trees from other places planted on the temple land, then ordered a special building to be erected for the occasion. It is said that around 1,300 women, including the feudal lords' consorts, were invited to this extravagant celebration.

## Summer: Sake on the Rocks

During the hot summer months, people enjoy drinking sake that has a fresh and light flavor—ideally ice cold out of a glass cup. But another good option is an aromatic sake on ice! At this cold temperature, the sake will admittedly not make much of an impression on your nose, but your palate will enjoy a firework of aromas. And here is another option for some summer freshness: Spice up some junmai sake with shiso, peppermint, basil, or rosemary.

## Fall: Kiku Sake, Tsukimi Sake, Sake Day

In the old Japanese lunar calendar, September 9th is a feast day to drink sake with chrysanthemum blossoms—a flower symbolizing good fortune, health, longevity, and protection against bad luck. This custom is known as kiku sake. Tsukimi sake is also celebrated in the fall. Its history dates back to ancient times, when tsuki matsuri (moon rituals) were held to thank the gods for the fall harvest. In the Nara and Heian periods (eighth to twelfth centuries), the custom of kangetsu no yoi (moon watching parties), where sake is drunk while admiring the night sky, was introduced from China. Aristocrats in particular celebrated these two occasions. October 1st is traditionally considered Sake Day, and the entire month of October is considered the month of sake, as this is when the new rice is harvested and sake production begins. Another ancient custom begins in the fall: according to the lunar calendar, warmed sake is drunk from September 9th to March 3rd.

## Winter: O-toso, Yukimi Sake

On January 1st, Japanese people gather with families and friends to honor Toshigami-sama, the New Year's god, and ask for health and happiness in the coming year. For the occasion, sake is infused overnight with a variety of herbs and spices, such as cinnamon and sansho pepper, to make a special drink called o-toso. This infused sake—and the New Year's Day tradition it was made for—was introduced to the Japanese imperial family from ancient China during the Heian period (794–1185), then became known to the wider public. Another special role sake plays in winter is to honor the first snowfall. This involves a method of drinking known as yuki-wari-zake, in which snow is packed tightly into a cup and the sake is poured over top to make yukimi sake (snow viewing sake). And, of course, winter is also the best time for warm sake, heated gently in earthenware carafes. —

# WHAT IS
# SAKE PAIRING?

**Sake is not just an exquisite soloist,** but also a versatile talent within the culinary orchestra. With its nuanced aromas and full-bodied flavor, premium sake steals the show as an excellent accompaniment for Japanese delicacies and dishes from other parts of the world. Similar to wine pairing, sake pairing is all about finding the right combination. Or, as sommelier world champion and Master of Sake Markus Del Monego puts it, it's about creating harmony between the notes of sweet, sour, salty, bitter, and umami in dishes and beverages.

## Dialogue with Food

The art of combining wine with food has a long tradition in Europe, and this tradition is upheld by sommeliers. Compared to wine, sake does not have much acidity or tannins, so it does not clash with food; this is why there is no tradition of recommended pairings in Japan. Even in upmarket kaiseki restaurants, there are often only a few different types of sake on offer—those that the owner or chef happen to like—and, frequently, the same one or two types of sake will be served throughout the meal, or, more rarely, a different sake is served with each dish. The profession of sommelier in Japan had also up until now mainly been focused on serving wine in Western restaurants, but in recent years, the Japan Sommelier Association has started to branch out into the field of sake pairing, and some kaiseki restaurants and upmarket sushi restaurants now employ sommeliers who are responsible for wine and sake. Together with Hitoshi Utsunomiya, Marie Chiba is also developing new, scientifically designed sake pairings.

The umami of sake connects and harmonizes the various types of flavors contained in all types of dishes. Sake is free! It can be enjoyed without rules or dogma. So, experiment with different sakes until you find the harmony that pleases you most. A successful pairing is all about knowing the flavor characteristics and qualities of the dishes and the beverage, and seeking out how all of these can be brought into dialogue with each other.

## Why Does Sake Go Well with Washoku?

Sake is basically liquid fermented rice. It thus makes an excellent accompaniment for traditional Japanese cuisine (washoku), which is usually based on fresh ingredients, does not contain much oil, and is typically seasoned with dashi broth and fermented products like soy sauce and mirin. (For more information about Japanese cuisine, see pp. 226–229.) Sake has a natural sweetness, umami, and a mild acidity, so there is a synergetic effect when it is combined with the umami of washoku. The rice sweetness of sake also perfectly harmonizes with the sweeteners mirin and sugar. But sake does not actively add its own seasoning to dishes—it assimilates into them and merges with their aromas without adulterating their character.

## Does Sake Go Well with French Cuisine?

Yes! Two distinguishing characteristics of classic French cuisine are its great variety of sauces and its use of animal fat (lard and butter). If we compare their flavor components, French cuisine is mainly defined by saltiness, various kinds of fat (cream, butter, and animal fat), umami, and acidity (wine and vinegar), whereas Japanese cuisine is based on saltiness (soy sauce, miso, sea salt), sweetness (mirin, sake, sugar), and umami (dashi).

French cuisine is a style of cooking that is perfected through the addition of various flavor components, and the wine that accompanies a meal is also viewed as one of these components or as a condiment. A dry Riesling paired with grilled fish brings in some fresh acidity, just like lemon does in other dishes. A well-aged Bordeaux wine made from Cabernet Sauvignon and Merlot grapes has berry and spicy notes, as well as velvety tannins, and brings depth and piquancy to meat dishes. By bringing the aromas, acidity, and tannins of wine into play, French cuisine attempts to bring the aromas of the dishes and of the wine into harmony with each other.

Sake can be paired with French cuisine in a similar manner. An aromatic junmai daiginjo sake goes well with a grilled steak because the aromas of the beverage absorb the qualities of the beef fat and lend the whole dish a piquancy reminiscent of aniseed and herbes de Provence. Sake also goes very well with dairy products such as butter, cream, and cheese; the umami and mild lactic acid in sake barely affect their flavor, but rather contribute to releasing it. A sweet kijoshu acts like a Sauternes when combined with blue cheese or foie gras. The umami of sake extends the flavor of the dish and underscores its seasoning.

## Sake Pairing in Europe

For some time now, many young sommeliers have been enthusiastically trying to create new dialogues between various food dishes and beverages, especially with natural wines and craft beer. In this context, sake pairing, too, is now practiced in many restaurants. In order to find new sake pairings and support the know-how of sommeliers, a sake pairing contest has been set up with the support of sommelier unions in Germany, Austria, and Switzerland, and in 2021 and 2022, more than 90 sommeliers created their own individual pairings out of a selection of premium sakes. The Master of Sake Pairing 2021 was the Austrian Maximilian Steiner (Hotel Steiner, Tyrol); he received this prize for his pairing of swordfish/broad bean cream/cucumber and pioppino mushrooms with a Tedorigawa u yoshidagura sake. In 2022, the title went to Angelika Grundler (Restaurant Pavillon in the Hotel Baur au Lac, Zürich) for her pairing of sweetbread saltimbocca with a chanterelle ragout and a sauce Gribiche with a Hatsumago Kimoto Tradition sake. You can view the descriptions of around 200 sake pairings at **sake-pairing-contest.com**— from oysters to foie gras, cheese and pizza, to roast venison— which prove that sake complements more than just Japanese dishes.

## Regionality and Cross Culture

Just like wine, sake varies according to the region it is produced in (see pp. 138–153). In Japan's mountain regions, a sweet and strong sake is favored to go with salty specialties, yet people in the coastal regions drink a fresh and light sake with fish and seafood.

Chefs in Europe and the United States are increasingly using Eastern ingredients, condiments, and cooking methods; Asian fusion and Nikkei cuisine, developed by Japanese immigrants in South America, are now particularly popular. The menus in such establishments are colorful and diverse, and diners are often expected to share a range of small dishes with the other people at their table; for example, sashimi, beef tataki, teriyaki chicken, and prawn dumplings will all be served simultaneously. Should you pair all these dishes with an all-rounder sake, often offered as the house sake? Or should you choose an aromatic and expressive sake for the starters, then a traditional, robust sake for main

dishes? You can do either. Another delicious example of cross-culture cuisine is ceviche with Japanese sashimi, South American lime, and chili—which pairs excellently with a light, fresh-tasting sake.

## Similarity or Contrast?

A pairing can be successful when the sake and food dish have similar aromas or intensities of flavor, such as when a sea bream carpaccio is combined with a fresh and light sake. However, it is sometimes more interesting to bring together a sake and a dish that contrast with each other, such as, for example, Parma ham with a sweet Katsuyama Lei junmai ginjo, whose aromas are reminiscent of melon (and therefore of a popular Italian antipasto). The saltiness and mild umami of air-dried ham are complemented by the sweetness and fruity notes of the sake, and the flavors of the two mutually enhance each other. Similarly interesting interplays can be obtained by combining grilled rosemary lamb chops with a highly aromatic daiginjo; the flowery ginjo aromas act like a condiment for the meat. In addition, the alcohol in the sake enhances the fresh rosemary notes and contrasts nicely with the smoky notes of the meat. —

# 8

## ADVANTAGES OF SAKE PAIRING

### 1. Sake enhances the flavor of food components
(herbs, spices, etc.).

### 2. Sake mollifies sharp flavors
(saltiness, acidity, bitterness, spiciness) and combines different elements of flavor; for example, the sweetness of sake tempers the salty flavor of soy sauce.

### 3. Sake complements the flavor of food dishes
(acts like a sauce or condiment).

### 4. Sake covers up undesired aspects
(the smell of fish, etc.).

### 5. Sake emphasizes umami in the dishes.

### 6. Sake does not fight against food dishes
but rather imbues them with complexity and harmony.

### 7. There are no impossible combinations
that might lead to unpleasant gastronomic experiences, unlike with wine, which is sometimes very difficult to combine with dishes that are high in iron or zinc, such as liver, tuna fish, mussels, and seaweed. Since sake barely contains any iron, this problem does not arise.

### 8. Sake cleans the palate
and leaves behind pleasant aromas and umami.

# 8

## TIPS FOR A HARMONIOUS SAKE PAIRING

### 1. Let yourself be guided by the intensity of the flavors
Sake with a rich flavor pairs best with hearty dishes, whereas a light sake goes well with refined dishes.

### 2. Let yourself be guided by the aroma
A sake should be in harmony with the range of aromas in a dish. A strong sake with smoky aromas pairs well with grilled dishes, whereas a fresh sake with aromas of green apple, citrus fruit, and herbs will suit a lighter dish, such as fish carpaccio with rocket.

### 3. Let yourself be guided by the terroir of the products
Sake from breweries in the coastal region of Japan goes well with fish and shellfish, while sake from the interior tends to go better with hearty dishes.

### 4. Let yourself be guided by the degree of maturity
Young sake pairs well with fresh vegetables, fruit, and cream cheese, whereas an aged sake will combine well with pickled vegetables, dried fruit, and mature cheese.

### 5. Take exclusivity into account
An exclusive sake requires a partner of equal rank. Drop sake, the purest version of daiginjo or junmai daiginjo, goes well with caviar or truffles, and Kimoto junmai daiginjo, with its silky texture and distinctive acidity, is the perfect fit for Kobe beef.

### 6. Find an all-rounder sake
There are sakes that easily pair with a wide range of dishes, such as sushi, yakitori, asparagus with hollandaise sauce, or fish and chips. One for all! You should always have a bottle of this easy going sake in your refrigerator.

### 7. Create a contrast
An aromatic sake for a hearty meat dish, or a sweet sake to go with mature cheese—an opposition between a sake and a dish can create an interesting contrast in which the individual elements also complement each other. This can then give rise to a third flavor, and that is the best sake pairing—a marriage, you might say!

### 8. Construct a dramaturgy in the menu
You are your own sake sommelier, and you are staging a series of culinary duets! You might start, for example, with sparkling sake for a toast at the beginning of the meal, then serve a fresh and light sake with a low alcohol content to go with goat cheese mousse, an aromatic daiginjo to go with raw king prawn aromatized with orange, a smooth junmai ginjo with fish with beurre blanc, a strong Kimoto junmai daiginjo to accompany a main course of venison, and a sweet kijoshu with a chocolaty dessert.

# HARMONY WITH FOOD

**What goes particularly well with sake?** The basic principles of sake pairing are as follows: light sake for light dishes, strong sake for strong dishes. When selecting a sake to enjoy with food, the ingredients in the dish are an important factor, but you should also consider how it has been prepared. Both the sake and the dish can have various nuances that influence the pairing—as can your personal preferences, of course. To make it easy, here is a list of dishes that go especially well with sake.

# RAW FISH AND SEAFOOD

## Raw Oysters with Lemon
**Suitable Styles of Sake:**
A. Sparkling,
B. Light and fresh
C. Fruity and mild
**Why?** The light, fruity notes and sweetness of the sake will enhance the salty, milky flavor, lemony aroma, and umami taste of the oysters and mellow their mineral flavor.

## Maguro Sashimi (Tuna Fish Sashimi) with Soy Sauce and Wasabi
**Suitable Styles of Sake:**
B. Light and fresh
C. Fruity and mild
F. Traditional and umami
**Why?** The umami of the fish, soy sauce, and sake will mutually enhance each other. Sake seems fruitier and milder when it is combined with a salty, malty soy sauce. The green, sharp notes of the wasabi will give the pairing refreshing accents, and the sake will mask the tuna's metallic notes.

## Salmon Tartare with Grated Lemon Rind, Parsley, and Olive Oil
**Suitable Styles of Sake:**
B. Light and fresh
C. Fruity and mild
D. Aromatic and expressive
**Why?** The sake will enhance all the spicy notes in the dish and define its flavors more clearly. In addition, an aromatic, expressive sake will introduce some spiciness and refine the flavor of the dish with its creamy texture.

## Sole with Ponzu Sauce or Sole Ceviche
**Suitable Styles of Sake:**
A. Sparkling
B. Light and fresh
C. Fruity and mild
**Why?** The delicate umami of the sole will be elegantly uplifted by a sake without overly strong rice notes. A sake with a fresh acidity (usually malic acid) will connect with the citric acid in the dish.

## Sushi with Ika (Squid), White Fish, Shrimps, Mussels, and Salmon
**Suitable Styles of Sake:**
B. Light and fresh
C. Fruity and mild
**Why?** These various sushi bites will pair well with a compatible, not dominant, light and fruity sake with discreet aromas.

# FISH ROE

## Caviar
**Suitable Styles of Sake:**
A. Sparkling
E. Complex and refined (excluding kimoto sake)
**Why?** Caviar has a mild, buttery, nutty flavor. The aroma of the sake will merge with the fish roe and uplift it. There will be a pleasant interplay between the fruity sweetness of the sake and the salty butteriness of the caviar.

## Wild Salmon Caviar
**Suitable Styles of Sake:**
D. Aromatic and expressive,
E. Complex and refined (excluding kimoto sake)
**Why?** A highly aromatic sake will harmoniously round off the saltiness and oil of the fish roe. The oil in the roe will extend the fruity aromas of the sake.

# EGG DISHES

## Chawan Mushi (Stacked Eggs with Dashi Broth)
**Suitable Styles of Sake:**
B. Light and fresh
C. Fruity and mild
**Why?** The refined flavor of the chawan mushi will be gently enhanced by a light and fruity sake with a low alcohol content.

## Quiche Lorraine
**Suitable Styles of Sake:**
C. Fruity and mild
**Why?** The sake perfectly complements the mild mixture of egg and cream, the salty, fatty bacon, and the light, toasty notes of pastry, becoming fruitier in the process.

## Tortilla
**Suitable Styles of Sake:**
F. Traditional and umami
**Why?** The mild egg flavor is complemented by the crispy fried potatoes and the strong garlic note. A mild Junmai accompanies the dish with similar intensity, bringing out the umami flavor and the spicy note.

# COOKED VEGETABLES, FISH, AND MEAT WITH VARIOUS SAUCES

## With Teriyaki Sauce (e.g., Yakitori Skewers and Salmon with Teriyaki Sauce) or with Miso Sauce (e.g., Unagi with Miso)
**Suitable Styles of Sake:**
D. Aromatic and expressive
F. Traditional and umami
G. Aged
**Why?** Teriyaki sauce consists of soy sauce, mirin, and sake and has malty-sweet notes, so it pairs well with a strong and expressive sake. If the basic ingredients of a dish are fatty, such as in the case unagi (eel) or pork belly, a kimoto or yamahai sake with strong acidity will make a good pairing.

## With a Buttery Sauce or a Hearty Meat Sauce (e.g., Fried/Roasted Pike with Nut Butter)
**Suitable Styles of Sake:**
D. Aromatic and expressive
E. Complex and refined (including kimoto sake)
F. Traditional and umami
**Why?** An aromatic sake pairs well with butter and other types of animal fat and acts as a condiment, enhancing the umami of the dish. An aromatic sake will make an appealing contrast to a hearty meat sauce, while a kimoto sake or a sake with a more traditional style and umami will underscore the flavor of the dishes.

## With a Creamy Sauce or Béchamel Sauce (e.g., Asparagus with Hollandaise Sauce or Scallops au Gratin)
**Suitable Styles of Sake:**
C. Fruity and mild
F. Traditional and umami
**Why?** Mild dishes pair well with a sake that has a similar intensity or mildness; here, the fruity or rice notes of sake complement the dishes' milky notes.

# DEEP-FRIED VEGETABLES, FISH, POULTRY

## Shrimp and Vegetable Tempura
**Suitable Styles of Sake:**
B. Light and fresh
C. Fruity and mild
F. Traditional and umami
**Why?** Deep-fried tempura batter is crispy and encloses the fine aroma of the ingredients it contains. For tempura with salt and lemon, choose a light and fresh sake to enhance the freshness of the citrus fruit and cleanse the fat of the tempura, or choose a fruity sake to amplify the fruit flavors. For tempura with tsuyu dip, choose a warm, traditional sake; the umami of the pairing will add complexity to the dish, since the sauce itself also contains a lot of umami (dashi, soy sauce, mirin, and sake).

## Karaage Chicken

**Suitable Styles of Sake:**

B. Light and fresh

D. Aromatic and expressive

F. Traditional and umami

**Why?** Chicken marinated in soy sauce, mirin, and ginger has a strong umami flavor. A lighter or fruity sake complements the dish and also cleanses your palate. On the other hand, a traditional sake will amp up the umami flavors.

# BEEF OR GAME STEAK

## Medium-Rare Steak with Rosemary Jus

**Suitable Styles of Sake:**

F. Traditional and umami

D. Aromatic and expressive

E. Complex and refined (kimoto junmai daiginjo)

G. Aged

**Why?** The combination will enhance the umami. The sake is strong enough for the meat's smoky notes and fat. The animal fat will be made more digestible by the acidity of the kimoto or yama-hai sake, and the rosemary aroma will become stronger, making the dish spicier and more flavorful. An aged sake with caramel, cocoa, or spicy notes will add complexity to the dish.

# CHEESE

## Brillat-Savarin Cheese, Mozzarella, Fresh Goat Cheese

**Suitable Styles of Sake:**

A. Sparkling (especially sweet-and-sour types),

B. Light and Fresh

C. Fruity and mild

**Why?** A sparkling sake with a slightly sweet-and-sour flavor and low alcohol content has a similar acidity to cheese and can add some fruity notes to it. In addition, the light fizziness of the sake will loosen up the thick consistency of the cheese.

## Hard Cheese (e.g., Mature Comté, Beaufort, or Parmesan)

**Suitable Styles of Sake:**

C. Fruity and mild

D. Aromatic and expressive

F. Traditional and umami

**Why?** A fruity or traditional sake will enhance the umami of a mature cheese and add stimulating, fruity notes.

## Pungent Cheeses (e.g., Gorgonzola, Roquefort, or Smear-Ripened Cheeses Such as Munster)

**Suitable Styles of Sake:**

D. Aromatic and expressive

G. Aged

H. Sweet and aromatized

**Why?** A strong-flavored cheese should be paired with a sake that has distinctive aromas and residual sugar, which will act similarly to a forest honey paired with gorgonzola or a sweet wine paired with Roquefort.

# DESSERT

## Wagashi from Sweet Cooked Beans

**Suitable Styles of Sake:**

C. Fruity and mild

H. Sweet and aromatized

**Why?** Wagashi is a Japanese confection, usually made out of boiled beans and agar-agar; it has an elegant sweetness. A fruity and mild sake will add fruity notes to the wagashi; a double-brewed kijoshu will give it a complex sweetness and depth.

## Mousse de Champagne

**Suitable Styles of Sake:**

A. Sparkling

H. Sweet and aromatized

**Why?** This fine, cream-based mousse can be gently and deliciously paired with a light sparkling sake without any aggressive acidity.

## Chocolate Cake

**Suitable Styles of Sake:**

G. Aged

H. Sweet and aromatized

**Why?** An aged sake with distinctive notes of dried fruit, nuts, caramel, and spices will give chocolate cake a pleasant complexity and depth.

# WASHOKU — KEY ELEMENTS OF JAPANESE CUISINE

**The Japanese word *washoku* means "harmony of food."**
In 2013, washoku, referring to traditional Japanese cuisine
in all its diversity—from kaiseki menus to dishes served in
humble izakaya bars in the Edo period, such as sushi, soba,
and tempura—was included by UNESCO in its Intangible
Cultural Heritage List.

Japanese cuisine is based on the principle of ichiju sansai: the extremely healthy harmony of one soup and three dishes accompanied by rice. A distinction is made, however, between everyday cooking, which varies from one region to the next, and kaiseki cuisine, the country's haute cuisine, which developed out of tea ceremonies and the practice of providing hospitality to the medieval aristocrats and samurais of the Edo period. At all times, however, this concept is about more than just the food itself; the know-how and traditions connected to its preparation and meticulous presentation are equally important.

## The Rule of Five

Japan's traditional cuisine aims to appeal to all five senses: colorful vegetables and strips of pork belly shiny with fat in a steaming bowl of ramen feed the eye, the strong aroma of meat enchants the nose, the tongue feels the hot, thick texture of the dish, as well as an explosion of umami, and slurps of relish reach our ears. In addition, washoku always includes five tastes (gomi): salty, sweet, bitter, sour, and umami, as well as five colors (go shiki): black, white, green, yellow, and red. Moreover, five types of food preparation must be included (go ho): raw, boiled, deep-fried, grilled, and steamed.

## Rice as Staple

In Japan, everything revolves around rice. Japanese people place rice at the center of their meals—at the center of their lives, even. Traditionally, they already eat a bowl of rice and miso soup for breakfast, accompanied by a few salt-preserved vegetables (tsukemono) and/or salted plums (umeboshi) with nori seaweed. The rice is usually boiled in water and unseasoned. Chewing makes it grow sweeter in one's mouth, and it mixes well with the saltiness of the umeboshi, becoming "seasoned on the palate" (konai-chomi). When eating, each individual can determine the flavor of the dish themselves through the amounts they put into their mouths, so, despite its simple components, the dish is never boring.

In kaiseki, Japan's haute cuisine, rice is served after a sequence of dishes, as a main course (shushoku) with miso soup and something savory. In everyday cooking, all dishes are laid out at the same time, but rice is at the center of the meal. There are also specific rules about where to place the dishes: rice on the left-hand side, miso soup next to it on the right, and then other dishes above these two, in as well-balanced a formation as possible. Ideally, to satisfy the rule of five, there should be three additional dishes, such as chikuzen-ni (boiled vegetables), sanma no shioyaki (grilled saury with grated radish), and wakame no sunomono (sour cucumber and wakama seaweed). The dishes and contents of the miso soup can vary daily, but in the middle of the table, there will always be some shiny, boiled white rice.

## Seasonal Food from Land and Sea

In Japan, vegetables and fish are stars of almost every meal. There are currently 150 different types of vegetables farmed in the country, and around 4,200 species of fish live in the seas surrounding the island nation. Soybeans and other pulses, mushrooms, wild vegetables, kelp, and poultry are also traditional foodstuffs. The abundance of edible treasures from the water, mountains, and fields changes according to the season. In spring there are bamboo shoots, mountain vegetables, tai (sea bream), sawara (Spanish mackerel) and katsuo (skipjack tuna). Summer is the time of cucumbers, tomatoes and edamame, ayu (sweetfish), hamo (pike conger), and sea eel. The fall offers, among other things, matsutake mushrooms, sweet potatoes, kakis, sanma (saury), oysters, scallops, and salmon. In winter there are shungiku (chrysanthemum greens), Chinese cabbage, buri (yellowtail amberjack), monkfish, cod, zuwai crab, fugu (pufferfish), and much more. Traditionally, meat only rarely finds its way to the table; in the past, it was only in the mountain regions that people ate wild boar and venison. It was not until after the Meiji Restoration (around 1867) that people started to eat beef and pork. Meat is usually sliced thinly and boiled, such as for shabu-shabu or sukiyaki. There is also the tradition of shojin-ryori (a vegetable diet) in Japan, in which vegetables and tofu play the leading roles. Good examples of shojin-ryori dishes are grilled eggplant and boiled furofuki daikon radish, each served with dengaku miso (miso glaze) or a tempura of seasonal vegetables.

## Water and Dashi

Water plays an important role in Japanese gastronomy; it is used not just to brew sake, but also to boil or steam rice and other ingredients and to make tea, miso soup, and the legendary dashi stock. Japanese cuisine is also known for its so-called "subtractive aesthetic" and flavors composed of saltiness and umami, which are achieved in large part by the addition of water, especially in dashi stock, which typically combines kombu (seaweed) and dried bonito flakes. The combination of various amino acids in the stock has a synergetic effect that increases the umami flavor, and this flavor is not just modified by adding further ingredients (e.g. plant-based ones), but also by the character of the water. Soft water tends to bring out the flavor in a dashi, while hard water prevents the flavors from unfolding.

# UMAMI FROM FERMENTED CONDIMENTS

Typical condiments in Japanese cuisine include fermented products such as soy sauce, miso, mirin, sake, and rice vinegar. They provide all five basic tastes, thanks to their umami and, occasionally, further factors such as sweetness, saltiness, and acidity. Their common denominator, umami, is created by koji and the aging process. Japan's warm and humid climate provides a good environment for fungi to grow in and has naturally encouraged a culture of fermentation. The deep, complex umami taste in fermented condiments and dashi still defines Japanese cuisine to this day.

Rice, koji, and soybeans are the main ingredients required to produce fermented condiments, which are traditionally fermented and aged for over a year in wooden barrels made from Japanese cedars. Industrial production has created completely different processes in recent years, but products made this way contain less natural umami and flavor. In contrast, a craft that has been passed down and refined from generation to generation, together with some house yeast that may have been developing in a brewery's historic premises in wooden barrels over 150 years, will give a condiment complex and unique flavors.

## Miso

This is one of Japan's favorite condiments. It is produced by fermenting and aging steamed or boiled soybeans together with koji and salt and is often used to make miso soup and boiled dishes. Different types of miso are used depending on the region, and their flavor varies according to their ingredients and how they are combined. The most popular type is reddish kome miso, made using soybeans and koji rice; this is produced all over the country. Mame miso, however, is mainly produced in Aichi, and owes its intense, acidic flavor to the duo of soybeans and soy koji. Mugi miso, in contrast, is mainly produced using soybeans and barley koji; it has a sweet aroma and is particularly popular in Kyushu.

## Soy Sauce

Koji made out of steamed soybeans and roasted wheat provides the base for this famous condiment—a fermented liquid that is used both as a marinade and for dipping and cooking. There are five types of soy sauce: koikuchi (dark), usukuchi (light), tamari, saishikomi, and shiro (white), and different types are favored in different regions. Dark soy sauce accounts for over 80 percent of production in Japan and is the type that is used most often. It contains an equal balance of soy and wheat and has a high level of umami. Light soy sauce has a higher salt content than the dark variety and is less fermented and aged. It is used to make dishes in which the color of the ingredients is supposed to be emphasized. Saishikomi is double brewed and less salty than koikuchi, with a very strong umami flavor. Tamari is made almost entirely out of soybeans and is characterized by its umami taste and richness. White soy sauce contains more wheat than soybeans; thus, it has a high sugar content and does not keep for long.

## Rice Vinegar (Kome-zu)

This condiment is used to give dishes such as sushi and sunomono a certain acidity. Rice vinegar is produced by fermenting sake with acetic acid bacteria. It makes ingredients softer and can be added to ponzu (a soy sauce seasoned with lemon juice) to give it a richer flavor. Aka-zu, the milder type, is mainly used for edomae sushi; produced using aged sake lees, it makes ingredients keep for longer. Historically, rice vinegar was very important, since it helped preserve rice and fish without a refrigerator and therefore enabled the development of sushi. Kuro-zu (black rice vinegar) is produced in Kagoshima in small clay containers following a specific fermentation procedure; it has a strong flavor.

## Sake

Just like wine in French cuisine, sake is a basic condiment in Japanese cuisine, used to give dishes a gentle sweetness and umami. As a marinade or condiment, it also removes unpleasant smells, making dishes smoother and enabling them to keep for longer. Before the emergence of soy sauce, and especially during the Edo period (1603–1867), so-called "iri sake" (sake boiled with salt or umeboshi) was used as a condiment.

## Mirin

Produced by fermenting steamed rice and kasu-shochu (shochu

mixed with sake lees), mirin is a very versatile condiment. Its alcohol content comes to around 14 percent, and it has a rich, nuanced but gentle sweetness, which goes well with nimono (boiled vegetables). In addition, mirin contains many types of amino acids, so it can add complex variations of umami taste to different foods. It is also used in marinades and to glaze meats and fish, such as salmon teriyaki.

# OTHER CONDIMENTS

## Sea Salt
Sea salt has been used for many years to season grilled foods and sashimi, pickle vegetables, and make dried fish.

## Sugar
Sugar is an essential component of Japanese cuisine, usually used in combination with soy sauce, salt, miso, and other ingredients, and even in stews. Japanese confections are made using special wasanbon sugar, which is produced according to a traditional procedure and has a gentle sweetness; it is somewhat similar to European icing sugar, but with a creamy color. Before sugar cane was farmed on Amami Island, this sweetness was obtained using koji or malt.

## A Formula for Seasoning
A large number of Japanese dishes can be prepared using a simple combination of basic condiments such as soy sauce, miso, mirin, and sake, as well as dashi stock. It is thus extremely important to pay attention to the quality of the individual condiments used. As much as possible, use products that were made following traditional methods—these will have natural aromas and umami tastes.

The base sauce, made by mixing soy sauce, sake, and mirin in equal proportions, is the first golden ratio; it can be used to make yakitori or salmon teriyaki, among other dishes. If you add dashi stock, you have a plethora of further possibilities. For boiled fish, the rule of thumb is 6 parts dashi stock and 1 part each soy sauce, mirin, and sake; use 8 parts dashi for nimono, 4 parts dashi for tempura sauce, and 12 parts dashi and 1 part each soy sauce, mirin, and sake for soba and other noodle soups. Use these proportions to start, then adapt the seasonings to suit your taste.

If you have concerns about the alcohol content, heat up the mirin and sake before using them so the alcohol evaporates.

To make a delicious sesame sauce, mix together 1 part each miso, sake, mirin, ground sesame seeds, and water; this tastes wonderful with fried vegetables or as a dip.

The two basic sauces described above can also be combined with rice vinegar and vegetable oil to make a salad dressing. Mix in yuzu, green shiso, and sansho for extra flair.

## Fragrant Garnishes
Herbs, citrus fruits, plants, and flowers give Japanese cuisine a touch of seasonality and diversity, but the rule is to only use one suikuchi (fragrant garnish) per dish. For example, yuzu rind releases a soft fragrance when the lid is taken off a soup bowl, and it is meant to be held up to one's lips when eating the soup. Sesame seeds, nori seaweed, chives, ginger, wasabi, mustard, and pepper sansho (Japanese mountain pepper) are used at appropriate times of the year to enhance various soup ingredients. Shanso leaves and flowers bring a taste of spring; in summer, green shiso, green yuzu, and myoga (the buds of a vegetable plant) are used; and early fall is the time for sudachi lemons, mitsuba, and chrysanthemum flowers. In late fall and winter, yellow yuzu and ginger make their appearances. Cherry leaves, bamboo grass, oak leaves, and kaki leaves are also used in Japanese cuisine to aromatize (and develop) dishes. Shiso flowers and leaves, just like chrysanthemum flowers, are used as a garnish for sashimi, and the same applies to wafer-thin slices of daikon radish. Daiginjo sake, with its fruity aroma, can also be used as a condiment. —

# Hironori

ORYOURI FUJII ✿✿ RESTAURANT
IWASE, TOYAMA PREFECTURE

Iwase was famous during the Edo and Meiji periods (1603–1912) for its shipping companies, and the extensive restoration of many of its narrow streets has revived the flair of that time period. Since 2019, one of its historic trading houses has been home to Hironori Fujii's two-Michelin-starred kaiseki restaurant. Fujii, who comes from the Toyama Region, is in his late 40s and spent many years working in various famous ryotei in Kanazawa and Kyoto.

I am standing outside the classic wooden gate to his restaurant, Oryouri Fujii. When you step through its white linen curtain, you come into a beautiful garden, complete with a koi pond and trees that burst into a glorious play of color in the fall. Water patters onto the cobblestones, which lead up to the single-story restaurant building. A woman in a kimono greets diners with a bow, a smile, and the greeting, "Irasshaimase (welcome)!" You then remove your shoes and are led into a room with a long low table. I settle down onto a zabuton (Japanese cushion) on a tatami mat and stretch my feet under my table. In front of me are the cold kitchen and a window open-ing out onto the garden. On the table in front of me is a black lacquered tablet with cedar wood chopsticks and a shallow, vermilion-lacquered sake cup. Once I have wiped my hands with a warm oshibori (towel), sake is poured from a bottle inscribed "freshly pressed" into the cup, then offered to me. The kaiseki ritual has begun.

The term *kaiseki* is now used to refer to Japan's haute cuisine; it consists of several courses and is traditionally enjoyed with sake. Rice, which for Japanese people is an essential part of any meal, is not served until the end of a kaiseki meal. There are 11 dishes on the menu that Oryouri Fujii hands me when I visit, handwritten in black ink on Japanese paper. I choose an appropriate sake accompaniment to go with them; the list is exclusively composed of sake from the neighboring Masuizumi Brewery. Hironori's restaurant does not have a sommelier, so every time he changes the menu, the whole staff spends a day tasting different sakes with the dishes in order to decide on appropriate pairings.

A linen curtain marks the entrance to Hironori Fujii's Kaiseki world.

## 1 | INOKO-MOCHI WITH KARASUMI + SAKE MASUIZUMI "DO YOU KNOW"

"Please choose your sake cup." The young man who is responsible for tableware takes the cover off a wooden box on the counter, and I see a colorful palette—almost a jewel case, in fact—of taizo glasses: lapis lazuli, gold, red, and crystal. I hesitate and, in the end, opt for a white cup with a spiral pattern. The kanji character for the first sake on the menu means "Do you know," and it is apparently produced using isehikari rice from the organic rice terraces in Toyama City. The first dish to be served is wrapped in washi paper, tied up in red and white paper string, and decorated with yellow-green gingko leaves: a rice cake in the shape of a wild boar.

According to the Chinese calendar, November is the month of the wild boar, and it is said that eating inoko-mochi will fend off all illnesses. My little cake is composed of steamed, slightly warm sticky rice with a sweet potato core and is coated with mullet roe (karasumi). Thinly sliced, it first releases smoky aromas; however, when I chew it, it develops a unique, iodine-like flavor combined with a delicious, bitter umami. The accompanying sip of sake is also warmed up by the inoko-mochi, so the sweetness of the rice and sake enhance each other, and the saltiness of the karasumi is made rounder. A good start!

## 2 | TURNIP AND SHINJO ZUWAI CRAB DUMPLINGS KOMBU-DASHI + MASUIZUMI PERO

The cover of the black-lacquered bowl in front of me is adorned with a gold relief of chrysanthemums on the inside; as it is removed, the scent of a fine broth with a hint of yuzu rises up into the air. In the clear stock, I see a boiled turnip and a white dumpling made out of zuwai crab meat. "This cup was made specially for our fall season in Wajima, on the Noto Peninsula, and this soup stock, which is seasoned only with a little salt, was made solely out of kelp and the brewing water from Masuizumi," explains Hironori Fujii. When I break up the little turnip with my chopsticks and press it onto my tongue, it releases sweetness and saltiness, and the crab dumpling disintegrates in my mouth.

Usually, shinjo fish dumplings are made out of puréed white fish or crab meat, with yam or egg white as a binding agent. But those at Oryouri Fujii have a texture in which you can still feel the fibers of the crab meat—they seem to barely contain any binding agent at all. I tell the head chef that I have never eaten such a delicious shinjo. He responds: "It was quite a bit of work to obtain this exquisite, loosely bonded texture." His words suggest a light-heartedness that signals how much he enjoys this experimentation. The cold sake that accompanies the soup only contains 12 percent alcohol, but it has a clear sweetness and acidity. It is usually difficult to combine sake with soup, but in this case the two fit perfectly together.

## 3 | SASHIMI OF WILD BURI + MASUIZUMI GENTEI DAIGINJO

## 4 | SASHIMI OF AORI-IKA + MASUIZUMI R KIMOTO NAMAZAKE YAMADA NISHIKI

Buri (yellowtail amberjack) from Toyama Bay is a winter delicacy that fattens with every cold snap. It has a firm structure and is served with wasabi soy sauce and a spicy radish soy sauce. Its umami is enhanced by the dark soy sauce—just like that of the gentei sake that is served with it, which has a wonderful ginjo aroma and a creamy texture reminiscent of cantaloupe. And the squid, refreshingly prepared with the juice of green sudachi lemons and sea salt from the coast near Suzu, is poetry for the eyes, thanks to the precise furrows that have been cut into it with a knife. With every bite, my mouth fills with the sweetness and flavor of the raw aori-ika, and I appreciate the structure achieved by the generous lactic acid aroma of my warm Kimoto Namazake. The combination of cold sashimi and slightly tempered sake is a surprising success. Hironori says, "Usually you would not drink nama sake warm. Aside from the master brewer's recommendations, however, we always strive to find how best to pair each sake with each dish."

Ingredients, cooking methods, and crockery harmonize with the seasons.

## 5 | KOBAKO CRAB MARINATED IN SOY SAUCE + SAKE MASUIZUMI KIJOSHU NO KIJOSHU

Kobako is a female snow crab; it is smaller than its male counterpart and carries eggs in its shell. This one was marinated at length in a stock made with soy sauce, and the shell was then filled with the roe, dyed black by the soy sauce, and a little crab meat. The luxurious, golden-brown, thrice-brewed Kijoshu sake is a perfect pairing for this dish—it bewitches you with its aromas of honey and caramel and its honey-like texture. Its complex, nuanced sweetness, which is reminiscent of that of wasanbon sugar, is not sustained, however, and surprisingly light. This sake is reminiscent of mead but with some umami, so it is finer and more pleasant. The complex aromas of the sea and of soy sauce, the saltiness of the dish, and the sweetness of the sake perfectly complement one another.

## 6 | HASSUN + IWA 5 ASSEMBLAGE 2 & ASSEMBLAGE 4

Hassun are the jewels of kaiseki cuisine and the essence of Japanese cuisine—bite-size, beautifully arranged starters that express the Japanese appreciation of beauty and seasonality. Hassun was born out of the idea that diners should be able to enjoy their drinks first without wondering what they should eat. The composition laid out in front of me on a large plate is decorated with yellow and vermilion-red kaki leaves, as well as beautiful, slightly golden gingko leaves and dark green pine needles. The small dishes I have been offered include eggplant dengaku (eggplant with miso glaze), carrots with white miso, salmon roe marinated in soy sauce, duck breast, pear wrapped in prosciutto, and monaka (rice waffles filled with walnut miso).

The two sakes that are paired with the hassun are assemblages from the years 2021 and 2023. Number 2 has a golden glow and is slightly darker than Number 4, having been aged for longer. Both creations perfectly complement the dishes, enhancing the dining experience and underlining the dark miso flavor.

Despite the different aromas of the various dishes, the IWA 5 kimoto sakes go well with each individual creation; they amplify the flavors of the ingredients, temper their saltiness, and complement their umami. These combinations bring to mind an expert dancer in a tuxedo, creating wonderful dances with a series of different partners, each with its own unique character. Once the round dance of the hassun has come to an end, I take one more sip of Assemblage 4. My first impression is one of a gentle aroma with nuances of marzipan, hazelnut, coconut, violet, nori seaweed, white pepper, and sweet pepper, mixed with a clear acidity and minerality. When warmed on the tongue, this sake becomes milder and fuller with hidden fruity notes and a subtle bitterness. Its finish shimmers with notes of white and sweet pepper. Superb!

## 7 | ROASTED KAMASU WITH MATSUTAKE MUSHROOMS + MASUIZUMI YUHO JUNMAI GENSHU

Kamasu (barracuda) is a lean fish, but it grows fat in the fall. Its thick filet is cut up into three pieces, wrapped around a frayed matsutake mushroom, skewered, and grilled over a charcoal fire. Matsutake mushrooms grow in pine forests and have an aroma of pinewood and earth. Since they have a very brief season, they are only used by the most exclusive restaurants and are regarded as they most precious autumn ingredient in Japan.

With kamasu, a halved sudachi lemon works a small wonder: if you press it over the fragrant fish and then take a bite, the fish's juices and fat run out. Thanks to the warmth from your mouth, the aroma from the mushroom filling is then released—and the fibers of the semi-raw matsutake stems become crunchy as you chew them. The succulent taste of the fish is intensified by the fresh acidity of the sudachi lemon, and in addition, the zest of the citrus fruit gives the dish a green, peppery note. The junmai sake further enhances this taste experience, intensifying the aroma of the mushrooms, and its subtle (rice-based) sweetness also complements the delicacy of the other ingredients. Sipped on its own, the Yuho comes across as rather simple; it gains substantially from being paired with the food, however. Exquisite!

Seasonal specialties from Toyama: kobako crab and matsutake mushrooms

## 8 | SEMI-DRIED ANPO-KAKI, NAMASU + MASUIZUMI LINK 8888

Anpo kakis (persimmons), a specialty from the Toyama Region, have the consistency of dried apricots yet none of their acidity. They are dried semi-raw for around a month, so their water content is only half of that of fresh kakis, which gives them a jellylike consistency and a complex sweetness. Hironori Fujii covers the fruits with a sesame cream, lending slightly salty and nutty notes, and beds them on soured namasu made out of lightly-salted carrots and daikon radish. The accompanying Link 8888 rice wine was produced using Masuizumi sake aged for over 10 months in old Chivas Regal whisky barrels, which give it its smoky caramel and coffee notes. As you eat, it develops nuances of chestnuts and fruitcake in your mouth. It is surprising to taste such complex layers of sweetness and bitterness in a Japanese pairing of sake and food.

## 9 | SATOIMO (TARO) + MASUIZUMI SHIRAHAGI ON THE ROCKS

After the intense flavors of the previous dish, here comes a pleasant, simple one with taro root in a seaweed and bonito broth. The taro owes its gentle and mild flavor to the good quality of the soil in Nanto, where it grows, and to the water from the Tateyama Mountains. The accompanying Shirahagi sake is served with ice cubes made from the Masuizumi brewing water. The ice melts slowly, reducing the alcohol content of the drink. The coldness of the sake and the warmth of the taro dish make for an exciting contrast.

## 10 | FUKIYOSE GOHAN + MASUIZUMI FUNAHASHI

The rice in this dish, cooked in earthenware pots, is mixed with autumnal delicacies such as sweet potatoes and gingko nuts. The accompanying Funahashi, which is brewed using the popular koshihikari table rice, has a full-bodied flavor. Before being served, this sake is first warmed up to 60°C (140°F), then cooled down to 45°C (113°F) in order to enhance the succinic acid that defines its flavor. To go with it, aside from the rice dish, I am served miso soup and tsukemono (fermented vegetables)—a delicate combination, which the sweetness of the mild sake harmonizes with perfectly.

## 11 | SAKE DESSERT

In the past, a kaiseki menu came to an end with the serving of rice and miso soup, perhaps followed by some fruit and tea. Nowadays, though, a sweet dessert is often served, just like on a western menu. At Hironori Fujii, ice cream made with Mauritius rum and the kasu (lees) of a Junmai Daiginjo Platinum is served, followed by autumnal chestnut bonbons and green tea.

Final verdict: This two-hour-long meal was a unique, impressive experience. Its courses were composed using the products of the land and waters of the Noto Peninsula, which are only available in this season and in this location. Equally impressive were the numerous sake "pictures" from Masuizumi, complemented by the IWA duo. It was wonderful that they were not just tailored to the aromas of the dishes, but also encouraged to reveal their potential by being served at different temperatures and in different types of glasses. —

*Yuzu, soy sauce, konbu: basic ingredients of Japanese cuisine*

In the winter, Japanese cuisine is full of the flavor of yuzu.

A clear morning breeze in the historic geisha district of Kanazawa

# Yoshihiro

AOYAMA

A FEAST FOR ALL SENSES — SAKE. FOOD. PAIRING.

It is noon on a sunny November day in Aoyama, a classy neighborhood of Tokyo in which art, architecture, haute couture, and the finest satoyama cuisine play big roles. "I called this dish *gokoku hojo*, which means 'rich harvest' in English, to express the desire for a rich harvest and gratitude for it. Sawara, Spanish mackerel, from Fukuoka, is the main ingredient, and it is enriched with various rice-based components," says Yoshihiro Narisawa, the head chef and owner of the two-Michelin-starred restaurant that bears his name near to Tokyo's National Art Center and the vast Meiji-jingu Gaien Garden. The warm light of late fall falls onto the white tablecloths through a large window.

When I remove the washi paper cover from the plate in front of me, a fragrant, white mist rises up. The filet of sawara is surrounded by grated red and green radish; on the slightly inclined sides of the plate, green and pink sauces alternate in a circle. The whole thing looks like a three-dimensional painting. "The composition represents a satoyama scene; it refers to terraced rice paddies in the morning mist and the ocean spreading out on the edge of the paddies. The mist is created using a special kitchen implement made out of rice straw and cherrywood chips; it is reminiscent of the fragrance that is released when the rice straw is burned on the paddies after the fall harvest. I start by marinating the fish in sake kasu and then grilling it over charcoal. The two types of radish are seasoned with citrus. The base for the pink sauce is made out of koji with a white paste, colored and aromatized with Japanese herbs such as red shiso and pickled plums; for the green sauce, I use green shiso and sansho leaves. The garnish consists of

Yoshihiro Narisawa puts satoyama on the plate in his restaurant.

# We would be delighted if our restaurant could help them understand the wealth and delectability of our regional food culture.

brown and black puffed rice. This is a dish that draws on the three components of aroma, aspect, and story," explains Yoshihiro.

The sawara is fatty, and its umami is intensified by marinating it in the sake lees. Its smoky aroma blends with the fresh fragrance of the shiso and sansho leaves in the two sauces. When you eat it, the mild acidity of the ponzu and the subtle sweetness and spiciness of the grated daikon radish refreshingly cleanse your tongue of the fatty, salty, and roasted aromas of the fish. The interplay among these contrasting aromas and flavors is complex and fascinating.

To drink, I am served Masuizumi Bo, a pure sake produced using a rice variety called yamadabo, the mother of the famous yamada nishiki sake rice. This sake has a dense texture on the tongue, releasing a discreet aroma of white blossoms and white peach, as well as an elegant rice flavor. It underlines the

individuality of the contrasting ingredients in the harvest dish by adding aromatic notes and combining them all into an even more exquisite experience. Just like the sake, the koji and the kasu that Yoshihiro Narisawa uses in his kitchen come from the Masuizumi Brewery.

"In Japanese rice farming culture, absolutely nothing must be thrown away. It is part of Japanese cuisine that you have to use the whole rice plant," explains Yoshihiro.

"The ash that is created by burning the weeds and rice straw on the paddy improves its soil. Koji, miso, and the vinegar that we use for our dishes are all made out of rice," explains the acclaimed chef.

Five of the seven beverages that are offered at Narisawa to accompany the menu are sake; the remaining two are wines from Toyama. It is rare for a Michelin-starred restaurant in Tokyo to offer so much sake as meal pairings. In fact, when I visited

The scent of rice straw smoke is reminiscent of autumn in rural Japan.

Various sakes accompany the Narisawa's fine cuisine.

this same restaurant eight or nine years ago, I was mainly offered foreign wines and only a few sake options. Has his philosophy changed?

"We use high-quality Japanese ingredients in our restaurant," answers Yoshihiro. "I very often travel to rural areas to visit producers, and I often buy directly from vegetable farmers, fishers, or breeders. The basis of my cuisine is a dashi stock made out of konbu seaweed and katsuo skipjack tuna. We also work with other cooking techniques from French, Italian, and Chinese cuisine. What goes well with fine Japanese ingredients and aromas is a good sake, don't you agree?"

The chef, who was born in 1969, has developed his own genre of cuisine, which he calls "the innovative satoyama cuisine." It expresses the rich food culture of these cultured landscapes and the wisdom of Japanese ancestors. Yoshihiro's grandfather and father both worked in the food industry, and he himself initially devoted himself to Japanese cuisine. At the age of 19, Yoshihiro went to spend eight years in Europe, then continued his training in countries such as Switzerland, Italy, Spain, Portugal, Monaco, and France. After returning home, he opened up his first restaurant in the city of Odawara and started to engage with local producers. As he worked, he became increasingly aware of the significance of satoyama.

People from all over the world who sympathize with Yoshihiro's philosophy now come to visit the restaurant he opened in 2003 in Tokyo, with its large glass façade and minimalistic, modern design of grey, white, and black colors. The first thing his guests see as they are led to their table is the Japanese flag: a red sakazuki sake cup placed in the center of a sheet of handmade white washi paper. Once the sake has been poured into the cup, the meal can start. The Narisawa food menu provides a short explanation of the meaning of the sakazuki aperitif, which relaxes the stomach and the spirit, and which is sometimes also found in traditional kaiseki restaurants. In addition, there is a graphic description of satoyama and information about the origin of the ingredients used in the dishes. But will visitors from overseas and other countries understand the depth of the culture of satoyama? "Tokyo is the gateway for people from abroad," says Yoshihiro with a smile, "and we would be delighted if our restaurant could help them understand the wealth and delectability of our regional food culture, and perhaps even encourage them to travel out into the countryside. We have producers here who produce such wonderful vegetables and meats and such excellent sake. When we compile our dishes, we always have our customers, our diners in mind. Many visitors to Narisawa are generous and educated, but we take care not to impose my enthusiasm for the satoyama landscape and its cuisine onto them. I became a chef because I can make people happy with my cooking. Eating is the happiest activity for human beings." —

245

# Tokyo by night

TOKYO

In Japan, the end of the working day traditionally marks the beginning of sake time. Allow me to take you on a tour of some of the finest watering holes in the country's main metropolis.

### Day 1 in Tokyo, 7:00 p.m. in Roppongi, Eureka!

It is a February evening in Tokyo, shortly before 7 p.m. Many workers have already enjoyed their first after-work sake one hour earlier. The reason for this lies in the very word *sake*: the second part of the character used to write it means "rooster" in the Chinese zodiac calendar and represents the time span between 5 and 7 p.m. In the past, the temple bell was rung exactly in between these two hours.

I am standing at the Roppongi crossroads, where two major roads meet: the elevated highway and the one that leads to Tokyo Tower. Roppongi is an urban nightlife district, and my destination here is the Eureka! restaurant. This modern izakaya is located in an area where the flashy advertising signs become rarer and rarer. It has a glass façade, so you can see into its almost full interior.

Marie Chiba, the owner of the restaurant, smiles from behind the U-shaped bar and welcomes me with a bottle of sake in her hand. She is a sake sommelière, known for her innovative ways of combining the beverage with food. It's not for nothing that her restaurant is called Eureka!, after Archimedes' joyful exclamation: "I've found it!"

This evening, patrons crowd into the venue, which looks more like a modern bar than a traditional Japanese restaurant. Two fashionably clad young women, a man and woman who seem to work in the media, and a couple from Hong Kong who are on a sightseeing trip sit nearby. The daily specials are written up in chalk on a board, but Marie is also happy to advise her guests. Before the first drink is served, I am offered a small bowl of soup made with soy milk and shallots as an amuse-bouche—this wonderful creation warms my body and soul.

Marie chats with the various groups of diners at the 20-seat bar, explaining her pairings and serving them sake, which is poured out until the guest says, "No, thank you, no more." The owner of the Eureka! moves briskly, giving instructions to the kitchen and the other sommeliers and keeping an eye on everything. I now have in front of me a ham cordon bleu with gorgonzola and black garlic—and, to go with

Fun, pleasure, and good conversations—at the Eureka!, sake provides the right mix.

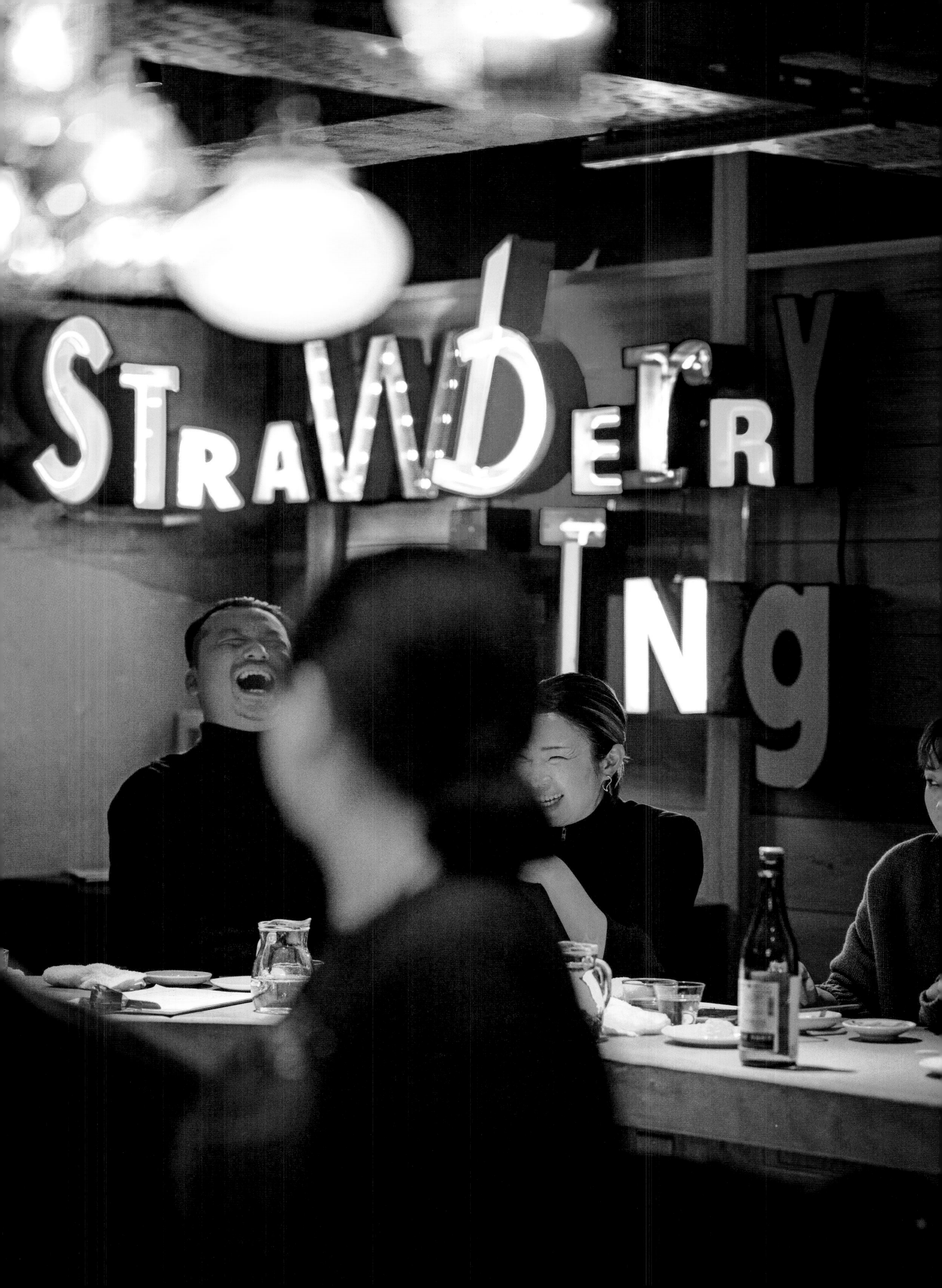

Food is arranged in small portions, like tapas.

it, a doburoku (unfiltered farmer's sake) from Tono. "This is our classic," explains Marie. The sweetness and creaminess of the sake make a wonderful contrast to the salty, crispy cutlet, and the black garlic gives the depth to the whole experience. The sweetness and umami of the sake temper the dish's saltiness, sourness, and other spicy notes.

The next pairing is authentically Japanese. To go with yellowtail amberjack (buri) and wild vegetables with soured white miso, I am given a Jokigen nama sake from Shiga Prefecture, which has been aged for five years at -5°C (23°F). The bitterness and crunchiness of the wild vegetables and the rich, sweet-and-sour sauce taste of spring. The silky and creamy sake gently adapts to the dish's aromas and gives it a light sweetness and umami. After the hearty previous pairing, this is a quiet combination and welcome change. The sake isn't fighting—instead, it underscores the dish's aromas and gently enfolds them without adulterating its own flavor.

As my visit to the Eureka! nears its end, I order some okan (warm sake). Marie has selected a Kaze no Mori Alpha 8 Earth from Nara for me—a sake brewed with ultra-hard water and roasted, unpolished brown rice. She pours it into a tin jug, dips it in hot water, and explains, "The higher its temperature, the more buttery a sake made from brown rice will become, so I'm raising its temperature to 65°C (149°F). As I do this, I whip it with a little frother, to let some air into the sake." After a few minutes, the jug is dipped into cold water so it cools quickly. "This way, the sake stays both airy and full-bodied." Now, Marie transfers the sake to a ceramic carafe and warms it up slowly in a bain-marie that is a little cooler than the previous one. As she does this, she keeps putting her nose close to the carafe to check how the sake's aroma is developing—a very elaborate procedure aimed at obtaining the best possible flavor.

In the past, izakaya and kappo restaurants had staff who were specifically responsible for warming the sake and serving it tempered according to its type and to each patron's preferences—from lukewarm to hot. Here, this ancient izakaya ritual is expertly adapted by Marie for a contemporary sake bar.

The Eureka! owner now carefully pours the sake she has twice warmed and cooled into a specially designed ceramic cup. The beverage has a caramel-like aroma and tastes of roasted brown rice, nut butter, and caramel. Its texture is smooth on the tongue and its flavor diffuses as though it were gently melting, but its aftertaste is pure. Wonderful!

## 9:15 p.m. in Hibiya, Bar Folklore

The night in Tokyo is just getting started. I take the subway from Roppongi to Hibiya, a rather refined neighborhood full of international luxury brand stores such as Hermès and Louis Vuitton. A cold wind is blowing as I get out and walk up the narrow staircase to the street. I remember my mother telling me that when it is cold and windy in Tokyo, it is snowing in the mountains of her home of Niigata. I hurry to a fancy arcade underneath the historic elevated railway, which was inspired by the ones in Berlin. This is where Shuzo Nagumo opened his Bar Folklore; his cocktails, mixed using regional sakes as a base, are said to be unique.

The atmospheric, slightly hidden bar has such a low doorway that you have to stoop to get in; with its ancient wood cladding and its clay-plastered walls, it is reminiscent of a tea ceremony room. Although it is only dimly lit, I spot many bottles bearing Japanese characters on its shelves, as well as beautiful glasses and ceramic objects. The atmosphere is calm, with a relatively small number of patrons. Once I have taken my seat at the bar, I am handed a warm oshibori (towel).

Shuzo Nagumo, who has just served a young woman at the back of the room, comes over to greet me and says, "First of all, I want to make you a Solar Flare: a mixture of yamahai sake from the Noguchi Institute, vodka with tonka beans, white port wine, our own distilled kyara wood extract, caramel butterscotch liqueur, and coffee." I can't wait.

Soon afterwards, I have before me a long-stemmed cocktail glass containing a golden, gleaming liquid and coffee ice balls. Shuzo explains, "This cocktail was created on the occasion of the 500th anniversary of a kodo (the way of aromas) school.

A FEAST FOR ALL SENSES — SAKE. FOOD. PAIRING.

A FEAST FOR ALL SENSES — SAKE. FOOD. PAIRING.

The Solar Flare: a sake-based cocktail with fragrant kyara wood

254

Kyara is a very expensive, fragrant wood and is only used in small quantities, but it has a strong presence."

The second cocktail, the Bouquet, is prepared using Sake Tedorigawa, jasmine pearls, and elderflower liqueur—a wonderful mixture that makes me feel like I'm receiving a kiss from the sweet morning dew. A young woman sitting quietly in the back of the room gazes musingly into her glass; her beautiful black hair comes down to her shoulders, and her elegant cream cashmere sweater suits her perfectly. She seems to be enjoying her cocktail pairing and her time alone, though she occasionally chats to Shuzo and to the barkeeper. Her personality and the refined flavor of my second cocktail start to merge with each other in my mind, staying with me long after the elegant young woman has left the bar. A beautiful finish for my first Tokyo sake evening.

## Day 2 in Tokyo: 6:15 p.m. in Shinbashi, Kuri Sake Bar

The next evening, my first stop is in the neighborhood of Shinbashi. Unlike the sophisticated, urban atmosphere of Roppongi yesterday, this area is a post-work destination for many office workers. Many yakitori—typical grilled meat restaurants—have set up shop here underneath the elevated railway, not far from the station bearing the same name and close to the Marunouchi business district and Kasumigaseki government offices. As a result, even when I arrive, shortly after 6 p.m., the air is already full of white smoke and the smell of burned soy sauce.

A few streets further, there is a colorful variety of venues: standing bars with red lanterns above their entrances, ramen kitchens, kappo restaurants with bottles of sake in their entrances, izakayas specializing in seafood, Spanish bars, karaoke bars, sushi bars, restaurants serving specialties from Niigata, and trendy cafés. The neon lights of yet more venues shine out from the upper floors of the buildings.

A group of four men in dark suits stops outside a popular motsunabe joint. After briefly consulting with each other, they walk in. This restaurant specializing in pork offal fondue is cheap, and it does not offer any particularly good sake; most of the patrons are drinking hoppy (a beverage made out of cheap shochu) or beer. So, I hurry on past to my favorite sake bar, Kuri, in the Shinbashi Ekimae Building, which, as well as offices, houses around 70 restaurants and bars. In the small venues on the basement floor, which are often only three meters (10 feet) wide, and whose tables and chairs protrude across the corridors, the atmosphere is usually animated and jolly.

In Kuri, at the other end of the basement floor, the atmosphere is a little calmer, more relaxed. This is a self-service, standing bar, where sake lovers congregate. The prices for the 30 types of sake on offer range from 150 to 800 yen for portions of 45 or 90 milliliters (1.5 or 3 ounces). I ask the owner, Hironobu Kurihara, for a recommendation, and soon I am served a glass each of Hizirism kassei-shubo from Fukushima and W-Aiyama, a junmai muroka nama sake from the Watanabe Shuzo Brewery in Gifu—for a total of 500 yen, equivalent to a little over three dollars. Kassei-shubo is an experimental sake, since shubo is the precursor of the mash and is only sold to a limited number of sake retailers. Its sweet and sour flavor and refreshing bubbles remind me of cider. Suddenly, I spot a familiar face at the bar: John-san! John Gauntner, the American sake ambassador, a Sake Samurai and author of many books about sake, is chatting to Hironobu in fluent Japanese. I have known John for many years, since we are both members of the International Wine Challenge jury. We chat a little and swap news about the industry. John has been living in Tokyo since the end of the 1980s. "I sometimes drop into Kuri on my way home," he explains with a smile before taking his leave. "Matane (see you soon)!"

Alone once more and starting to get hungry, I leaf through a magazine on the table and discover a tip about a yakiniku joint near Kanda station, just two stops away from Shinbashi. I decide to check it out. "Thank you, Hironobu-san! I'll be back soon."

## 7.18 p.m. in Kanda, Yakiniku Rokkakai

The tiny yakiniku bar is called Rokkakai and is located underneath the tracks of the Kanda elevated rail station. It has no door; instead, you enter the bar through an opening in a transparent plastic curtain. In the middle of the room is a table with two charcoals grills. As I walk in, hesitantly, shortly after 7 p.m., there are already five people—clearly regulars—standing around the cooking surfaces. Pieces of meat are sizzling appetizingly over the fires. The bar owner is standing at the head of the table and has set up four magnum bottles of sake in front of him. Noticing my hesitancy, he says, "You can order meat from 500 yen per plate, the sake is also 500 yen a glass. Pick one of these four bottles." I opt for the Tatsuriki Junmai-Dragon.

He fills up a large, teacup-like drinking vessel to the rim for me. "Cheers to our new guest," cries the landlord, and all other persons present also raise their guinomi cups, smile, and clink glasses to welcome the newcomer. The sake is delicious, fruity, and easy to drink. I quickly lose my initial nervousness and feel welcome in this company. It is also pleasant to smell the scent of the slowly grilling meat as I enjoy my sake—and a plate fresh, raw meat and cleansed offal is soon set before me. As I grill the meat on one of the two communal shichirin grills using disposable chopsticks, one of the regulars explains to me that I should not grill it for too long, and that I would do best to season it only with rock salt and lemon, rather than with yakiniku sauce, as is often done. An excellent tip!

When I lift the hot meat to my mouth, its smoky aromas rise up into my nose, and from the first bite the fat dissolves in my mouth. I sip my room-temperature sake, whose fruitiness mixes deliciously with the rich beef fat, and the lemon aroma refreshes my palate.

By this point, more regular patrons have arrived; 10 people are now crowding around the grill table. Every entrance is a new opportunity to raise a glass to someone. It's fun—even for a newcomer like myself. Most yakiniku restaurants only offer beer to drink. "Why," I ask the landlord, "does the Rokkakai specialize in sake?" He laughs: "It's very simple—because Morita, the owner, loves sake. When he was still working as an architect and was also a professional boxer, he wanted to open a restaurant for his boxer colleagues, where you could eat your fill of tasty meat without spending too much money—and where, at the same time, he could offer them good, affordable sake. Hayato Morita, who later on will look in on the Rokkakai in person, was rewarded for this concept, which has been a success for over 15 years, by the Japan Sake Brewers Association Young Council, which gave him the title of Sake Samurai." Being a Sake Samurai myself, I am overjoyed at this happy coincidence, for, since 2007, there are only five or six people a year who are named Sake Samurais out of a mass of candidates from all over the world. Together with Marie and John, that therefore makes four of us in this short time in Tokyo. Clearly, a passion and love for sake brings people together everywhere.

## 9:15 p.m. in Asakusa, Kappo Restaurant

I liked the Rokkakai a lot, but now I want to have another, quiet drink. So, around 9 p.m., I take the Ginza line subway from Kanda to Asakusa, a journey of only 10 minutes. Here, not far from the Senso-ji Temple, the atmosphere still harkens back to the 1960s and 1970s; next to the entrance to the Kappo restaurant is a menu handwritten in ink on Japanese paper. The word kappo literally means "cutting and cooking." Restaurants of this kind are usually small and cozy, and you only find out about them through word of mouth, so I know I won't likely come across people from other parts of the city here, let alone foreigners, and I assume everybody will be speaking only Japanese.

I enter through a white curtain. The elderly landlord behind the counter on the right-hand side looks at me through his reading glasses and says, "Welcome, you can take a seat wherever you like." There are three people sitting at the bar, who seem

The figure of the tanuki is seen as a lucky charm in the restaurant business.

to be regulars. They are sharing their food and chatting to each other: a couple in their mid-60s, who look like they own a store in the neighborhood, and a younger woman in a navy-blue blazer. I take a seat at a small table. The chef brings me a warm towel and a tsukidashi, a small composition of starters. I'm not very hungry after the grilled meat I had earlier, but I still order the daily special: shirako (cod milt) pickled in ponzu vinegar, a winter specialty, and kawaebi no kakiage (small, deep-fried river prawns).

There are only four types of sake to choose from: three from Niigata and one from Gifu. It seems like the owner only offers people his favorite sakes. I ask for some Gokujo-Yoshinogawa-Junmai from Niigata, my parents' hometown. It has the mild sweetness of boiled rice and feels clean and refreshing in the mouth: a light and clear Niigata-style sake. This restaurant is a one-man operation, but nevertheless, my sake comes quickly. So, I start with the tsukidashi: smoked duck breast, marinated wakame seaweed and crabmeat, salami and broccoli with yuzu miso, all offered in tiny portions. While I sip at my sake and eat the food, I remember the trips I would make to Asakusa with my family when I was

still a child. During the Edo period (1603–1867), Asakusa was the most affluent nightlife district near the historic Senso-ji Temple, and to this day its narrow alleys are lined with small traditional restaurants and izakaya, which reflect the lifestyle of its common people.

In recent years, many foreign tourists have been coming here, but at night the neighborhood is deserted because it does not have many hotels. The food that is placed on my table next brings a smile to my face: the shirako is freshly-cooked and lukewarm, and a creamy mass flows into my mouth when I bite into it. The river prawns are crisply deep-fried in sesame oil and sprinkled with salt; they make the Gokujo Yoshinogawa junmai seem fruitier and more full-bodied. I alternate between taking a sip of sake and a bite from one dish, then another. My chopsticks dance on my tongue, just like the aromas—a delicious interplay. I enjoy the fresh shirako, which is only ever available for one month of the year, and I think about how, when you have good sake and good food, you can also be happy without another person by your side. Content and exhilarated, I walk back home through the Tokyo night. —

# Japanese Sake Journey

## A winter tasting tour through Japan with local experts

SENDAI

IWASE

HAKUSAN

SHINMINATO

KYOTO

HIMEJI

KURUME

MIYAKI

TOKYO

OSAKA

TARA

### Day 1 — 8:05 a.m., Tokyo Station

It's early morning in Tokyo Central Station; commuters push through in droves. For me, this marks the start of a sake tour, during which I will visit breweries in Kansai, Kyushu, and Hokuriku to see up-close how daiginjo is produced. I move through a stupendous flow of travelers, as if I am surfing a wave. Tokyo-eki is one of the most important stations in Japan; every day, up to 4,100 trains drive in and out of it. In addition, it has a shopping and dining center spanning two underground floors, as well as hotels and offices, so it can practically be thought of as a complete city in its own right.

Bento box stores line the way to the platforms for the Tokaido Shinkansen trains to Kyoto and Osaka. Since there are no restaurant cars on Japanese trains, I buy a classic Shumai Dumpling Bento from Kiyo-ken and a bottle of warm hojicha tea and hurry to the boarding area. The Shinkansen trains run every five minutes. I board my train and take my reserved seat on the right-hand side in the direction of travel. All the way to Yokohama, the tracks are lined with office buildings up to 20 stories high and multi-story residential buildings. But then, we gradually come to a rural area, and the Pacific Ocean becomes visible on the left-hand side. Almost 30 million people live in the greater Tokyo area! After Mishima Station, Mount Fuji becomes clearly visible at last, with its white cap of snow—it's said to be a lucky sight.

### 5:28 p.m., Pontocho in Kyoto

Having visited the Yasaka Shrine, which is also worshipped by many geishas, I walk down the wide road towards the west, where the sun is just setting.

In Tokyo's dense urban space, many people long for the wide open spaces of the countryside.

Kyoto may be rich in tradition, but it also has a modern side.

Sake tastes even better when you're chatting to the head chef.

It's easy to find your way in Kyoto, where the streets are all laid out in a checkerboard pattern. As I stand on the bridge over the wide Kamo River and look around, the Yasaka Shrine glows red. To the right of the bridge begins Pontocho Alley: it is about half a mile long, lined on both sides with geisha houses and restaurants. Dimly lit side alleys lead to hidden ryotei restaurants, which you cannot enter without a recommendation from a regular.

Kyoto has a long tradition of kaiseki cuisine, but also of wonderful, simple fare known as obanzai. The dishes take a lot of time and effort to prepare, usually using seasonal ingredients from local farmers. Together with the two companions I have brought with me today, I am now standing in front of a famous obanzai restaurant in the middle of Pontocho Alley. Although it has only just opened, its 30 seats are already occupied. Good thing I booked! The menu promises a host of specialties; I find it hard to decide what to choose. But there are three of us, so I can order plenty. For a start, I order sashimi of tai sea bass, sweetly cooked ayu fish, sesame tofu, tamagoyaki (omelet), cooked taro root, and nuta with kujo leek. The restaurant only offers two types of sake from the Kamotsuru Brewery in Hiroshima: daiginjo in a 1-go (180-milliliter/6-ounce) bottle and a taru sake aromatized in a small sugi barrel.

The 60-year-old owner and head chef of the restaurant, dressed in white, is presently slicing sashimi at the counter, while two other cooks work in the kitchen behind him. The five waiting staff are deft and take people's orders quickly and efficiently. There is a lively, pleasantly jolly atmosphere. The taru sake has been poured out of a wooden barrel into a 2-go (360-milliliter/12-ounce) tokkuri carafe, and its cedar wood aroma is not as strong as I expected.

Our six dishes are served in close succession on a small table. In this kind of restaurant (koryori-ya or izakaya), it is customary to share various dishes with other people and enjoy them all at the same time. "Kanpei!" We clink our o-choko cups together. The fresh sea bass sashimi has the right bite and the right sweetness. The tamagoyaki contains a lot of dashi stock; the mirin also gives it a sweet flavor and umami. Eating the warm omelet with the cold, grated daikon, made salty by the soy sauce, creates an interesting contrast. The freshwater ayu fish has also been slowly cooked in soy sauce and mirin, and its bones are so tender that you can eat them as well. The kujo spring onions, which are still firm to the bite in a nuta miso sauce, are also a beautiful combination—and the taru sake underscores the flavor of all the dishes and gives the meal a woody accent.

## 9:30 p.m., Dotonbori in Osaka

Wow, it's bright here! The huge, brightly colored neon signs are reflected in the river and make the night seem like day. A variegated crowd of people flows onto the bridge over one of the few remaining canals. Two young men are rapping a cappella to a bass rhythm, and a Korean couple are taking a selfie in front of the famous huge neon advertisement for Glico. Although they are only a one-hour train ride away from each other, the difference between the calm, noble atmosphere of Kyoto and the popular, dynamic spirit of Osaka is overwhelming.

Osaka is also known as the city of kuidaore (food fanatics). The neighborhood of Dotonbori in particular is defined by a host of venues—from takoyaki, okonomiyaki, and kushi-age street-food and takeout restaurants to upmarket kappo and fish establishments.

Osaka is a scintillating city—it seems to call out, "Look here!" Already, the façades of various venues lure the eye with large, colorful advertisements. Here, an orange, luminescent giant spider crab with legs a meter long; there, a colossal spotted octopus hugging the logo above the entrance of a takoyaki bar with its tentacles. This octopus draws us in as if by magic. Once we are seated, we each order takoyaki—eight fried octopus balls coated in a special batter, doused in brown sauce and mayonnaise, garnished with bonito flakes, dancing in steam. The fresh, hot balls look delicious, but we don't want to burn our mouths so we wait patiently, sipping pints of draft beer. Sake is not on offer here, unfortunately. The takoyaki in Tokyo are famous for being crunchy on the outside and soft as butter on the inside, while those from Osaka are soft on the outside and tenderly melting on the inside. In any case, the bitterness of the cold beer refreshes our mouths.

We soon get some refreshment from above, too: it starts to rain. Still, we wander onto Hozenji Yokocho, a quiet cobbled alley lined with long-established little restaurants, including several that specialize in unagi (eel dishes). In this neighborhood, which developed out of the street food stands that used to cater to visitors to the small Hozenji Temple nearby, you can still feel the atmosphere of old Osaka. A couple walks out of one of the restaurants on the other side of the street. The woman, who is wearing a kimono, hands the man an umbrella; as he takes it, he pulls her in closer to him so she doesn't get wet. The lights of the restaurant are reflected by the glistening cobblestones.

## Day 2 — Himeji in Hyogo, She'll Be Kobe Beef Restaurant

The Himeji Castle in Hyogo Prefecture is registered as a UNESCO World Heritage site. Ryusuke, the kuramoto of Tatsuriki Brewery, has chosen the nearby She'll Be steakhouse for our dinner together. It was founded by the second generation of the Uramoto family of butchers, who can look back on 50 years of history as Kobe beef retailers. Hyogo is renowned for its beef, and She'll Be is famous for only serving the very best quality of meat, from class A5-10 upwards. We are greeted by the head chef, Michaiki Uramoto,

in a private room on the second floor of the restaurant, which only has seating for six people. He tells Ryusuke, "You have brought us your best sake today, so we have prepared a Chateaubriand and an A5-12 class sirloin steak of Kobe beef, which is only produced by a small number of cows per year." He proudly shows us the marbled meat. "We always buy a half cow of the best quality and let it mature for 40 to 60 days in our refrigerated cellar."

Ryusuke now places on the table the Tatsuriki Junmai Daiginjo Akitsu Kimoto he has brought with him, as well as a green bottle without a label, which he filled this morning with fresh shizuku collected in drops from the daiginjo mash. "The best sake for the best meat"—certainly an excellent alternative to the red wines from five major French châteaux, which She'll Be has in stock. To start, the Tatsuriki kuramoto now pours the Daiginjo Shizuku into wine glasses, and we clink glasses with the head chef. Wafts of ripe melon and pear rises up from the sake; it seems to have a stronger aroma now than it did this morning, when we tasted it out of kikichoko cups in the cold ginjo cellar. It still contains a bit of carbonic acid from its fermentation, which mixes with its creamy texture and has a pleasant feel on the tongue. A wonderful kick-off to our meal!

Unlike in other teppanyaki restaurants, you don't hear the loud sizzle of the grill at She'll Be. Uramoto-san explains: "If you grill meat at a high temperature, its surface develops these scratches, so-called burn marks. We set the temperature of the grill to just 70° to 80°C (126° to 144°F) so the meat cooks slowly." As we watch the head chef grill the Chateaubriand, we alternate between the kimoto, which has a creamy, elegant body after aging, and today's freshly pressed daiginjo, with its glorious fruity notes. I am astonished at how different two sakes produced out of the same rice—a top-class yamada nishiki—can taste. "The sirloin cut is taken from the central part of the

265

Kobe beef: an aged treat from the very best stock

Michiaki Uramoto cooks the meat gently, at a low temperature.

Just watching the yakitori skewers being prepared is enough to fire up your senses.

cow's back. It is the muscle that sits on the cow's backbone, and it is characterized by its fine marbling. Sirloin has a juicy texture and tastes slightly sweet," explains Michiaki Uramoto as he cuts up the meat for us. The sirloin is quite fatty but wonderfully tender. The daiginjo continues to blossom, releasing a spicy aroma of lily flowers and aniseed, which goes well with the fat in the meat and acts like a fruit sauce. The kimoto sake makes a very different impression; due to the way it is produced, it has a certain mature flavor with an astringency similar to that of red wine. The lactic acid in the kimoto mixes with the fat in the meat, fills up the mouth with umami, and gives it a long, sustained aftertaste. What a joy!

## Day 3 — Kurume in Fukuoka, Kurume Kushi Yugen Restaurant

I take the Shinkansen from Himeji to Kurume in the afternoon. Because I forgot to book a seat, I have to stand in the middle of a completely overcrowded carriage for the two-and-a-half-hour journey, which means I can't enjoy the view as the train runs along the coast of the Seto Inland Sea. On top of that, the tracks go through an underwater tunnel between Honshu and Kyushu, so I don't really get the feeling that I've crossed the strait. At Kurume Station, I am greeted by Sotaro Kinoshita, the 10th generation kuramoto of the Amabuki Sake Brewery. He suggests we go and eat some yakitori, the specialty of Kurume, once I have left my luggage at the hotel. The restaurant, Kurume Kushi Yugen, is just a few minutes' walk away from the hotel and has a modern, café-like atmosphere with glass walls facing the street. As we walk in, we immediately spot a charcoal grill station with shrimp and fish skewers lying in its ashes. There is another grill station behind the bar.

We sit down at a table toward the back, and Sotaro immediately starts to order. The restaurant is completely full this Sunday evening—the voices and laugh-ter of the diners mix with the sizzling of the skewers. Yudai Suzuki, the restaurant owner and a friend of Sotaro's, comes over to us with a bottle of Amabuki Cho Karakuchi junmai sake. He pours it into a pre-cooled glass. Cho karakuchi means "extra dry," and this sake has a clear flavor and barely any sweetness, like smooth vodka, with a full body that only the yamada nishiki rice variety can offer. This combination is what makes the Cho Karakuchi so unique.

The scent of the freshly grilled yakitori rises up into our noses. *Yakitori* literally means "chicken grilled on the skewer," but liver and other offal can be served as well as meat. Everything is seasoned with sweet soy sauce. There is a clear contrast between the strong, dry sake and the salty, malty sauce, but the discreet umami of the sake and the heft of the chicken seem to pair well: the overall result is har-monious. Next, we are served, among other things, a king prawn grilled whole and seasoned only with salt. Sotaro removes its head and shell and squeezes some fresh lemon juice onto the prawn meat. The aromas of the shellfish, as well as its sweetness and umami, are deliciously enhanced by the dry junmai.

A woman sitting with three friends at the table next to ours strikes up a conversation with us. "That prawn looks delicious. Would you like to try our Akita sake with it? We'd be delighted if you would!" The four all live locally. I look at the bottle they have offered us: it's a sweet Kijoshu Hinotori, from the Ar-amasa Brewery, which is very popular with people in the know. It is rich and has a lot of umami. It would go well with the yakitori, but it is too overbearing for the grilled prawn—almost a dessert. Once we have taken our leave from the bar owner and the wom-en at the table next to ours, Sotaro asks whether we should go and get another drink. "In Kurume, you do hashigo sake: bar hopping." He takes me to Gyoza Sobei, a simple snack bar that is very popular with locals. Although the evening has a wintery chill to it,

In the Kurume Kushi Yugen, unique aromas from the grill will make your mouth water.

A favorite meeting point for over 50 years: Gyoza Sobei in Kurume

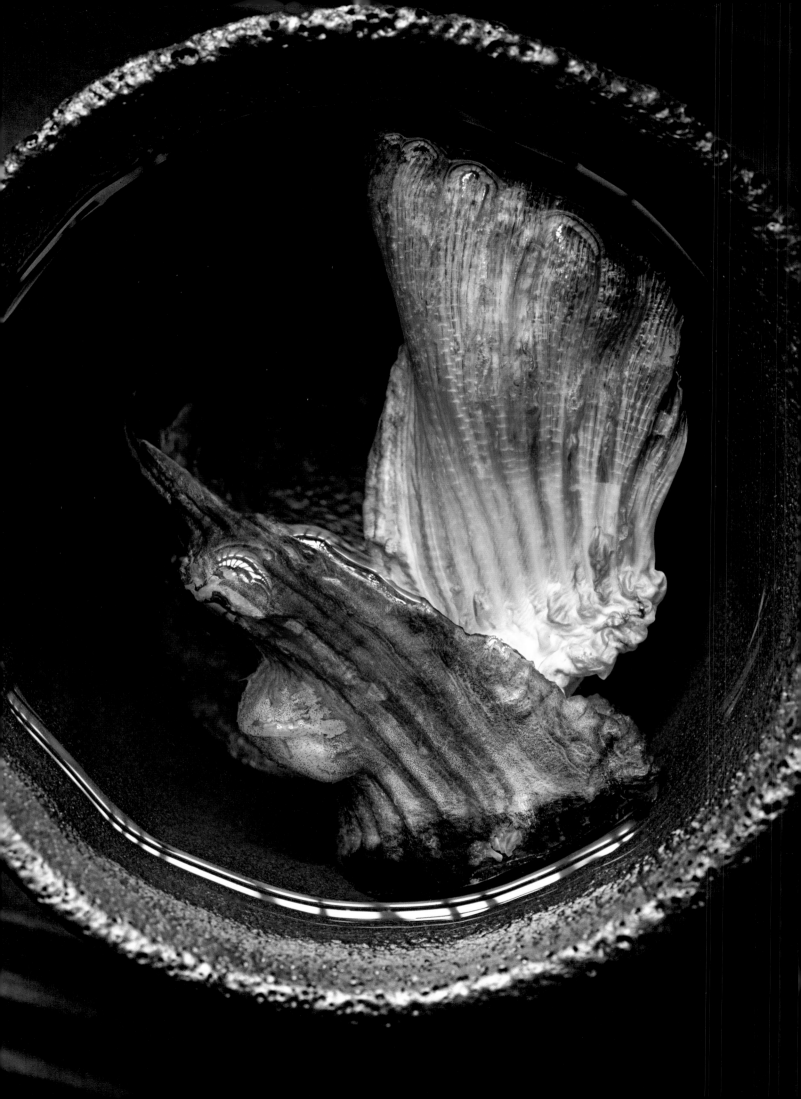

Hire sake: served hot and flavored with grilled fins

there are about 15 people sitting around a large table outside the restaurant, drinking merrily. We prefer to drink our last glass indoors in the warmth, accompanied by a few gyoza.

## Day 4 — Miyaki in Saga, a Fugu Feast

Yesterday, I relaxed in a big onsen bath in my hotel and had a good sleep afterwards. Now it's 7:30 a.m., and Sotaro Kinoshita is picking me up to take me to the Amabuki Brewery. Once we have crossed over the Chikugo River, which is also the border between prefectures, the landscape changes; the winter rice paddies of the Saga Plain stretch out before us like a black and green carpet. Sotaro explains, "Here, in one of Kyushu's biggest rice farming areas, some of the fields are not burned down as usual after the harvest in the fall, in order to use the mix of ashes and straw as fertilizer. Instead, they are planted with wheat or barley, which can be harvested in March."

The Amabuki Brewery, too, is surrounded by rice paddies. It includes a series of buildings where rice is polished and brewed and sake is aged and bottled. We walk into the brewery cellar, which was built a good hundred years ago and is adorned with a splendid carving of the wind god. Having viewed the production area, we go to a restaurant called Uoki to pick up some fugu (puffer fish) dishes. This long-established restaurant, which is just a few minutes' drive away, exclusively procures wild fugu fished out of Amakusa, on the west coast of Kyushu. The restaurant owner and head chef, Noriaki Nagahara, lifts a living fugu from the tank and shows it to me. "He is earmarked for this evening's diners," he explains, and replaces it lovingly in the water. "I've already prepared one for you to take away. The ponzu sauce that goes with it is homemade too. Enjoy."

Back in the brewery, we head for the dining hall in the main building. Its table has a retractable charcoal grill built into it. Sotaro unwraps our packet, revealing a large, beautiful koimari ceramic dish, on which puffer fish sashimi is arranged in the shape of a chrysanthemum flower. In the middle of the dish are thin strips of puffer fish skin, chives as delicate as threads, sudachi lemons, and red momiji oroshi (grated radish with chili). You can see the beautiful, vermilion-red, green, and blue painted design on the dish through the gossamer-like sashimi. "This has been in the family for generations," explains the Amabuki kuramoto, "and it is supposed to be several hundred years old. 300 years ago, the feudal lords in this region did not just promote rice farming, but also ceramic manufacturing. Koimari ceramics were exported and became collector's items for kings and dukes in Europe."

Sotaro now places an earthenware pot full of konbu-dashi broth on the iron frame above the charcoal fire, and asks, "Why don't we start with the fugu-sashimi while we wait for the broth to boil?" We clink our glasses, which are full of hot hire sake that was poured into our cups over a grilled puffer fish fin. Just like a hearty dashi broth, hire sake served this way whets the appetite.

Using our chopsticks, we pick up two or three thin slices of fugu-sashimi, dip them in the ponzu made out of soy sauce and citrus fruits, and place them in our mouths. The texture of the fugu is firm to the bite; chewing it brings out the sweetness of the fish. Fantastic! The hire sake adds smoky notes and enhances the dark aromatics of the soy sauce in the ponzu seasoning.

"The hire sake is too strong for our fine fugu-sashimi," says Sotaro, and he pours a new, slightly chilled sake into my wine glass. Oh, it's my favorite: Amabuki Kimoto Junmai Daiginjo! This sake is brewed using omachi rice and rhododendron yeast. Its aroma is reminiscent of white blossoms, and it has an elegant umami and acidity. Meanwhile, Sotaro also places a tall ceramic cup of the same sake in front of me, tempered to 40°C (104°F). Served in this

The union of two art forms: the finest fugu sashimi is served on an antique Koimari platter.

A culinary moment with the kuramoto family of the Amabuki Brewery

way, the Kimoto junmai daiginjo makes a completely different impression: it tastes milder and smoother. I feel warmed up, as if someone has placed a light scarf around my cold shoulders. As well as its aroma of flowers, the warm junmai daiginjo releases notes of steamed rice and something lactic; it beautifully emphasizes the flavor and sweetness of the puffer fish.

I thank Sotaro heartily for the great sake and delicious food. By this point, Sotaro's father, Takefumi, has come to keep us company. He has just been taking guests from Taiwan on a tour around the Amabuki Brewery. Sotaro removes the cover from the earthenware pot: steam rises up, and the broth bubbles with chunks of fugu, Chinese cabbage, shiitake mushrooms, tofu, and other ingredients. The dish is called fugu-chiri and is a winter specialty that many Japanese gourmets are enthusiastic about. But not everyone gets to experience fugu-chiri in such a unique setting, and with a kuramoto by their side. I fish a chunk of fugu and a little Chinese cabbage out of the pot and place it on my small koimari plate. The chilled junmai daiginjo acts like a delicious sauce to accompany the fugu. I am overcome with happiness. "You can call the puffer fish fuku instead of fugu," Takefumi Kinoshita says to me with a smile. In Japanese, the word *fuku* means "happiness."

## Day 5 — Tara in Saga, Oyster Grill

The sky is clear and blue this morning. Sotaro Kinoshita picks me up in his car at 10 a.m., and we drive about an hour and a half to the Ariake Sea, a shallow bay with a large tidal range on the western side of Kyushu Island. As the Amabuki kuramoto explains to me, it is rich in vegetation and houses many native breeds of fish and shellfish. "Nori seaweed from the Ariake Sea is famous, but [the area] also has thriving oyster farms, many of which run their own restaurants near Tara on the west coast." Many Japanese food lovers believe that Ariake oysters are the best in the world; it is said that they become stronger due to the tidal range and taste better because many

rivers flow into the bay and bring with them nutrients from the woods, enriching the plankton the oysters eat.

It was low tide an hour ago, so we can't take a boat to the place where the oysters are farmed. "Let's go straight to the oyster shack," says Sotaro. The Yueimaru oyster shack has a store selling oysters and other seafood, as well as drinks, and you can then prepare the food yourself on the grill in its restaurant. The weather is warm and sunny, so we take a seat on the terrace. As the oysters, shrimps, and scallops that we selected start to cook on the table grill, their delicious scent mixes with the sea breeze—a wonderful moment. With the blue sky above us and blue sea in front of us, it's hard to believe it's actually February.

The oysters known as takezaki are relatively small, but I'm surprised when I open them; their meat has hardly shrunk in the heat, and its intense, natural, slightly sweet flavor is enchanting. The Ariake Sea, in fact, does not just have a large tidal range, but also a lower salt content than most other seas.

Sotaro opens two cup sakes he has brought with him. "These cup sakes were produced at the request of an American retailer, and I selected two types: a light junmai, which also goes well with sushi, and a yamahai junmai sake that is popular in tonkotsu ramen restaurants, which is brewed with marigold yeast and has a strong flavor." I sip them both. The grilled oysters that are sprinkled only with a bit of lemon already make a good pairing with the sushi sake, and the umami flavor of the soy sauce–seasoned seafood is enhanced by the yamahai junmai. Grilling on the shore of the Ariake Sea is a spectacular experience. A refreshing sea breeze caresses my hot cheeks.

## Day 6 — Hakusan in Ishikawa, Ryokan Wataya

My day in Kanazawa starts at a slow pace. The journey yesterday from Kyushu to here took six hours and was very tiring, so I don't set off for the Tedorigawa Brewery until the afternoon. After my visit there, I

drive towards Mount Hakusan, which is viewed as holy, together with Kuramoto Yasuyuki Yoshida. "The Hakusan massif does not just supply vital water for the inhabitants at its foot, but also the brewing water for Tedorigawa," explains Yasuyuki on the way. Our first stop is at the Shirayama Hime Shrine, at the start of the still-snowy pilgrim trail leading to the Hakusan. Then, we continue to the Ryokan Wataya restaurant. It is over 150 years old and has one Michelin star.

Satoko Wada, the sixth-generation owner of the Ryokan, welcomes us in with a warm smile; she is wearing a beautiful, discreet kimono. We take off our shoes and follow her through a red-carpeted, labyrinth-like corridor into a large tatami room with a low table and chairs. There is an inset fireplace, its coals glowing already, on the floor by a window in the corner. Our host says, "We are in the mountains and don't have anything very special to offer you, but we hope that you will enjoy our hearty kaga cuisine, which has been passed down from generation to generation, and which uses river fish, wild vegetables, and game." Satoko pours out the sake Yasuyuki has brought along, a Yoshidagura U Yamahai Junmai, into our wine glasses. She serves us on her knees, and her movements are wonderfully elegant. The rustle of her kimono, the aroma of the excellent sake, and the warmth of the charcoal fire, which I can feel even from a distance, intoxicate me before I have even tasted the sake.

Our meal begins with warm sesame tofu—a typical winter dish. But the green paste made out of fukinoto, the flower buds of a mountain vegetable, introduces small accents that announce spring, a peculiarity at this time of year. Our warmed ceramic bowls are glazed in earthy and green tones and fit perfectly with the color scheme of this appetizer.

Next, we are served a white soup of daiginjo sake kasu in red bowls with deep-fried char, carrots, and radish in the shape of red and white plum flowers, steamed green leaves, and thinly-sliced leek as a filler. Plum trees start to blossom in mid-February, but spring comes late here in the mountains, so it is a lovely idea to express the longing for it in a dish which is a little ahead of its season. The two mild, warm dishes go perfectly with the cool, sparkling yamahai sake, which, with its fruity, juicy flavor and fresh acidity, tastes like white wine. Its alcohol content is only 13 percent, which is very much an advantage when paired with the soup.

A cook is now grilling huge mushrooms and iwana char on long skewers in the recessed fireplace. "The Wataya speciality is grilled food, and everything is prepared right in front of the diners: ayu trout from early summer to early fall and iwana in fall and winter," explains Satoko Wada. From time to time, you can hear the charcoal snap, and a spicy scent fills the room. As the fish cooks, we discuss which sake would go best with it and the rest of the menu. Time flies by as we indulge in an unforgettable cortège of delicacies. My best pairings are a warm, classic yamahai junmai with the unagi eel in a bamboo leaf; a mild, fruity, and elegantly smooth Shukon junmai ginjo to go with both the konbu jime sashimi of iwana and the grilled version of this same fish; an aromatic junmai daiginjo Honryu with the grilled mushrooms; and an amber-colored, complex 1996 junmai daiginjo with rich aromas of cocoa, dried plums, and soy sauce to go with the venison steak. We have exclusively enjoyed products from the region around Hakusan this evening, and, while we did not climb up the holy mountain itself, we have certainly made our way to a culinary summit.

## Day 7 — Train Journey from Kanazawa to Toyama

It's only half an hour on the train from Kanazawa to Toyama Bay, where for the next few days I will be a guest at the Masuizumi Sake Brewery in the small port city of Iwase. At first, the tracks take you along the

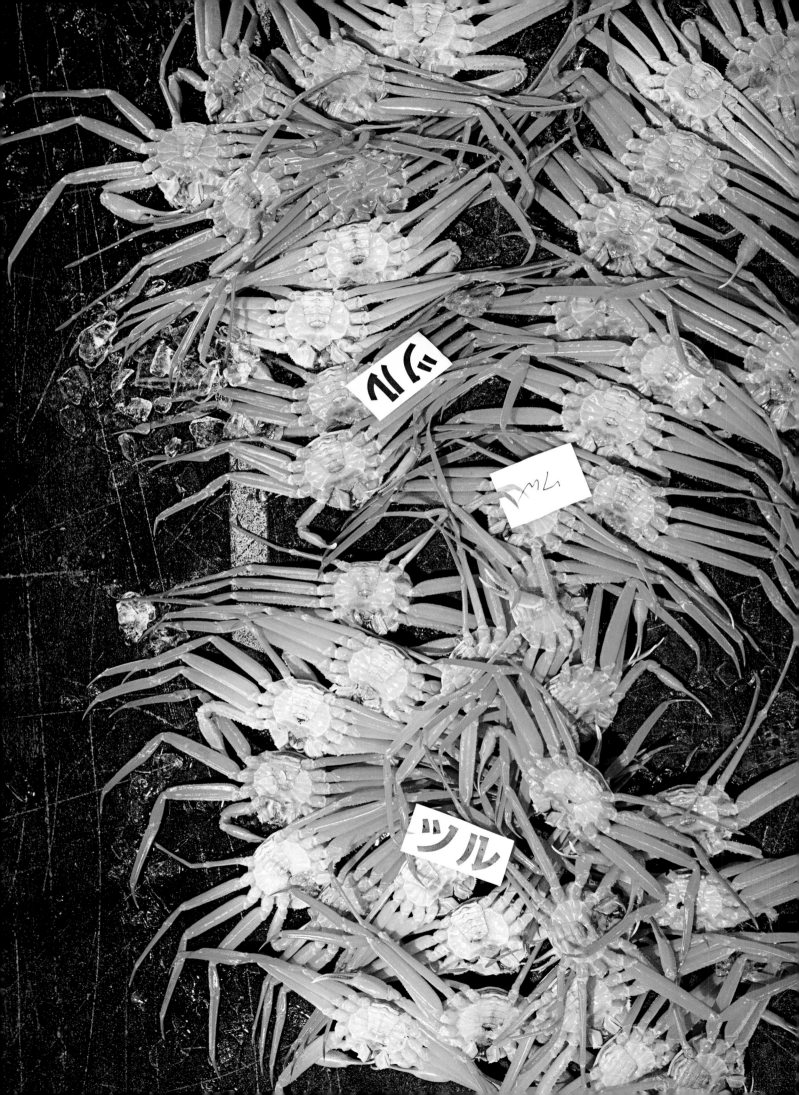

Zuwai crabs are sorted according to their size before being auctioned.

edge of the Noto Peninsula, which projects like an arm into the Sea of Japan. The scenery on the way changes from hills to plains, then to Toyama Bay on the left-hand side; to the right are the snow-covered summits of the Tateyama Mountains. A magnificent landscape! It is also crisscrossed by several rivers, which bring nutrients from mountain forests down to the sea.

Toyama Bay is known as a "natural aquarium;" its coast falls off steeply, plunging to a depth of 1,200 meters (3,937 feet), where cold water fish and snow crabs live. At around 300 meters (984 feet), however, flows the warm Tsushima Current, in whose environs a multitude of warm water fish are at home.

## Day 8 — 12:55 p.m., Shinminato in Toyama, Crab Auction in the Fishing Port

When I hear that a midday auction for zuwai-gani (snow crabs) is taking place in the fishing port of Shinminato in Toyama Bay, I make a spur-of-the-moment decision to go and take a look. The memory of the delicious crabs I once ate in the Oryouri Fujii in Iwase makes my mouth water all over again. When I arrive at the building shortly before 1 p.m., the crab auction has already started. Hundreds of orange-red snow crabs are lying on their backs in neat rows and organized into different blocks, covering the floor of the modern hall; their long legs are still moving back and forth. The most exclusive and expensive specimens, honzuwai-gani, are labeled with a certificate of origin attached to their claws.

There are around 20 buyers in the hall this afternoon. While they wait for the bell to ring announcing the next lot, they stroll around the displays of crabs, evaluating them. Then, they rush toward the auctioneer, who begins mumbling something almost incomprehensible into his megaphone; when they are interested in buying something, the buyers bid with a hand signal. If they are successful, staff members pack the auctioned crabs into plastic bags and bring them out to a truck. The auction ends after about an hour; now, the cleaning of the auction hall begins.

The zuwai-gani must be transported directly to the restaurants or cooked immediately, since otherwise they become too soft. Snow crabs are a pricey treat, particularly at the start of their season in November, when a honzuwai gani menu in a ryotei restaurant in Tokyo or Kyoto can cost 150,000 yen ( about 1,000 dollars) per person. I am astonished that there are people who are prepared to spend so much money for the first snow crabs of the year.

It's just a few steps from the auction hall to Shinminato Market, where customers can buy and eat fresh fish and seafood. A tent has been put up at the entrance; inside, crabs that have just been auctioned are cooked in a pot. I buy a medium-size zuwai-gani and some sake and walk into the market building. "What a day," I think to myself. What bountiful treasures are offered up by nature in Toyama! Just like the group of market visitors next to me, I start to remove the crab legs from the shell. "Oishii! (delicious!)" Nothing more eloquent can be heard from the neighboring tables, either, because they are all busy snapping off and consuming the extremities of their crabs. I always take a sip of sake between bites. The bottle I bought is not from Masuizumi, admittedly, but it's an excellent pairing for the sweet, lukewarm crab meat. After I'm finished with the legs and claws of the zuwai-gani, I break open the main shell and pour the sake in. Its aroma mixes deliciously in my mouth with the spicy marine essence of the boiled crab.

## 6:00 p.m., Iwase in Toyama, Banshaku with a Toji Master Brewer

"We'll soon be having dinner with the brewers— would you like to join us?" asks Kiichiro Hatanaka, the toji of Masuizumi Brewery. We go into a small refectory equipped with a kitchen; the brewers come

in one after the other from their work stations and sit down at the table. There are ten of them, five on each side. The toji takes the seat at the head of the table. I have met some of the brewers when visiting the brewery in previous years, so many of the faces are familiar to me now.

Several crates with unlabeled magnum bottles are stacked up on one side of the refectory, to be served after the end of the working day. They are full of Masuizumi Karakuchi sake, a futsushu. It has a clean, refreshing flavor but feels elegantly full-bodied in the mouth—the perfect accompaniment for our evening banshaku, since it pairs well with all kinds of dishes.

The contents of the first bottle have already been transferred into a stainless steel kettle and warmed over an open fire. One of the brewers goes round and pours the warm sake into small beer glasses that everyone holds in the center of the table. Hatanaka-san calls out, "Otsukaresama! (good work)," and we smile and raise our glasses. The sake, which is slightly warmer than body temperature, slips smoothly down our throats and warms our cold bodies. The jovial conversation with the toji makes me forget my nervousness about being an outsider, and I start to feel like a member of the brewery.

This evening, the long table is laid with boiled rice, miso soup, sashimi from Toyama Bay, oden, and pickled vegetables. The sashimi is placed on the table in small packages; it is from a nearby supermarket, but it's much fresher and tastier than what you are given in expensive restaurants in Tokyo. "Buri (yellowtail amberjack), amaebi shrimp, and squid." A brewer sitting across from me identifies these various marine treasures. "The buri is delicious because it's a wild fish from nearby Toyama Bay and has been supplied directly from the market." Oden is a popular winter dish, in which various fish pastes, daikon radish, deep-fried tofu, and boiled eggs are cooked in a broth seasoned with soy sauce. The steaming pot is placed in the middle of the table, and its contents are shared among everyone, with those who are sitting closest to the pot passing some oden to their colleagues sitting further away. Naturally, the toji is served first.

The kettle with warm sake is handed around and now arrives at the toji. He invites me to raise my glass and pours some for me. I take a sip and then pour a little sake from the kettle into his glass. After perhaps an hour, several brewers suddenly stand up and say, "Gochiso-sama (Thank you for the food)." "We're now going to do the final work, checking on the koji." I follow the men through the dimly lit, unheated production hall to the koji chamber. While they monitor the rice, I try a little of the fresh, warm koji—the best dessert for this banshaku evening.

## Day 11 — Iwase in Toyama, Cave Yunoki Restaurant

I have now already spent three days—some on my own and some with company—in Iwase, in order to try out the best of Japanese cuisine, including kaiseki and soba. This city has developed into a gourmet destination around the Masuizumi Sake Brewery, and in order to find out whether sake can also be paired with French cuisine, I am now due to visit the one-Michelin-starred restaurant Cave Yunoki, which was opened in 2009 in the old Mori shipping family's warehouse complex.

I walk into it through a wooden sliding door in the middle of these historic premises. The dining room, with its high ceiling supported by shining black columns and girders, is illuminated only by a skylight. A big wooden table in the middle of the room and a sofa in front of a glowing red chimney create a warm, relaxed atmosphere, as if you had been invited round to a friend's house. The kitchen behind the counter, in contrast, is lit like a theater

285

Squid from Toyama Bay

At Cave Yunoki, the ingredients, crockery, and sake come from the local area.

stage. The head chef, Eiju Yunoki, who grew up near a fishing port in Toyama and spent many years studying French cuisine, smiles at me from his kingdom of pots and pans and tells me, proudly, "Of course we almost exclusively use ingredients from local fishermen, hunters, and farmers, but we also want to create a quality that can only be experienced here, thanks to our Masuizumi sake, drinking vessels made by ceramic and glass artists in Iwase, and the whole atmosphere in this warehouse, which is over 100 years old."

The way the Michelin-starred chef sprinkles salt onto meat with his fingertips, his precise movements in the kitchen with its open charcoal grill station, and how he explains the dishes to diners at the counter all make you feel like you are watching a theatrical performance. To start with, I am served a raw oyster resting on a block of salt with herb aspic; the arrangement, presented on a ceramic cylinder, is simple and beautiful, like an objet d'art, and it goes perfectly with a glass of freshly-pressed Masuizumi Platinum. The milky oyster meat is gently encased in the fruity aroma and rice notes of this nama sake. Its salty, mineral oyster notes and the sweetness of the sake come and go in my mouth like waves, leaving behind a wonderful aftertaste. For a moment, I can feel the sea billow inside this dimly lit warehouse.

The next dish, honkatsuo (skipjack tuna), is arranged on a beautiful glass plate made by the artist Taizo Yasuda; its gold dust trimming spreads out like a halo around the fish, which has only been briefly grilled on the skin side, so the latter is crispy with smoky aromas, while the raw flesh is tender and buttery. It is served with marinated kinjiso leaves, which have a green surface and a purple underside, as well as a caramelized beetroot sauce. The sake that accompanies this dish is a limited-edition Kimoto R2 Masuizu-

mi Shiboritate. The complex acidity and umami of the full-bodied, unpasteurized sake wonderfully enhance and complement the flavor of the skipjack tuna.

As a main course, we are served wild nihon-shika (venison) from Kurobe, deep in the Tateyama Mountains. The meat has been grilled slowly on all sides over the charcoal embers, then arranged on a black, tablet-like plate made by the ceramicist Gaku Shakunaga, accompanied only by fanned-out maitake mushrooms and a dark red sauce—a simple, appealing presentation. The meat is perfectly cooked. From its outside, with fragrant, smoky aromas, through its juicy, pink middle to its still-red core, every piece has a different texture and flavor. If you chew it slowly, all of these components combine to form a delicious whole.

This dish is paired with a Masuizumi 8888 Link sake, a junmai daiginjo that has been aged in Chivas Regal barrels and has complex aromas of vanilla, dried fruit, and coffee, as well as a rich flavor. It makes an excellent partner for the meat's smokiness and strong, gamey aroma. It acts like a complex sauce, completing the straightforward umami flavor of the venison and raising it to a new level. I have eaten the best venison of my life at Eiju Yunoki and experienced the best sake pairing for it. After lunch is over, every cell in my mouth still holds the memory of this delectable combination—and neither my head nor my heart will ever forget it.

## Day 12 — 10:00 a.m., Sendai in Miyagi, Morning Market & Shozan Restaurant

"Delicious, sweet tangerines—try them!" "Tuna fish from Aomori—cheap and tasty!" The vendors at the Sendai Asaichi, the morning market of the biggest city in the northeast of Japan, are merrily and loudly advertising their wares. Locals and tourists scrimmage around here in equal numbers today. One and a half hours away from Tokyo on the Shinkansen, Sendai is the gateway to the large region of Tohoku, and up to 60 merchants and businesses offer vegetables, fruit, seafood, and other articles at the Sendai Asaichi. I discover various citrus fruits like tangerines, yuzu, and ponkan, winter vegetables such as hakusai (Chinese cabbage), daikon, taro root, and leek, as well as displays of mackerel, perch, cod, plaice, crabs, oysters, salmon roe, and several kinds of tuna fish, from red ones to large fatty ones. A land of plenty!

With me is Euka Isawa, the daughter of the kuramoto of the traditional Katsuyama Brewery. The Isawa Clan is not unknown in the culinary world of Tohoku; aside from its 300-year-old sake brewery and various other ventures, it runs a cookery school. Euka often used to shop at the morning market as a child with her grandfather, Heiichi. "Nameta garei (flounder) with roe is very popular in Sendai," she explains. "You have to have it when you're sharing a meal to mark the end of the year with your family or staff, because it is said that flounder will bring you happiness in the new year." Euka and I first attend to the topic of oysters this morning; we get enormous ones opened for us at a stand and enjoy them with just a few drops of lemon. Wonderful!

After our visit to the market, we drive to Shozan, a newly opened restaurant in what used to be the Katsuyama Brewery premises. In 2005, Katsuyama moved its sake production to a rural suburb, since building developments had negatively impacted the water quality in the inner city of Sendai. Euka is not involved in sake production. Instead, in addition to numerous other projects, she runs the Shozan. She also works as a sommelier and recommends sake to go with dishes that reflect the essence of European cuisine.

She suggests something light for our lunch: to start, some air-dried ham and mozzarella, paired with a Katsuyama Lei that smells of ripe melon. The saltiness of the ham combines perfectly with the thick texture, sweetness, and elegant umami of this sake.

For our second course, we have some katsuo skipjack tuna from Kesennuma, cooked at a low temperature and served with ground sesame seeds and finely chopped Japanese herbs (myoga and shiso), paired with a Katsuyama Ken. This junmai ginjo sake has a very balanced aroma and very clear umami flavor. The fruity aroma of the Ken combines with the soft, creamy texture of the skipjack tuna and gives it a fine structure, all while enhancing the dish's sesame notes and fresh, herbal aroma.

Euka's most recent project is a microbrewery for Doburoku in a newly established gastronomic arcade in Sendai Station. "Every day, 18 liters of sake fermentation mash are newly-prepared in glass containers and set out in a display window so every passerby can observe the fermentation process, which takes about 10 days." Fittingly, the small establishment is called Fermenteria; there, everyone can experience the wonder of fermentation while they purchase and drink some freshly made sake.

## 8:00 p.m. at Home in Tokyo

My tasting tour has now come to an end, and I have returned from Sendai to Tokyo, to my house near Asakusa. I open a bottle of Masuizumi Karakuchi. This is the sake that I drank at the banshaku with the toji and staff of the brewery. As I take sips from my glass, I remember the many encounters and discussions I had during my journey, as well as the wonderful sake pairings I was lucky enough to experience. —

With Fermenteria, her micro-brewery, Euka Isawa is sparking a new interest in sake culture.

A feast for the eyes as well: uni (sea urchin)

# SAKE AROUND THE WORLD

Where you can drink, buy, learn something about, or observe sake production.

## NORTH AMERICA

### CANADA

## Vancouver
**Artisan Sake Maker**
1339 Railspur Alley, Vancouver, B.C. V6H 4G9
A small sake brewery founded in 2007 by the Japanese Masa Shiraki on Vancouver's Granville Island. The brewery now farms its own rice and brews sake exclusively using Canadian ingredients.
**artisansakemaker.com**

### USA

## Los Angeles
**Sake School of America**
843 East 4th Street,
Los Angeles, CA 90013
School Director and Sake Samurai Toshio Ueno offers a range of sake and shochu courses with diplomas such as the WSET Level 3 Sake and the J.S.A. Sake Diploma.
**sakeschoolofamerica.com**

## New York
**Brooklyn Kura
(sake brewery, shop, bar)**
BrooklynKura.com34 34th Street, Brooklyn, NY 11232
Founded in 2018 by two Americans, Brian Polen and Brandon Doughan, this brewery produces handcrafted sake using rice from the USA. It is also a bar and shop.
**brooklynkura.com**

**Decibel (bar)**
240 East 9th Street,
New York, NY 10003
A legendary sake bar with an underground atmosphere and 75 different kinds of sake.
**sakebardecibel.com**

**Sakagura (restaurant)**
211 East 43rd Street B1,
New York, NY 10017
A restaurant in the authentic izakaya style, which has been introducing NYC to premium sake since 1996.
**sakagura.square.site**

## San Francisco
**True Sake (shop)**
556 Hayes Street,
San Francisco, CA 94102
The first specialized sake dealer in the USA. Its owner, Beau Timken, is a Sake-Samurai and co-chair of the International Wine Challenge.
**truesake.com**

## SOUTH AMERICA

### BRAZIL

## São Paulo
**Shin-Zushi (restaurant)**
R. Afonso de Freitas, 169,
Paraíso, São Paulo 04006-050
Sushi in the traditional Japanese style.
**instagram.com/shinzushioficial**

**Yorimichi (restaurant)**
R. Otávio Nébias, 203, Paraíso, São Paulo 04002-011
An izakaya restaurant that is very popular with sake fans; has a wide range of premium sakes.
**yorimichiizakaya.com.br**

### PERU

**Maido (restaurant)**
Ca. San Martín 399,
Miraflores 15074
Chef Mitsuharu Tsumura's Nikkei cuisine was ranked number six on the "World's 50 Best Restaurants" list in 2023.
**maido.pe**

**Osaka (restaurant)**
Av. Pardo y Aliaga 660,
San Isidro 15073
An upmarket Japanese restaurant with several branches in South America and Miami.
**osakanikkei.com**

## ASIA PACIFIC

### AUSTRALIA

**Tetsuya's Restaurant**
529 Kent Street,
Sydney, NSW, 2000
This restaurant, which was opened by the Japanese Tetsuya Wakuda in 1989, has been listed several times as one of the "World's 50 Best Restaurants." Wakuda's restaurant, Waku Ghin, in Singapore has been awarded two Michelin stars.
**tetsuyas.com**

# CHINA

## Beijing
**Sake MANZO (Restaurant)**
1/F, 21st Century Hotel,
40 Liangmaqiao Road,
Chaoyang, Beijing
One of the first sake restaurants
in Beijing.

## Hong Kong
**City Super (shop)**
Times Square, Basement 1,
Causeway Bay, Hong Kong
Excellent range of sakes
at good prices.
**online.citysuper.com.hk**

**Hong Kong Wine Academy
(school)**
Everglory Centre, Unit 1205, 1B
Kimberley Street, Tsim Sha Tsui,
Hong Kong
Cofounder Micky Chang is a Sake
Samurai and offers courses at this
institute that lead to the WSET
Level 3 in Sake diploma and the
J.S.A: Sake Diploma International.
**hkwineacademy.com/en**

## Shanghai
**Soul You (Restaurant)**
L101B, 1Lou 01B, 345 Tiyulu,
Pudongxin, Shanghai
You can buy and drink over 20
different sakes by the glass from
vending machines in this yakiniku
restaurant.

# JAPAN

## Kobe
**Fukuju (brewery, shop,
tasting room, restaurant)**
1-8-17 Mikagetsukamachi,
Higashinada, Kobe, Hyogo
658-0044
About 20 minutes in a taxi from
Shin Kobe Station. Reservation is
necessary to visit the brewery.
**enjoyfukuju.com/en/**

## Kyoto
**Gekkeikan Okura Sake
Museum (museum, shop,
tasting room)**
247 Minamihama-cho,
Fushimi, Kyoto 612-8660
The museum is located in
the famous sake center of
Fushimi and presents the
history of sake production.
**gekkeikan.com/museum/**

**Sake Hall Masuya
(restaurant, bar)**
298-2 Ichirensha-cho,
Nakagyo, Kyoto 604-8146
A modern izakaya restaurant
with a wide selection of sake.
**masuya.kyoto/sakehall/**

## Tokyo
**Ginza Kimijimaya (shop, bar)**
1-2-1, Ginza, Chuo,
Tokyo 104-0061
There is a changing list of 10
different sakes to try by the glass
here, and the staff are all trained
to give good recommendations.
**kimijimaya.co.jp/shop/ginza**

**IntertWine K×M Yamajin
(shop, bar)**
Azabudai Hills Market,
1-2-4 Azabudai, Minato, Tokyo
Two of the best Japanese sake and
wine experts, Kenichi Ohashi MW
and Motohiro Okoshi, offer innovative pairings in their bar.
**intertwine-km.jp/en**

**Japan Sake and Shochu
Information Center
(shop, tasting)**
1-6-15 Nishi-Shinbashi,
Minato, Tokyo 105-0003
The tasting bar offers a changing
selection of around 50 sakes, shochu, and awamori
**japansake.or.jp/sake/en/jss/
information-center**

**Jyuku to Kan (shop, bar)**
7-16 Sanban-cho, Chiyoda,
Tokyo 102-0075
Nobuhiro Ueno, one of the most
famous experts for aged sake,
celebrates various tempered aged
sakes in his upmarket salon.
**sakematured.com**

**Sake World (courses)**
Sake Samurai John Gauntner regularly offers the Sake Professional
Course. His magazine, *Sake Today*, has readers around the world.
**sake-world.com**
**saketoday.com**

# TAIWAN

## Taipeh
**Hana Bi (restaurant)**
No. 1-3, Ln. 20, Sec. 2, Zhongshan
N. Rd., Zhongshan, Taipeh
Sake Samurai and importer
Michael Ou's izakaya restaurant.

**Kanpai (restaurant)**
Sake-Samurai Shoji Hiraide is
the owner of over 60 yakiniku
restaurants in Taiwan and China.
The daily 8 p.m. cry of "Kanpai!"
and the communal drinking here
are lots of fun.
**kanpaiyakiniku.com.tw/en/
branch**

# EUROPE

**Sake & Shochu Academy
Europe (school)**
Yoshiko Ueno-Müller has been
offering various sake courses for
sake enthusiasts and sommeliers,
leading to diplomas such as the
WSET Level 3 Sake or the J.S.A.
Sake Diploma, since 2005.
**sake-academy.eu**

## AUSTRIA

### Vienna
**Mochi (restaurant, bar, shop)**
Praterstrasse 15,
1020 Vienna
The Berliner Eddi Dimant and the Austrian Tobi Müller have embodied their love for Japanese cuisine and sake in Vienna in the form of a restaurant, ramen bar, takeaway deli and catering service.
**mochi.at**

## FRANCE

### Paris
**WAKAZE (restaurant, shop)**
31 rue de la Parcheminerie,
75005 Paris
This sake brewery, which was founded in 2016 in Japan by Takuma Inagawa, produces experimental sakes using French rice in a suburb of Paris. The sake is served in the restaurant in the Quartier Latin (where you can also buy it by the bottle).
**wakaze-sake.com**

## GERMANY

**Ueno Gourmet
(online shop for Germany, Austria and Switzerland)**
This company, which was founded in 2005 by Yoshiko Ueno-Müller and Jörg Müller, is one of the most renowned importers for premium sake, offering approximately 150 different varieties.
**japan-gourmet.com**

### Berlin
**893 Ryotei (restaurant)**
Kantstrasse 135/136,
10625 Berlin
Behind the graffitied windows is a modern izakaya restaurant with a wide range of sakes.
**www.893ryotei.de**

**Restaurant Tim Raue**
Rudi-Dutschke-Strasse 26,
10969 Berlin
This two-Michelin-starred ürestaurant has been offering over 20 different sakes to go with its dishes since 2010.
**tim-raue.com**

### Frankfurt
**Masa (restaurant)**
Hanauer Landstrasse 131,
60314 Frankfurt am Main
Modern kaiseki cuisine with good sake recommendations; awarded one Michelin star.
**masa-frankfurt.de**

### Hamburg
**Nikkei Nine (Restaurant, Bar)**
Neuer Jungfernstieg 9–14,
20354 Hamburg
A Japanese refuge that is also inspired by elements of Peruvian cuisine in the famous Four Seasons Hotel. Its signature sake cocktail, "Yuzu Sansho," has many fans.
**nikkei-nine.de**

### Munich
**Tohru in der Schreiberei
(restaurant)**
Burgstrasse 5, 80331 Munich
The Munich-born, half-Japanese Tohru Nakamura offers two-Michelin-starred cuisine that brings together the best of his two cultures. Everything on the menu can be paired with sake.
**schreiberei-muc.de/tohru**

## GREAT BRITAIN

### London
**Hedonism Wines (shop)**
3-7 Davies St, Mayfair,
London W1K 3DJ
This renowned wine shop in the upmarket neighborhood of Mayfair offers a wide range of premium sakes and tableware.
**hedonism.co.uk**

**Kanpai London Craft Sake**
(brewery, restaurant, bar)
48 Druid Street, London Bridge,
London SE1 2EZ
Tom and Lucy Wilson were so inspired by Japanese drinking culture that they founded the first sake brewery in Great Britain in 2016.
**kanpai.london**

**Wine & Spirits Education Trust (school)**
The biggest wine school in the world has developed its first WSET sake courses in three levels (Levels 1 to 3), offering them in its own school in London, as well as in partner schools all over the world.
**wsetglobal.com**

**Zuma (restaurant, bar)**
5 Raphael Street, Knightsbridge,
London SW7 1DL
The most successful restaurant concept for modern Japanese cuisine in the world, including 20 locations in London, New York, Dubai, and Bangkok.
**zumarestaurant.com**

## SPAIN

### Barcelona
**Dos Palillos (restaurant, bar)**
Carrer Elisabets 9,
08001 Barcelona
Albert Raulich, the former head chef of cult restaurant El Bulli, and his wife Tamayo have created a fusion of Spanish tapas culture and Asian cuisine with sake.
**dospalillos.com**

# GLOSSARY

## Japanese words and technical terms

**Aged sake**

Sake that has been left to mature in tanks, bottles, or barrels for one year. Depending on the quality of the sake, how it is stored and for how long, it will develop different flavor profiles. In general, aged sake develops a darker color, more intense aromas (such as honey and spices), and a full-bodied texture. In Japanese: koshu, jukusei-shu

**Aji 味, Ajiwai 味わい**

Flavor

**Ama sake, Amazake 甘酒**

A sweet, nutrient-rich, nonalcoholic rice-based beverage made from koji (also see Kasu sake)

**Amakuchi 甘口**

Sweet-flavored sake

**Amami 甘味**

Sweetness; one of the five basic tastes (go-mi)

**Amino acids**

Molecules responsible for the body and umami of sake

**Aminosan-do アミノ酸度**

Amino acid content

**Annual Japan Sake Awards**

In Japanese: Zenkoku Shinshu Kanpyokai; the biggest and most important contest for ginjo-shu produced in the previous winter season. This competition, which has been held every year in April/May since 1911, is organized in conjunction with the National Research Institute of Brewing and the Japan Sake and Shochu Makers Association. Each brewery may only register one ginjo-shu for the contest. Outstanding brands of sake are rewarded with a gold medal.

**Aru-ten アル添**

Sake that contains brewing alcohol; futsushu (non-premium sake) and non-junmai types of sake in the premium class (honjozo, ginjo, daiginjo) are included in this category

**Atoaji 後味**

Aftertaste, lingering note

**Atsu-kan 熱燗**

Sake heated to a temperature between 45° and 55°C (113° and 131°F)

**Awamori 泡盛**

A traditional distilled spirit from Okinawa made with black koji rice

**Bin-hiire 瓶火入れ**

In-bottle pasteurization

**Bodaimoto 菩提酛**

A brewing method developed in the middle ages

**Brewing alcohol 醸造アルコール**

An alcohol with a neutral aroma and flavor that is distilled from molasses, among other things, and is added to many types of sake. In Japanese: jozo arukoru

**Brewing Society of Japan**

An organization that was founded in 1906 to support research and further development in brewing technology. The Brewing Society organizes conferences and training courses and distributes cultured yeasts (kyokai-kobo) for the production of sake, soy sauce, etc; in Japanese: Nihon Jozo Kyokai.

**Daiginjo 大吟醸**

Premium sake in the highest-quality class

**District**

Specific areas within certain regions and prefectures in Japan (for the purpose of this book: Hokkaido, Tohoku, Kanto, Koshinetsu, Hokuriku, Tokai, Kinki, Chugoku, Shikoku, and Kyushu, including Okinawa); in Japanese: chihou

**Doburoku どぶろく**

The unfiltered, original form of sake, which has been brewed and enjoyed by the Japanese people since they started cultivating rice. The grains of rice do not dissolve entirely in this beverage, so it resembles liquid rice pudding.

**Flower yeast 含み香**

Yeast cultures for sake, isolated from flower blossoms (including begonia, abelia, rambler rose, and Nadeshiko carnation); in Japanese: hana kobo

**Fukumi-ka**

Aromas detectable on the palate; aftertaste or retronasal aromas

**Fushimi 伏見**

A neighborhood of Kyoto known as the second largest historical sake production site in Japan. The sake brewed with soft water in Fushimi is smooth, thus known as "ladies' sake" (onna sake).

**Futsushu** 普通酒
Standard, non-premium sake

**Genmai** 玄米
Unpolished brown rice (polishing ratio of 100 percent)

**Genshu** 原酒
Sake directly from the press, which has not been diluted with water

**Ginjo** 吟醸
Premium sake made of rice with a polishing ratio of under 60 percent

**Ginjo-ka** 吟醸香
Floral and fruity aromas of premium ginjo sake

**Ginjo-shu** 吟醸酒
A general term for premium sake produced using rice with a low polishing ratio and brewed at low temperatures: daiginjo, junmai daiginjo, ginjo, junmai daiginjo

**Ginjo-zukuri** 吟醸造り
A production method for ginjo, a premium sake, which involves highly polished rice and slow fermentation at an extremely low temperature of between 5° and 11°C (41° and 52°F)

**Go** 合
A Japanese unit of measurement for volume (180 milliliters/6 ounces); see Units of measurement

**Go-mi** 五味
The five basic tastes (amami, sanmi, shibumi, karami, nigami); traditionally used in East Asia to analyze the flavors of dishes or beverages

**Gohyakumangoku** 五百万石
A rice variety from the northwestern regions of Japan, used to brew light, dry, highly refined sakes

**Gosei seishu** 合成清酒
Literally "synthetically produced sake"; an alcohol created without rice or fermentation, developed as an ersatz for sake during World War II

**Guinomi** ぐい呑み
Large sake cup

**Hanami** 花見
Cherry blossom festival

**Happo-shu** 発泡酒
See Sparkling sake

**Heishi** 瓶子
Sake carafe on an altar

**Hi-ire** 火入れ
The pasteurization of sake

**Hine-ka** 老ね香
The unpleasant, musty smell of many old sakes

**Hinoki** ひのき
Japanese cypress tree

**Hito-hada** 人肌
The ideal temperature for warm sake (around 35°C/95°F)

**Hiya** 冷や, **Hiya-sake** ひや酒
Literally "cooled sake"; sake at room temperature

**Hiyaoroshi** ひやおろし
Sake that has only been pasteurized once and enjoyed after maturation in the fall

**Hon-nama** 本生
Unpasteurized sake; see Nama sake

**Honjozo** 本醸造
Premium sake with a fresh flavor profile, produced with the addition of brewing alcohol

**International Wine Challenge (IWC), Sake Section**
The biggest and most important wine challenge in the United Kingdom, which has included a sake section since 2007. The jury is half Japanese and half non-Japanese, the challenge is supported by the Japan Sake Brewers Association Junior Council, and it is viewed as the most important sake competition outside of Japan.

**Issho-bin** 一升瓶
A sake bottle with a volume of 1 sho (1,800 milliliters/61 ounces)

**Izakaya** 居酒屋
A simple restaurant and bar with a relaxed atmosphere, where various small dishes are offered to accompany sake

**Japan Sake and Shochu Makers Association (JSS)**
In Japanese: Shuzo-Kumiai Chuokai; the central alliance of sake breweries, composed of 47 prefectural associations

**Jinja** 神社, **Jingu** 神宮
Shinto shrine

**Jizake** 地酒
Sake with a regional character from a small brewery

**Jo-on** 常温
Room temperature

**Jomai** 蒸米
Steaming rice; a production step in making sake

**Joy of Sake**
The biggest public sake tastings outside of Japan with over 500 types of sake, organized every year in Honolulu and New York; visitors can taste ginjo-shu and junmai-shu sakes that have been registered with the U.S. National Sake Appraisal

**Jozo** 醸造
The Japanese word for the brewing and fermentation processes of miso, soy sauce, and sake, which appears in the names of some sake categories (e.g. honjozo) and in the company names of many breweries

**Jukusei** 熟成
The aging of sake—usually for six to twelve months in steel tanks—before being bottled

**Jukusei-ka** 熟成香
Pleasant, nuanced aromas
of aged sake

**Jukusei-shu** 熟成酒
see Aged sake

**Junmai** 純米
Sake made without the addition
of brewing alcohol

**Junmai-shu** 純米酒
General designation for premium sake without any added
brewing alcohol; this class includes junmai daiginjo, junmai
ginjo, and junmai sakes

**Junmai daiginjo** 純米大吟醸
Premium sake made of rice with
a polishing ratio of under 50
percent

**Junmai ginjo** 純米吟醸
Premium sake made of rice with
a polishing ratio of under 60
percent

**Kagami-biraki** 鏡開き
A barrel opening ceremony at a
special gathering, such as a
wedding or company jubilee

**Kaiseki** 懐石/会席
Traditional Japanese haute cuisine, served as part of a ceremonial tea or to show hospitality

**Kakemai** 掛米
Rice used in preparing a mash

**Kakishibu** 柿渋
A tannin extracted from the kaki
fruit, used for impregnation and
disinfection; kakishibu is used to
disinfect pillars in sake production halls and wooden equipment used during production.

**Kanpai** 乾杯
A toast, similar to "cheers!" or
"to your health!"; literally "dry/
empty your cup."

**Kann sake, Kann-zake** 燗酒
Warm sake

**Kann-zukuri** 寒造り
Traditional sake production in
wintertime

**Kaori** 香り
Aroma, bouquet

**Karakuchi** 辛口
Sake with a dry taste

**Karami** 辛味
Saltiness, spiciness; one of the
five basic tastes (go-mi)

**Kashira** 頭
An employee who manages
kurabito (brewery workers) and
works as the toji's assistant

**Kassei-nigori** 活性にごり
Unpasteurized sake with active
yeast

**Kasseitan** 活性炭
Activated charcoal, used to
clarify sake

**Kasu** 粕
Sake lees; the solid byproduct
of pressing the mash

**Kasu-buai** 粕歩合
The proportion of lees (kasu)
compared to the volume of rice
used; in ginjo-shu, the proportion of lees increases, sometimes
to over 50 percent

**Kasu sake** 粕酒
A popular, low-alcohol winter
beverage (also known as "fake
ama sake"), which is made by
heating sake lees with sugar and
water

**Katakuchi** 片口
Sake carafe with a wide mouth
and a spout

**Kijoshu** 貴醸酒
Sake produced using finished
sake instead of water; also
known as twice-brewed sake

**Kiki sake** 利き酒
Sake tasting

**Kikichoko** 利きちょこ
Sake cup for tasting

**Kime** きめ
The texture of sake; kime ga ko-
makai describes a fine, silky texture, and kime ga arai describes
a coarser texture

**Kimoto** きもと
The traditional method of
making the starter mash for
sake by pounding together a
mixture of koji rice, rice, and
water (yama-oroshi) to produce
natural lactic acids

**Kire** キレ
The aftertaste of sake; kire ga
aru describes a quick aftertaste
in the positive sense, and kire ga
warui describes a long aftertaste,
which is perceived as obtrusive
according to Japanese standards

**Kobo** 酵母
Yeast

**Koji** 麹
see Koji rice

**Koji-kin** 麹菌
A kind of mold fungus (in Latin:
Aspergillus oryzae) used to make
traditional fermented products such as sake, soy sauce,
and miso; the enzymes created
by koji-kin break starch into
glucose (sugar) and protein into
amino acids (e.g. glutamic acid,
the key to the taste of umami)

**Koji rice** 麹米
Rice fermented using koji mold,
containing (among other things)
the enzyme amylase; this is the
most important component of
the starter yeast and fermentation yeast for multiple parallel
fermentation

**Koku** 石
Japanese unit of measurement
(1 koku = approximately 180
liters/48 gallons); see Units of
measurement

**Koku** コク
A rich and dense flavor, full body

**Kome** 米
Rice

**Kosa** 濃さ

The density, body of the sake

**Koshu** 古酒

Literally "old sake"; according to Japanese law, sake that is older than one year after pressing; see Aged sake

**Kura** 蔵

Sake production facility, brewery, storehouse

**Kurabito** 蔵人

A brewery worker

**Kuramoto** 蔵元

The owner of a brewery

**Kuratsuki-kobo** 蔵付酵母

House yeast

**Kyokai-kobo** 協会酵母

Cultured yeasts, which are managed and distributed by the Brewing Society of Japan

**Kyubetsu Seido** 級別制度

A three-level classification system for sake, comprising tokkyu (premium), ikkyu (first class), and nikyu (second class); this system was abolished in 1989 and replaced by tokutei-meishou-shu

**Low-Alcohol sake**
低アルコール酒

Sake with a low alcohol content (below 13 percent)

**Maillard reaction**

The darkening of sake during aging; the result of sugar and amino acids binding to each other

**Main mash**

Fermentation mash, composed of rice, koji rice, water, and starter mash, usually prepared in three steps (see Sandan-shikomi) over the course of four days; in Japanese: moromi

**Masu** 枡

A square sake cup made of wood or painted wood with a capacity of 1 go (180 milliliters/6 ounces) or 1 sho (1,800 milliliters/61 ounces); traditionally used as a measuring cup

**Mike** 御饌

Food offered to the gods

**Miki** 御酒

Sake offered to the gods

**Mirin** みりん

A condiment often referred to as "sweet sake," made of rice shochu or brewing alcohol, sweet rice, and koji rice

**Miyama Nishiki** 美山錦

Rice from the northern regions of the country that are used to brew sake with a firm and fresh flavor profile

**Miyamizu** 宮水

Name for water from Nada district in Kobe, which was discovered in 1837 by the sixth generation of the Sakura Masamune Brewery and contains mineral nutrients that particularly stimulate the fermentation of sake

**Mizu** 水

Water, the main component of sake; since it makes up 80 percent of the beverage, water determines the body and overall character of a sake; soft water is particularly suited to the production of sake, especially if it contains no iron

**Moromi** 醪

Mash made of rice, koji rice, water, and starter mash; see Main mash

**Moto** 酛

Starter mash (see corresponding entry)

**Multiple parallel fermentation**

The unique fermentation process used to produce sake, during which koji mold constantly converts rice starch into sugar, while yeast simultaneously changes this sugar into alcohol.

**Muroka** 無ろ過

Unfiltered sake

**Nada** 灘

A neighborhood of Kobe, known as the largest sake production area in Japan; sake brewed with the medium-hard water in Nada (miyamizu) is strong and thus referred to as "men's sake" (otoko sake).

**Nama-chozo** 生貯蔵

Fresh-tasting sake that is only pasteurized one, during bottling; not a genuine nama sake (see corresponding entry)

**Nama sake, Nama-zake** 生酒

Unpasteurized sake, which must be kept refrigerated; not to be confused with nama-zume, which is only pasteurized once before aging, or nama-chozo, which is aged in a cold tank without pasteurization

**National Research Institute of Brewing (NRIB)**

In Japanese: Shurui Sogo Kenkyujo; an institute for research and development of alcoholic drinks and biotechnology, which provides training for brewery workers and sake merchants

**Nigami** 苦味

Bitterness: one of the five basic tastes (go-mi)

**Nigori sake, Nigori-zake** にごり酒

Naturally cloudy, unfiltered sake, which has a floury texture

**Nihonshu** 日本酒

The Japanese term for sake; since 2015, the terms *nihonshu* and *Japanese sake* have been protected by a Geographical Indication

**Nihonshu-do** 日本酒度

See Sake meter value

**Nodogoshi** 喉越し

Flavor, drinking sensation

**Nomiya** 飲み屋

Drinking establishment or izakaya

**Non-premium**

Regular, of ordinary quality; see Futsushu

**Noujun** 濃醇

Sake with complex, full-bodied flavor

**Nuka** 糠

Rice bran; a byproduct of rice polishing

**Nuru-kan** ぬる燗

Sake warmed to between 35° and 45°C (95° and 113°F)

**O-choko, Choko** ちょこ

A large wooden barrel made of Japanese cedar wood

**Oke** 桶

A large wooden barrel made of Japanese cedar wood

**Omachi** 雄町

Rice from the southwestern regions of the country, used to produce full-bodied, strong sakes

**Onna sake** 女酒

Literally "ladies' sake"; sake with a soft, smooth flavor profile

**Omiwa Shrine** 大神神社

One of the oldest Shinto shrines in Japan, known as a sake shrine

**Ori** 滓

Sediments in sake

**Oshaku** お酌

The custom of pouring sake out of a carafe into cups for other people; in Japan, it is considered improper to pour your own glass—this should always be done by someone else.

**Otoko sake** 男酒

Literally "men's sake"; sake with a strong, dry flavor profile

**Polishing ratio**

The percentage of rice grain that remains after polishing; the smaller a rice grain's polishing ratio, the higher quality, more refined sake it will produce.

**Prefecture**

Japanese administrative unit (ken); the prefecture with the most inhabitants is Tokyo.

**Premium sake**

In Japanese: tokutei-meishou-shu; a legally defined quality standard, based on the ingredients and production method. Premium sake is divided into six different classes (honjozo, ginjo, daiginjo, junmai, junmai ginjo, and junmai daiginjo).

**Regular sake**

See Futsushu

**Reishu** 冷酒

Cooled sake

**Roka** ろ過

Filtration of sedimented sake

**Sae** 冴え

The clarity of a sake

**Sakagura** 酒蔵

A sake brewery or production facility

**Sakamai** 酒米

Rice varieties that possess characteristics particularly suited to sake production, e.g. shinpaku.

**Sakana** 肴

Snacks and small dishes served as accompaniments to sake

**Sakaya** 酒屋

A store that sells alcoholic beverages

**Sakazuki** 盃

A sake cup

**Sakazuki-goto** 盃事

The exchange of sake cups to seal an agreement or as a sign of deference between two or more people.

**Sake** 酒

An alcoholic beverage; in a narrower sense, alcohol made with rice

**Sake brewery**

A business that makes sake; see Sakagura and Shuzo

**Sake meter value** 日本酒度

An indicator of how sweet or dry a sake is, determined by measuring the density of the sake compared to water; in Japanese: nihonshu-do

**Sake samurai** 酒サムライ

Since 2005, the Japan Sake Brewers Association Junior Council has awarded the "Sake Samurai" title to people who have contributed to the further development and spreading of sake culture. By 2023, hundreds of personalities from the worlds of gastronomy, education, media, and commerce have received this honorific title.

**-san** さん

A suffix added to names to indicate respect, e.g. Tanaka-san = Mr. or Ms. Tanaka

**San-do** 酸度

Acidity

**San-san-kudo** 三々九度

A ritual at wedding ceremonies, during which the bride and groom exchange small sake cups three times, then drink from them.

**Sandan-shikomi** 三段仕込み
The most widely used method to prepare the mash for sake production, which involves adding rice, koji rice, and water to the fermentation tank in three steps

**Sanmi** 酸味
Acidity; one of the five basic tastes (go-mi)

**Sanzoshu** 三増酒
Literally "triple-diluted sake"; sake that is produced with large amounts of brewing alcohol and additives, such as sugars and acids. This style of sake became popular during World War II and the period that followed it, but is now considered inferior.

**Satoyama** 里山
Mountains and forests located close to human settlements and connected to the lives of human beings; in a more general sense, an agricultural landscape shared by a community

**Seimai** 精米
The polishing of rice to produce premium sake; during this process, the external layers of the grains of rice are rubbed off, since they contain protein and fat that have detrimental affects on the flavor and color of sake

**Seimai-buain** 精米歩合
See Polishing ratio

**Seishu** 清酒
The legal Japanese name for sake; literally "clear sake"

**Senmai** 洗米
Rice-washing; a production step in making sake

**Shibori** しぼり
The pressing of the mash, during which the sake (see Genshu) and lees (see Kasu) are separated

**Shibumi** 渋味
Tartness, astringency; one of the five basic tastes (go-mi)

**Shikomi** 仕込み
Preparing the mash; a process in sake production

**Shinpaku** 心白
The opaque, white, starchy kernel of the rice grain, an indication of high-quality rice

**Shinseki** 浸漬
Soaking rice in water; a production step in making sake

**Shinshu** 新酒
A legally defined term for sake that has been pressed less than one year ago

**Shinto** 神道
A religion practiced exclusively in Japan and based on the country's own specific cultural background, e.g. the veneration of nature and ancestor worship

**Shizuku sake** 雫酒
Literally "drops sake"; an extra-virgin sake produced by transferring the mash to bags, then hanging them up and letting the sake drip out without pressing

**Sho** 升
Japanese unit of volume measurement, equal to approximately 1,800 milliliters (6i ounces); see Units of measurement

**Shochu** 焼酎
A typical Japanese distillate, produced out of cereals that are mostly rich in starch, such as rice, barley, or sweet potatoes; koji is used to ferment the mash

**Shoryakuji temple** 正暦寺
A temple in Nara where the medieval bodaimoto method was developed (see corresponding entry)

**Shubo** 酒母
Starter mash (see corresponding entry)

**Shuzo** 酒造
Sake brewery, sake production; often added on to the name of a brewery

**Shuzo-kotekimai** 酒造好適米
See Sakamai

**Shuzo-kumiai** 酒造組合
Regional association of sake breweries, organized within the prefectures

**Sokujo** 速醸
Simplified method for preparing the starter mash by adding lactic acid

**Sparkling sake**
スパークリング日本酒
Sparkling sake produced using natural fermentation or by adding carbon dioxide

**Special A district** 特A地区
The best rice paddies in Hyogo, according to the Village Rice System

**Starter mash**
A mixture of rice, koji rice, water, and yeast that is used to culture highly concentrated, healthy yeast; in Japanese: moto, shubo

**Sugi** 杉
A Japanese cedar tree

**Sugitama** 杉玉
A ball made of cedar branches and leaves and hung up above the entrance to a brewery

**Tachinomi** 立ち飲み
A drinking venue without any seats

**Tanrei** 淡麗
Sake with a clear and light flavor profile

**Tanrei-karakuchi** 淡麗辛口
A typical style of sake from Niigata, which has a slightly fresh and dry flavor profile

**Taru** 樽
A small wooden barrel

**Taru sake, Taru-zake** 樽酒
Sake aromatized in a wooden barrel

**Tezukuri** 手造り
A handcrafted product

**To** 斗
A Japanese unit of measurement, equal to approximately 18 liters (5 gallons); see Units of measurement

**Tobin** 斗瓶
An 18-liter (5-gallon) sake bottle

**Toji** 杜氏
A sake master brewer or production director

**Toji-shule** 杜氏流派
A regional association of toji, organized as a cooperative

**Tokkuri** とっくり
Sake carafe

**Tokubetsu** 特別
Literally "outstanding, higher, distinguished"; tokubetsu-junmai for junmai sake of outstanding quality

**Tokutei-meishou-shu** 特定名称酒
see Premium sake

**Tsumami** つまみ
Snacks to accompany sake

**U.S. National Sake Appraisal**
A competition that has taken place in the USA every year since 2001, during which more than 500 sakes are tasted and awarded prizes by 10 juries from Japan and the USA; the sakes registered for this competition are also available to taste during the Joy of Sake event series

**Umami** うまみ
A meaty, savory type of flavor discovered by Kikunae Ikeda; generally viewed as the fifth basic taste after sweet, sour, salty, and bitter

**Umeshu** 梅酒
Plum wine or liquor, traditionally it is produced at home using ume plums, sugar, and high-proof alcohol or sake

**Units of measurement**
The units of measurement from the old Japanese shakkanho system, still used for sake and rice today: 1 go = approximately 180 milliliters (6 ounces); 1 sho = approximately 1,800 milliliters (61 ounces); 1 to = approximately 18 liters (5 gallons); 1 koku = approximately 180 liters(48 gallons)

**Uwadachi-ka** 上立ち香
Aromas detectable through the nose

**Village Rice System** 村米制度
A system introduced in 1887 in Hyogo, in which district farmers and kuramoto independently draw up sales contracts

**Yama-oroshi** 山卸
The time-consuming pounding of koji rice, a traditional method for preparing a starter mash (kimoto) for sake

**Yamada Nishiki** 山田錦
A type of rice that grows in the southwestern regions of Japan and is the most popular variety of rice for producing premium sake with full-bodied, lively, and elegant characteristics

**Yamahai** 山廃
A simplified method for preparing the starter mash (kimoto) without laboriously pounding the rice (yama-oroshi)

**Yoin** 余韻
Echo, reverberation

**Yongo-bin** 四合瓶
The most widely used size of bottle (720 milliliters/24 ounces) for premium sake

# About the Author

Yoshiko Ueno-Müller was born in Tokyo and has lived in Germany since 1989, and she is the first woman, as well as the first person not living in Japan, to be able to call herself Master of Sake Tasting. She is also an IHK-certified sommelière and lecturer at the German Wine and Sommelier School, as well as a certified trainer and examiner for the WSET Level 3 Award in Sake and a Senior Judge at the International Wine Challenge. Moreover, she launched the 7 SAMURAI Chefs Project and the Sake Pairing Contest, in which leading representatives of European haute cuisine and top sommeliers take part. Yoshiko Ueno-Müller was named Sake Samurai by the Association of Sake Brewers for her services in promoting sake culture. The Japanese Ministry of Foreign Affairs also awarded her a special distinction.

Together with her husband, **Jörg Müller**, Yoshiko Ueno-Müller runs **UENO GOURMET**, a company that brings a select range of Japanese culinary products directly from their producers to Europe. In addition, she is the director of the Sake & Shochu Academy Europe (S.AK.E), which she founded together with her husband, and which offers further training courses such as the J.S.A. Sake Diploma International.

**japan-gourmet.com**
**sake-academy.eu**
**sake-buch.de/en**

SCAN ME

## Collaborators

**Markus Bassler.** A love of sharing food and drink moves the heart of this food photographer. He is at home at all the laid tables and in all the kitchens of the world. His newest hobbies: rice wine and kaiseki.
**markusbassler.com**

**Oliver Hick-Schulz.** Art director. foodie, globetrotter. Travels to the world's markets to ignite his inspiration for food. When it comes to cookbooks, his creativity knows no bounds.
**depoenk.de**

**Rita Henss.** Globetrotting word acrobat, as is evidenced by the 40 books she has written so far. Their main topic is culinary pleasure in all its forms—from West to East, street food through to Michelin-starred cuisine.
**ritahenss.de**

**Sanni Helm**
As an image editor, she works closely with photographers and clients to understand their vision. She knows how to creatively enhance photos while maintaining the integrity of the original image.
**helmapparat.de**

**Team UENO GOURMET** (Sayaka Hugot, Julia Lutter, Jörg Müller, Isabel Pichler, Eric Walsh) is one of the leading sake importers in Europe, and thanks to its qualified employees, this company has an excellent network including the most renowned sake breweries in Japan and numerous European restaurants.
**japan-gourmet.com**

# Acknowledgments

Writing a book about food requires a lot of energy, steady nerves, and a healthy stomach—and being surrounded by a good team and strong supporters. While working on this text, I met people who have inspired me and affirmed me in what I was doing. It was thanks to their wonderful help that I was able to complete my piece of sake time travel.

First and foremost, my thanks must go to my project team: I would like to thank **Oliver Hick-Schulz** for his unrivaled graphic design, and **Markus Bassler** for his touchingly beautiful photographs. The journey we took through Japan together was unforgettable and fascinating and provided an irreplaceable foundation for this book. I would like to thank **Rita Henss** for shepherding my texts into their final form and honing and polishing them. Many thanks to **Sanni Helm** for adding brilliance and depth to the photos.

I would also like to thank the team of **UENO GOURMET** and the **Sake & Shochu Academy Europe** for the short descriptions of the sakes and breweries.

I would also like to thank **Julie Kiefer** (Prestel Verlag) and her team for our pleasant collaboration.

This book would also not have come into being without the support I received from Japan. I would therefore like to thank the following breweries: **Amabuki, Daruma Masamune, Iwa, Katsuyama, Kaze no Mori, Mimurosugi, Nanbu Bijin, Niida Honke, Ninki, Shichiken, Tatsuriki, Tedorigawa**, as well as their kuramoto, toji, and employees.

I would like to give particular thanks to Kuramoto **Ryuichiro Masuda**, Toji **Kiichiro Hatanaka**, and their colleagues at **Masuizumi**. They invited us to their internal koshikidaoshi celebration and to their banshaku evening and showed us the fascinating culinary culture and art of the old trading port of Iwase. I would also like to thank **the artists and restaurateurs of Iwase**, as well as the **Tourist Office of Toyama Prefecture** and the people in charge of the fish markets in Himi and Shinminato.

For helping me with my sake diary in Tokyo, my thanks go to **Marie Chiba, Shuzo Nagumo, Hironobu Kurihara, Hayato Morita, and Yoshihiro Narisawa**, and for the tasting tour to **She'll Be, Kurume Kushi Yugen, Uoki, Yueimaru, Wataya, Oryouri Fujii**, and **Cave Yunoki**.

Thank you to **Takeshi Ueshiba** for his insight into the work of an oke barrel manufacturer, to **Shozo Tanaka** for sharing his knowledge about rice cultivation and cattle farming, and to koji expert **Akihiko Sukeno**. Many thanks, too, to the persons responsible for the **Omiwa Shrine** and **Matsuo Shrine** for letting us take part in the sake ceremony.

Thank you also to the two world champion sommeliers **Shinya Tasaki** and **Markus Del Monego** for the valuable information and advice they provided, as well as to **Shuzo Imada, Hitoshi Utsunomiya** (both Japan Sake & Shochu Makers Association), to **Takuji Takahashi, Nobuhiro Ueno, Haruo Matsuzaki, Taka Yamamoto, Ana-Lee Iijima, Yoko Yamamoto**, and **Kanako Kanki**.

For their cooperation with regard to the photography sessions in Germany, I would like to thank three restaurants in and around Frankfurt am Main: **Moriki, Masa**, and **Kaiseki Kentaro**.

And a very special thank you to my husband, **Jörg Müller**, who ceaselessly supported and encouraged me during the production of this book.

Thank you very much indeed! 心からの感謝を込めて
**Yoshiko Ueno-Müller**

## Further Reading and Information

**In English:**

*A Comprehensive Guide to Japanese Sake*, edited by Japan Sake and Shochu Makers Association, 2011

*J.S.A. Sake Diploma*, edited by Japan Sommelier Association, 3rd ed., 2023

*Japanese Sake: Service and Knowledge*, edited by Japan Sake and Shochu Makers Association, 1994/2021

*Understanding Sake: Explaining style and quality*, edited by Wine & Spirit Education Trust, 2016

**In Japanese:**

和食とワイン　田崎真也　高橋拓児　一般社団法人日本ソムリエ協会 2015
和食の文化史　佐藤洋一郎　平凡社新書 2023
最先端の日本酒ペアリング　千葉麻里絵　宇都宮仁 旭屋出版 2019
近江商人と北前船　サンライズ出版
山田錦物語　兵庫酒米研究グループ編著 2018
日本酒学講義　新潟大学日本酒学センター編　ミネルヴァ書房 2022
風の森を醸す　山本長兵衛　京阪奈情報教育出版 2021
Dancyu March 2023 プレジデント社
乾杯の文化史　神崎宣武編　ドメス出版 2007
日本の酒　坂口謹一郎著 1964/2007
江戸の料理と食生活　原田信男編　小学館 2004

**Websites:**

Japan Sake and Shochu Association
**japansake.or.jp**

National Research Institute of Brewing (NRIB)
**nrib.go.jp/English**

Sake & Shochu Academy Europe
**sake-academy.eu**

Sake Pairing Contest
**sake-pairing-contest.com**

© Prestel Verlag, Munich · London · New York, 2024
A member of Penguin Random House Verlagsgruppe GmbH
Neumarkter Strasse 28 · 81673 Munich

**Photo credits:** All photos by Markus Bassler, except:
p. 5 by ooyoo/iStock, pp. 8–9 and 113 by Takashi Sato (www.satophoto.net); p. 18 by Takeshi Sekiya (Sekiya Brewery Co., Ltd.); p. 114 by rssfhs/iStock

**Photos:** p. 1: Seeing, smelling, and tasting—the many pleasures of sake; p. 2: A winter treat: hot sake warms body and soul; p. 3: Sake brewers know how to throw a party; p. 4: A modern twist on the traditional kimono; p. 5: In the spring, cherry blossoms cover Japan in a rosy mist; p. 6: Artfully crafted: What will the sake from this cup taste like?; p. 7: The Masuizumi Brewery's vintage cellar: thirty years' worth of premium quality sake; pp. 8–9: Blue hour in Tokyo: When evening falls, it is time to enjoy sake.

Library of Congress Control Number is available; a CIP catalogue record for this book is available from the British Library.

**Editorial direction:** Julie Kiefer
**Design & art direction:** Oliver Hick-Schulz
**Editorial assistance:** Rita Henss
**Translation into English:** Kate McNaughton
**Copyediting:** Peggy Paul Casella
**Production management:** Luisa Klose
**Printing and binding:** TBB, a.s., Banská Bystrica

MIX
Paper | Supporting responsible forestry
FSC® C022120
www.fsc.org

Penguin Random House Verlagsgruppe
FSC® N001967

Printed in Slovakia

ISBN 978-3-7913-9304-9

**www.prestel.com**